NATIONAL
ECONOMIC PLANNING:
WHAT IS LEFT?

NATIONAL ECONOMIC PLANNING: WHAT IS LEFT?

DON LAVOIE
George Mason University

BALLINGER PUBLISHING COMPANY
Cambridge, Massachusetts
A Subsidiary of Harper & Row, Publishers, Inc.

International Standard Book Number: 0-88730-055-3 (CL)
0-88730-056-1 (PB)

Library of Congress Catalog Card Number: 85-7440

Printed in the United States of America

Library of Congress Cataloging in Publication Data

Lavoie, Don, 1951-
National Economic Planning: What Is Left?

  Bibliography: p.
  Includes indexes.
  1. Economic policy. 2. Economic development.
3. Industrialization. I. Title.
HD82.L297 1985   338.9   85-7440
ISBN 0-88730-055-3
ISBN 0-88730-056-1 (pbk.)

For my brother
John M. Lavoie (1959–1982)

CONTENTS

Acknowledgments   xi

Introduction   1

Chapter 1
Planning and the Radical Perspective   11

The Need for a Scientific-Radical Perspective   12
Is National Economic Planning the Answer?   17

Chapter 2
Coordination in Society:
Tradition, Market, and Planning   25

The Importance of Coordinating Processes   26
Tradition   30
Market   34
Planning   39
The Choices Before Us   45

vii

Chapter 3
The Knowledge Problem   51

Knowledge vs. Data: The Nature of the Problem   52
The Principle of "Mass Communication"   65
Scientific and Market Discovery Procedures   76

Chapter 4
Leontief and the Critique of
Aggregative Planning   93

The Critique of Aggregative Data Gathering   94
Leontief's Alternative: The Input-Output Method   105
The Leap from Data Gathering to Planning   112

Chapter 5
Planning From the Bottom Up?
The Myth of Economic Democracy   125

"Democratic" Planning as the Alternative to Planning
  by the Corporations   126
Why Planning? The Inevitability Argument   140
Band-Aids   146

Chapter 6
Reindustrialization: Shoring Up the
Economy's "Structural" Sectors   173

The Structure Metaphor   174
The Expert Coordinators   186
More Band-Aids   196

Chapter 7
What Is Left? Toward an
Alternative Radicalism   211

Planning as Reaction: War, Monopoly Power, and the Left   212
An Alternative to the Planned Economy   232

Appendix
Tacit Knowledge and the Revolution
in the Philosophy of Science   247

References   267

Index   281

About the Author   293

ACKNOWLEDGMENTS

I owe my understanding of the central argument of this book, which I call the "knowledge problem," to the Austrian economist Ludwig von Mises and his students, F. A. Hayek and Israel M. Kirzner, who had called it the "calculation problem." My renaming of the Austrian school's critique of planning should not be taken to mean that I consider my version substantially different. My purpose is only to try to indicate more clearly and in my own words what the original argument was getting at. The argument is theirs.

I must acknowledge the extent to which Michael Polanyi's ideas, including both his critique of planning and his general philosophical outlook, have shaped my own. In addition I should thank Ludwig M. Lachmann, whose patient, open-minded, and radical approach to scholarship in economics is a permanent source of inspiration.

This project was initially conceived and primarily sponsored by the Cato Institute of Washington, D.C. The support of the entire staff, and their patience, are very much appreciated. An anonymous referee for Ballinger Publishing Company is to be thanked for his careful comments. I am particularly grateful to Roy A. Childs, Jr., of Cato, who worked on the manuscript throughout much of the past two years. Whatever degree of readability the final draft has attained may be largely due to his effort.

The copy editing of the whole manuscript was done by R. N. Neff, Mark B. Foster, and Cynthia Benn. In addition, David Boaz, James Buchanan, A. W. Coats, Tyler Cowen, Lee Cronk, Tom DiLorenzo, Jim Dorn, Jack Douglas, Richard Ebeling, Richard Fink, Jack High, R. N. Neff, Tom Palmer, Jack Sanders, Sudha Shenoy, Mark Sunwall, and Karen Vaughn provided me with helpful comments on early drafts of some chapters. Special thanks are due to David Essex, Winston McCuen, Robert Rauth, Jr., and David L. Prychitko who helped with some of the research chores, and to Sandy Lore, Jane Williamson, Sharon Gable, and Gillian Jewell, who typed the manuscript in its several drafts. Financial and other assistance by the Liberty Fund of Indianapolis, Indiana, and the Center for the Study of Market Processes of George Mason University, Fairfax, Virginia, were very helpful for parts of the research. None of the above can be held responsible for the mistakes I have made. Most of all I would like to thank my wife, Mary, who has had to bear most of the costs of my preoccupation with this book.

INTRODUCTION

Whether it is called "reindustrialization," "national foresight capability," or "industrial policy" and whether its central agency is called a Reconstruction Finance Corporation, a Federal Capital Budgeting Office, or a National Investment Bank, the idea of national economic planning is in the air. Some Wall Street financiers favor using a planning agency to salvage the older, so-called sunset industries and the banking system; neoliberals want it to target "sunrise" industries; a major portion of the radical Left wants it to reorder the priorities of the economic system on behalf of the working class; elements of the Right want it to improve national defense or to coordinate tax-incentive schemes.

This book is a nonconservative critique of contemporary proposals for national economic planning. As Chapter 1 will elaborate, it is a critique that aspires to reject planning not in favor of some sort of reactionary defense of the status quo but rather on behalf of an alternative and, I believe, more scientifically sound radicalism. By "radicalism" I will mean any social philosophy ranging from Marxist to Jeffersonian which understands that our society is in serious trouble and demands a sharp departure from current policies. I will take for granted that the primary *goals* of radicalism are to transcend—through principled and concerted social action—war and militarism, political oppression, and special privilege, and to set in motion pro-

1

gressive forces that will begin to solve such difficult human problems as poverty, disease, and environmental decay.

Clearly my list of ultimate goals of the radical movement is somewhat personal and no doubt subject to debate, with the exception, of course, of ending the threat of nuclear war. Many goals one might wish to include, such as the resolution of our energy and health care problems, may be achievable as a consequence of the realization of listed goals. Others, like the abolition of gross inequalities of wealth and income, may be seen not as ultimate goals at all but rather as popular means favored for their presumed ability to achieve other more fundamental ends, such as the conquest of poverty. Since this book seeks a scientific examination of its subject matter, it will avoid debating the ends themselves and will concentrate on the effectiveness of alternative means for the attainment of what I will take to be largely agreed-upon ends.

Many of the leaders of the antiwar movement, such as Wassily Leontief and the editors of *The Progressive*, are also among the leading advocates of planning. It has been taken for granted that, in its resistance to militarism as with its other goals, the Left must rely on some form of national economic planning. I believe there is no question more urgent for radicals to answer than whether planning is in fact an appropriate means to attain these goals.

In a sense everybody is in favor of planning. But I will include under the heading of "planning" only those policy measures that involve concentrating power to shape the economy in a special government agency. The model for this agency could be a relatively modest attempt to control the economy, such as the Reconstruction Finance Corporation (RFC) in the 1930s or Japan's Ministry of International Trade and Industry (MITI); it could just as easily be an ambitious socialist attempt to run the whole economy. A critique of planning in this sense need not deny the truism that every rational human being would be wise to plan his own activities. Neither must it deny that society requires institutions such as courts and police which have to be deliberately planned by somebody. What is at issue here is whether the national government should try to increase its central control over economic activity in order to shape it to the goals of the Left. My conclusion will be that the ultimate *ends* of the radical movement will almost certainly be frustrated if national economic planning is chosen as the *means* for their realization. If this argument is correct, then by supporting the call for planning, most contemporary radicals in the world are acting as their own worst enemies.

Implicit in Karl Marx's critique of capitalism was the original conception of planning, requiring the complete abolition not only of private ownership of the means of production, but also markets, prices, and even money. These institutions were all to be replaced by a detailed, administrative control of the whole production process by a single hierarchical agency. This kind of planning I shall call "comprehensive planning."

Nowadays nearly all advocates of planning, including many who call themselves Marxists, explicitly accept the need for retaining market institutions in their schemes for setting up national economic planning agencies. This "noncomprehensive planning" includes virtually all of the practical experience with economic planning from Stalinist centralized variants to the moderate ones like the RFC and MITI. The whole critique of contemporary proposals for noncomprehensive planning in Chapters 4, 5, and 6 will involve an application of the same argument developed in the earlier chapters against comprehensive planning. It will be shown that the stated goals of those modern proposals—such as steering the economy—ultimately imply the very extreme notion of comprehensive planning. The critique of the market economy upon which planners base their argument presupposes that it is actually possible to scientifically control the causal development of a modern, technologically advanced economy. Planners of all stripes typically describe the present economy as "out of control" and reject halfway measures that shy away from doing whatever they seem to think necessary to bring the economy under the conscious control of some sort of planning institution.

All advocates of planning seem desperately to *want* comprehensiveness and rely profoundly upon its rhetorical appeal. The issue is not over whether comprehensiveness as such is desirable but rather what is *entailed* in the attempt to bring an entire technologically advanced economy "under control." The various advocates of planning to be discussed in the later chapters will answer, "more democratic institutions," or "more systematic funneling of investment monies to troublespots," or "more supply-side tax credit schemes," or perhaps just "more data." The earlier chapters, however, will assume that on this point Marx's answer was closer to the truth: To really control something as complex and interdependent as a modern industrial economy would require nothing less than the comprehensive direction of the detailed productive activity of the whole society. If this vast problem proves intractable, as it may well appear to be to most readers, with it will go all hopes for merely guiding a market economy. Each of the noncomprehensive proposals examined later will come up against the problem that it lacks the comprehensive scope to get the economy moving in the desired direction.

In a sense then, these earlier chapters are really not merely about comprehensive planning; they raise a fundamental objection to all proposals for increasing government's attempts to control the economy. The main purpose here is not so much to offer a critique of comprehensive planning, as to *explain* the knowledge problem by using comprehensive planning as a foil; the purpose of the later chapters will be to *wield* this analytical weapon against contemporary proposals for planning. The only way to make sense of the quintessential complaint of most planning advocates that "things are out of control" is to postulate that some workable way exists to bring such matters as are involved in a technologically advanced economy "under control." It is this postulate—held in common by comprehensive and noncomprehensive planners alike—that will be questioned.

My contention is that, although advocates of noncomprehensive planning have wisely abandoned comprehensive planning and accepted the need for markets in some sense, they have done so for the wrong reasons. At most they have realized that there is a political danger in concentrating so much power into the hands of a planning agency and that there is a need for using prices and profit incentives as important levers in the planning process. What they have failed to notice is that the competitive market is itself the primary source of knowledge about which goods are to be produced and which production methods are feasible; thus any attempt by a single agency to steer an economy constitutes a case of the blind leading the sighted.

In other words, the social function performed by a particular complex of legal and market institutions makes them indispensable tools for the solution of certain unavoidable economic problems involved in the day-to-day production and allocation of scarce resources. If we were unable to solve such problems, we would face the utter ruin of our economy. Individuals will lack the knowledge necessary to solve these economic problems unless such a complex of economic and legal institutions is permitted to exist. *If* this argument is accepted, any defense of an economic system, such as comprehensive planning, which explicitly aims at abolishing these very institutions, would be directly refuted by it. Moreover, any economic system, such as noncomprehensive planning, which seeks to interfere substantively with the way many of these institutions work would be at least running the risk of tampering with the very basis of our survival.

Before this challenge to planning can be posed, it is necessary to clarify the nature of the economic problems for which I claim it obstructs or prevents solutions. Why do we need to solve such problems in the first place? Only when we are satisfied that *some* kind of systemic solution to these problems is in fact necessary can we proceed to the question whether planning is adequate to the task. Chapter 2 will argue that a central challenge facing any economic system is the need to solve the day-to-day economic problems involved in allocating scarce resources. It will present an outline of the three fundamental organizing principles—which I will call Tradition, Market, and Planning—that have been used or proposed to meet this challenge. Although I will discuss these alternative processes in the context of their historical emergence and development, my purpose is not historical but theoretical. I make no pretense at adequately describing the vast expanses of history to which my analysis refers. Rather, I will summarize the nature of these three fundamental alternatives for economic organization and show why, in order to choose among them, we must examine their operating principles, especially those of the Market and Planning, more closely. Neither is my purpose at this stage to judge the relative effectiveness of Planning as compared with the other two principles but only to indicate some plausible reasons why this alternative seems attractive and scientific.

Chapter 3 contains the central argument of the book. A description of market processes is woven into a broad comparison between them and two analogous processes observed by modern biologists and philosophers of science: on the one hand how social insects coordinate their actions with one another, and on the other hand how members of the scientific community coordinate *their* actions with one another. Needless to say, I do not claim these processes to be identical; I only wish to indicate certain organizational patterns they all seem to share. I will argue that a similar sort of "knowledge problem" stands in the way of subjecting these biological, economic, and scientific processes to centralized comprehensive control.

In order to explain just what this knowledge problem is all about, it is necessary to distinguish between knowledge and data. Knowledge may be partly inarticulate—that is, unable to be articulated—

and therefore tacit and personal, while data is necessarily explicit, unambiguous, objective, and interpersonally communicable. While a planning bureau can gather data, it cannot gather the knowledge that would be needed for rational planning. Such knowledge is dispersed among market participants. It is embedded in their various skills and specialties, and is generated by their competitive contention with one another. Yet without such knowledge the planning bureau would be unable to justify intervening in ignorance into the workings of the market process.

If the modern approach to the philosophy of science (elaborated in the appendix) is valid, then the actual process of scientific discovery and progress is analogous to the process by which alternative methods of production are selected through rivalrous competition in a market economy. Thus the context or social process through which knowledge is generated—both in economic activity and in science—is all-important; where access to the fruits of this process is completely blocked (as with comprehensive planning), both the progress of our knowledge and our ability to solve important intellectual and economic problems would eventually, if the policy were consistently pursued, grind to a halt. If knowledge is dependent upon the process or context from which it springs, then any partial interference with either of them (as with noncomprehensive planning) may, if significant and persistent enough, threaten to subvert that knowledge itself.

The next three chapters will consider the proposals of several prominent writers who argue for a form of national economic planning that admits the need to retain market institutions. These writers concede that the problems of a technologically sophisticated economy are too complicated ever to be managed in total and in detail by any single agency and that prices, money, interest rates, capital markets, profit incentives, and so forth are necessary parts of the planner's tools. They still believe, however, that the basic problem is that our economic circumstances are "out of control" and need to be guided in an overall fashion by a central agency of some kind.

If these modern proposals reject the complete comprehensiveness of the engineering approach to planning, they also insist that a knowledge of and control over our economy *far more* comprehensive than anyone now has would be just the medicine it needs. The main idea of all these planning ideas (even the versions aspiring to decentralization) is to set up some sort of agency of the federal government vested with the responsibility of collecting extensive knowledge about our economy and exerting substantial influence over it. This planning bureau's agenda will comprise all our nation's overall economic problems.

Thus the main purpose of Chapters 4, 5, and 6 is to apply the *economic* argument presented in Chapter 3 to the leading modern proposals for national planning. The secondary purpose will be to show that these proposals have little to say to deflect the more familiar argument, the totalitarian problem, which raises doubts about whether a planning agency would be able in practice to avoid degenerating into *political* tyranny. While these proposals vary in the degree to which they appear sensitive to the dangers described in these two problems, even the most sensitive have remarkably little to say about how either of them can be overcome.

The major planning proposals of the contemporary American political scene can be grouped into three fairly distinct types. Unfortunately, the classification of noncomprehensive proposals into such types cannot be made by means of the sort of definite criteria by which they could all be distinguished from comprehensive planning proposals. Instead one finds a loose confederation of eclectic proposals, differing more by matters of emphasis and broad orientation than by inclusion of any particular policies or arguments. Some general ideas, like improving statistical collection methods or guiding the process of new capital formation, are common to all. But when these goals are made more specific, for instance in proposals to save the industrial base of the older cities or to funnel investment monies to newer high-technology industries, major disagreements arise.

I have therefore found it convenient to divide these proposals according to the characteristic *attitudes* of their adherents rather than by means of any specific policies. These attitudes will be brought out by (sometimes lengthy) quotations from the writings of these adherents themselves. Broadly speaking, the three major groups of proposals can be classified according to whether they concern themselves primarily with data collection, economic democracy, or the structural sectors of the economy. These three types correspond respectively to the ideas of the leading academic economist in favor of planning, Wassily Leontief (Chapter 4); the economic democracy movement of the more radically disposed planners such as Derek Shearer, Martin Carnoy, Robert Lekachman, Michael Harrington, and the editors of *The Progressive* (Chapter 5); and the reindustrialization proposals of the so-called structuralists led by Robert Reich and Felix Rohatyn (Chapter 6).

In letting the various proponents of planning speak for themselves, I have not been unaware that their terminology may prejudge the outcome of the policies they advocate. Nevertheless, the philosophy of science that forms the basis of my critique treats a theory as analogous to a pair of spectacles through which we try to make sense of the world. Hence it shows the impossibility of refuting a theory without first trying to see the world through its lenses. Only after we understand how these planning advocates see the world is it possible to contend, as I will, that their theoretical lenses give them a distorted view.

Even so, it may be said that there is an essential complaint against the status quo largely shared not only by all three variations on noncomprehensive planning but by comprehensive planners as well: Our society lacks an overall mechanism for controlling the flow of investment. As a result of this lack of control, irrational or undesirable uses of investment funds predominate and economic productivity consequently deteriorates. An important part of their solution to this problem, then, is the establishment of a special investment-guiding agency, modeled at least in some respects after the Reconstruction Finance Corporation that was set up during the Great Depression, as the main mechanism for the social control of investment. In the case of comprehensive planning virtually the whole of society is to be controlled by this agency. In the case of Leontief such an agency is needed to gather data in order to "rationalize" the policymaking process. In the case of the structuralists, it is the centerpiece of the whole argument. In the case of economic democracy advocates, other policies are thrown in as well. In all of their proposals this new RFC is to be given the crucial coordinating role to play in the planning process.

The advocates of all four versions of planning never tire of reminding us what a tremendously arduous task planning a modern economy is, but in doing so they are not responding to the central contention of the knowledge problem argument, which concludes that the way a modern economy works necessarily precludes its being rationally controlled. A modern economy can generate and disperse the knowledge its operation requires only by permitting a competitive process to operate in an unplanned manner. In short, our economic malaise cannot be blamed on the fact that our economy is out of control *because no modern economy could possibly be otherwise.*

It comes as no surprise, therefore, that there appears to be a wide chasm between the radical goals of the proponents of planning and the capabilities of any of the four varieties of planning to deliver on their promises. How do we explain this dichotomy between theory and practice? Chapter 7 provides a cursory overview of the historical development of the Left and its practical experiences with planning in order to suggest where in this development things went wrong. Comprehensive and noncomprehensive planning emerge from this account as successive and ultimately reactionary diversions of what began as a genuinely progressive movement, diversions which have not only wreaked havoc on the millions of human lives who have had to live under planned economies but which have also caused immense harm to the whole notion of popular ideological movements for radical change. A profound pessimism about social progress and often an escape into political apathy burden those who have come to realize that the Left as a political ideology has arrived at an intellectual dead end. In addition the conceptual straitjackets of the planning mentality have restrained modern radicals from seeing the fundamental nature of political struggle and prevent them from breaking out of the stalemate we face in the current political milieu between the Left and the Right.

The failure of the modern Left has been a tragedy, but it is not cause for pessimism. This failure was anticipated by the antiplanning elements of the early Left, and has been explained by their intellectual descendants as due only to the planning aspects of leftist ideology. It thus can be overcome only by a radical ideology that abandons planning but retains most of the other traditional hopes of radicals for a more rational, just, peaceful, and prosperous world.

The title of this book does not only ask, What is left of planning? It poses the further question, Given the failure of planning, what is the Left? Planning is not an end in itself; it has been proposed only as a means for the attainment of the progressive goals of the radical movement. Its failure suggests that what is needed is a completely different ideological foundation for the Left. It is not my intention with this book to undermine but to strengthen the radical movement, to help set it on a course that will make it more likely that one day its goals will finally be achieved.

1 PLANNING AND THE RADICAL PERSPECTIVE

In the first moments of a ten-thousand-megaton attack on the United States
. . . when the first wave of missiles arrived, the vast majority of the people in
the regions first targeted would be irradiated, crushed, or burned to death.
. . . In the ten seconds or so after each bomb hit, as blast waves swept out-
ward from thousands of ground zeros, the physical plant of the United States
would be swept away like leaves in a gust of wind. The six hundred thousand
square miles already scorched by the forty or more calories of heat per centi-
metre squared would now be hit by blast waves of a minimum of five pounds
per square inch, and virtually all the habitations, places of work, and other
man-made things there—substantially the whole human construct in the
United States—would be vaporized, blasted, or otherwise pulverized out of
existence. . . .

And this threat of self-destruction and planetary destruction is not something that we will pose one day in the future, if we fail to take certain precau-
tions; it is here now, hanging over the heads of all of us at every moment. The
machinery of destruction is complete, poised on a hair trigger, waiting for the
"button" to be "pushed" by some misguided or deranged human being or for
some faulty computer chip to send out the instruction to fire.

Jonathan Schell (1982: 56–57, 181–82)

The left is not for planning or public ownership or the democratization of
investment as an end in itself. . . .

Michael Harrington (1982: 422)

11

THE NEED FOR A SCIENTIFIC-RADICAL PERSPECTIVE

As Jonathan Schell's disturbing book *The Fate of the Earth* eloquently reminds us, our civilization has spawned a technology advanced enough to be capable of completely destroying that civilization, combined precariously with political systems so backward that such destruction is a distinct possibility.

But creating the definite risk of blowing us all up, a kind of "ultimate policy failure," is symbolic of the quite general failures of political policy, some of which, even if less final, are actually more likely to occur. Indeed, they have been occurring with numbing regularity. The systematic torture by established governments of dissidents for speaking and writing their ideas is not simply a risk or a possibility but an ongoing fact. Direct, brutal oppression combined with institutionalized corruption constitutes the modus operandi of most of the regimes of the "Third" and "Second" worlds, while the Western governments implicate themselves in this oppression indirectly by financially and militarily propping up these regimes.[1] Although such open oppression is relatively rare within the Western democracies (except for the special persecution of hated subcultural groups), it is supplanted there by a host of severe socioeconomic problems. The West faces problems with inflation and unemployment, falling productivity and investment, escalating crime and taxes, as well as decaying schools and other public services. And this only scratches the surface.

The peril in which modern civilization finds itself might be just cause for despair were it not for the ironic circumstance that in fact it was not an external force which brought us to the brink of destruction. Rather, it was the astounding rapidity of our own scientific progress. It has been the imbalance between our intellectual progress in the natural sciences and in the social sciences that has delivered us into a world where scientific developments in electricity and biology are diverted into the social production of electric prods for efficient torture and where nuclear physics becomes a threat instead of a benefit to civilization. As Jonathan Schell has written, "We try to make do with a Newtonian politics in an Einsteinian world." What humanity needs is a way of marshaling the progressive forces that have produced such startling advances in the physical sciences on behalf of a similar development of the social sciences and therefore ultimately of society itself. There is no reason why a species intelligent enough to produce computers cannot learn to organize its own society in such a way that they be used to solve social problems rather than to guide the missiles we aim at one another. Our ultimate social predicament should inspire not futility but rather hope that we can discover *why* our social institutions work so much less effectively than our machines and *how* we can set in motion a process for societal rejuvenation which matches our processes of scientific discovery.

It might be thought that there is one basic difference between scientific and social progress which inhibits the possibility of the former's being harnessed in service of the latter: the often lamented lack of a "social laboratory." Science, it is said, advances in the minds and practical experiments of a few great men; whereas, for society as a whole to change, great numbers of peoples—from a bewildering variety of cultural, linguistic, and moral backgrounds—must somehow all go along. There may already exist some brilliant social scientist who knows how to save humanity, but those ideas will never even be tried until enough human beings support them, yet how can we expect as many people to support such untried ideas as support the proven ideas of science?

There is an element of truth in this point. While the physical scientists can solve many problems by constructing relatively simple experiments to isolate causally the phenomena under study, social scientists have the more complex subtleties of human history as their only laboratory. In this realm an experiment, such as Lenin's attempt to institute central planning in the early years of the Soviet Union, may be seen as proving vastly different things to different observers. In the social sciences, it seems, interpretations of facts by means of complicated and often controversial theories are more decisive than the facts themselves.

However, as modern philosophers of science have shown, the physical sciences are not actually all that different in this respect from the social sciences. Even in the physical sciences, facts do not speak for themselves. They require interpretation by means of theoretical frameworks. Truth in the sciences cannot be established by rigorous proof; rather, scientists can only grope toward it in an unending process of mutual criticism and discovery. Even mathematics, once thought an impregnable citadel of certainty, is now a raging battlefield of controversy both among several competing and mutually incompatible schools of thought and among the individuals within each school. Science, then, like social change, involves an interpersonal process of persuasion. An idea in the mind of a great scientist does not become designated as a contribution to science until it achieves the consensus of the scientific community. This consensus is usually not achieved by the unambiguous demonstration of a new theory in an experiment. More often it is the result of heated arguments about the interpretations advanced by rival theories and subtle hints that the new theory somehow explains better.[2]

Science was once thought of as a logically unassailable structure standing above controversy and mere belief, but is now generally recognized by most philosophers of science as a body of beliefs to which a particular, highly respected subset of society adheres. Of course there are exacting standards within this scientific community and admission to its exclusive ranks is a most difficult endeavor, as anyone who has tried to get a Ph.D. or publish an article in a professional journal will attest. But the point is that science is not an uncontested body of unquestionable truths. It is only a more persuasively justified set of beliefs. It does not stand aloof from controversy. Rather, it *depends* on controversy so that its social consensus can be continually reformulated. It does not forsake commitment toward ideas (and the passionate belief in them) in favor of a dispassionate, workmanlike, discovery of facts—although that is what scientists often like to think they are doing. Science is actually an edifice of more firmly held, more persuasively defended, more clearly articulated beliefs, but nevertheless *beliefs*, most of which have never been and could never be conclusively demonstrated in laboratory experiments.

Some have viewed these developments in the philosophy of science as undermining what was once thought to be the bedrock rationalist foundation of our great heritage of science. But the achievements of science are no less permanent or wondrous for having been the result of an inarticulate social process. Our scientific heritage stands firmly in our libraries and universities and is embodied in our feats of engineering, unshaken by the logical quandaries of philosophers. Its justification lies in the values, methods, and standards that sustain it.

Rather than undermining our commitment to science, the modern philosophy of science should be seen as opening up for society the possibility of extending the fruits of the scientific discovery process to other as yet less developed, prescientific realms. If science does not always require *laboratories* but does require a process for the formation of a social *consensus*, then social sciences once thought crippled for their unique lack of the former and necessity for the latter can be liberated from their backwardness.

The last two centuries have produced many vain attempts by social scientists to mimic what were thought to be the exact, formal, experimentally proven methods of the natural sciences. Indeed, the intellectual roots of the notion of economic planning are in the confident attempts of nineteenth-century French rationalist philosophers such as Henri Saint-Simon and August Comte to build a complete science of society on the model of Newtonian mechanics. Since this effort was founded entirely upon a mistaken view of the nature of the physical sciences, it was in any case doomed to fail. But if social science is to flourish, it must be governed according to the standards appropriate to its own subject matter. Efforts to borrow analytical tools fashioned for the natural sciences have dominated and seem to have hampered the social sciences throughout this century.[3] Surely the path to scientific investigation of human action and social forces does not lie in a blind imitation of the sciences that study matter and energy. The general intellectual processes by which the natural sciences have made such phenomenal progress, however, are capable of adaptation to the study of society, if only society will devote the same intensity of intellectual effort to developing a scientific understanding of itself as it has to the scientific understanding of the physical world it inhabits.

Not that this task will be easy. The more one studies our social maladies, the more one suspects that our politics are not even Newtonian but are more properly designated Neanderthal. The problems are not merely Herculean challenges facing our existing social and political institutions. They seem so utterly immune to any policies we devise that they force us to call into question these institutions themselves. The same symptoms of failure (although to different degrees) seem to plague all societies of the world, whether they call themselves communist, socialist, or capitalist. And worst of all our leaders are still trying to play nineteenth-century war games in a world that is primed with the awesome destructive power to reduce itself, in Schell's words, to a republic of insects and grass.

In the face of this catastrophic performance of our political institutions, most of our intellectual leaders, whether of the Left or the Right, can be found busily debating the details of the established programs and quarreling about various methods of fine-tuning our society by means of the established institutions. But this world doesn't need a tune-up; it needs an overhaul, and needs it desperately. To hope that these stale and decrepit political institutions will, in their present form, be able to invent and implement imaginative solutions to the new and perhaps final human problem of the arms race, after they have so miserably failed in the face of far simpler challenges, seems unrealistically utopian.

But in a sense, what is wrong with these policy debates is precisely that they do not dare to be utopian enough. That is, they confine their attention to minor modifications in the established and badly rusted political machinery instead of trying to imagine the substitution of a fundamentally different approach altogether. What is needed is a radical perspective, both in addition to a scientific perspective and as a logical consequence of it. We need to locate the *root cause* of the social maladies we have endured and stop combating their symptoms. We need to elaborate an approach as different from our dominant political-economic paradigm as chemistry is from alchemy. We need to find a principled approach to social issues which will outline a clear goal of a peaceful, prosperous, and just society, and then seek consistent and feasible paths to its realization. We cannot afford to let ourselves be battered about by the winds of political fashion until by some unlucky turn of events we destroy our very cultural and economic existence.

Only principled social action, on the model of clear scientific thinking guided by a consistent set of ideas and deriving from these a clear direction for policy changes, can hope to straighten out the conflicting strands of policy we find ourselves tangled in. We must dare to imagine radical alternatives to the kinds of social institutions to which we have become so accustomed, and to explain why these new institutions would work qualitatively better than the present ones. Only a principled radical approach can effectively combine an uncompromising diagnosis of our contemporary social ills with a clearly articulated vision of what social health would look like. What is needed, in short, is a workable utopia. As F. A. Hayek (1973: 65) writes,

> Utopia, like ideology, is a bad word today; and it is true that most utopias aim at radically redesigning society and suffer from internal contradictions which make their realization impossible. But an ideal picture of a society which may not be wholly achievable, or a guiding conception of the overall

order to be aimed at, is nevertheless not only the indispensable precondition of any rational policy, but also the chief contribution that science can make to the solution of the problems of practical policy.

IS NATIONAL ECONOMIC PLANNING THE ANSWER?

The policy direction that social thinkers of a radical bent have most often advanced as the alternative mechanism for reconstructing society on a scientific basis has been the notion of national economic planning. The diagnosis of contemporary difficulties implicit in these proposals focuses on the essential problem of modern societies although it does not seem to resolve it. That problem is the fundamental contradiction between government, on the one hand, which claims to represent a conscious expression of and instrument for the social will, and society itself on the other, which seems ever to be struggling against its own supposedly democratic instrument. Actions taken by governments seem to reflect the conscious will of their own personnel, or of wealthy or powerful special interests, more often than the will of society as a whole.[4] Members of society in turn struggle both against one another and against the government either to gain control over this instrument of power for their own benefit (which modern economists call rent seeking) or to protect themselves from being victimized by that power (rent avoidance). (See Tullock 1967 and Krueger 1974.) In either case a whirlwind of activity revolves around government in the pursuit of control over its special powers, and considerable amounts of scarce resources are diverted from other uses to this struggle.

Our pervasive social problems may be viewed as symptoms of an underlying contradiction between that portion of the sphere of private decisionmaking that is often driven by acquisitive motives and embroiled in competition for scarce resources, and the sphere of public decisionmaking, equipped with a monopoly over coercive power, ostensibly driven by higher motives and reconciled to one conscious, internally consistent purpose. These two spheres combined produce a chaotic result in which the self-serving motives of the private sector strive to direct the apparatus of coercion of the public sphere. Failing that, the private sector attempts to counteract the policies undertaken by the public sphere. The government does not play the role of agent for the social will but simply joins in the self-serving struggles of the private sphere. The public sector interferes with the operation of the private sphere, making war with the private decision-making order, while the competing participants from the private sector respond and attempt to circumvent such interference, to engage in defensive maneuvers, to try to grab state power for themselves and use it against their competitors.

Karl Marx conceived of central planning as an attempt to resolve this inherent contradiction between the private and public spheres of society.[5] As in any genuinely radical perspective, his particular diagnosis of the problem is inextricably bound up with his utopia, his notion of a cure.[6] Marx saw the problem as being located in the competitive private sphere, the market system, where separate, divided, or "alienated" interests contend with one another for resources. He argued that, so long as democratic institutions tried to merge themselves with this competitive sphere, they would invariably succumb to it. The solution, then, was to eradicate competitive market relations and to replace them with a broadening of the democratically based public sphere to encompass all of social life. No longer would politicians stoop to being tools of special and conflicting interests, since the private sector would cease to exist as a separate component of society. All social production would be carried out by the "associated producers" in conjunction with a common plan. Production would no longer be a private act of war by some market participants against others in a competitive struggle for wealth, but would instead be the main task of the self-coordinated democratic institution.

According to this perspective, the coercive powers of governments will gradually become unnecessary, since the underlying cause of coercion—the contention or rivalry among members of society—will have been removed. Thus the reason for our pervasive social ills, culminating in the modern threat of total destruction in war, is perceived to be the fact that we have narrowly confined the function of democratic institutions to a tiny part of social life and have left the bulk of economic activity to the unplanned outcome of non-democratic private struggles for wealth in the market. The proposed solution is to widen democracy to the whole sphere of economics and completely abolish private ownership of the means of production, thereby eliminating the competitiveness of market relations as a basis for economic decisionmaking.

Marx was unfortunately averse to describing how his utopia was supposed to work. Nevertheless, one can still infer from his many indirect references to the communist society that some sort of democratic procedures would be constructed through which the goals of society could be formulated. After this is done, scientists would devise rational comprehensive planning procedures to implement these goals. Since this planning, to be meaningful and scientific, must obtain control over all the relevant variables, Marx consistently foresaw it as centralized and comprehensive. The commonly owned means of production would be deliberately and scientifically operated by the state in accordance with a single plan. Social problems would henceforth be resolved not by meekly interfering with a competitive market order but by taking over the whole process of social production from beginning to end.

Just as a chemical engineer faced with the problem of producing a new synthetic material would begin by developing an exact under-standing of the properties of the various elements at his disposal and then proceed to devise a step-by-step procedure to combine these elements in the appropriate way to yield the desired product, so would the "social engineer" proceed. A thorough compilation of the available elements (the factories, manpower, raw materials, and so on) and a rigorous study of their properties would be followed by a step-by-step plan to integrate these elements into a single production process.

This comprehensive or engineering model of planning will be shown to be the only completely coherent notion of planning advanced in the literature of radicalism, but even it is fundamentally flawed. The social engineering approach mistakes the economy for the rather mechanical process by which an individual technician solves a given problem, when the economic system is actually more like the overall social process of scientific discovery. Science and the market are not limited to the solving of given and well-defined problems by known procedures. They also involve the very process of conceptualizing the problems and discovering the procedures. The notion of comprehensive planning represents the nineteenth century's boldest attempt to apply its mechanistic view of science to society to yield a program for radical change. But it can no longer serve in a century that is, for good reasons, abandoning that view of science.

Though it still receives lip service by many contemporary planning advocates, this comprehensive, social-engineering conception of planning has been almost universally abandoned. Attempts either to implement this extreme view of centralized planning or to defend it from theoretical critique have proved utterly disastrous. In its place have flourished less consistent and usually less coherent notions of noncomprehensive planning, which still aspire—at least rhetorically—to the original goal of bringing the chaos of competitive markets under more rational control.

Unfortunately, attempts to implement or theoretically defend the various forms of noncomprehensive planning have been drastically disappointing, even if they have not been quite the unmitigated catastrophe of comprehensive planning. This fact alone does not, of course, preclude the possibility that some new variant on the idea of national economic planning may yet be devised which resolves the grave difficulties of all its predecessors.

But before we can confidently expect such a workable notion of planning to emerge, we would have to find that modern advocates have learned from the failures of the past. This does not yet seem to be the case. Of the contemporary advocates of planning who consider the issue of past failures, most blame them on a lack of attention to democratic values, on the fact that the wrong personnel have been in charge, on a lack of statistical data, or on the supposition that its principles were not carried far enough. These rationalizations are not supported by the factual record and the primary arguments raised against national economic planning—which I will designate the "totalitarian problem" and the "knowledge problem"—are more fundamental and are almost completely unaddressed in contemporary planning proposals.

In fact almost all planning proponents have paid a great deal of attention to and placed primary emphasis upon democratic values. The totalitarian problem of planning, which its critics have raised, was never claimed to be a consequence of the evil intentions of planning advocates, but rather of the kinds of institutions planning puts into place and the inherent dynamics of these institutions. The argument is that national economic planning involves *by its very nature* the concentration of immense political and economic power in a single agency. This agency would have to be capable of mobilizing the vast resources of a nation. Such concentration will naturally lend itself to abuse by those hungry for such power and eminently competent in its exercise. It does not matter who initially is put in charge or how much that person and his or her employees emphasize or love democracy. Nothing that contemporary planning advocates have said adequately addresses this institutional argument. Instead, we hear more sincere, more emphatic, and more eloquent assurances by planning advocates that *this* time democratic values will be preserved.

Even were this difficulty resolvable, there remains another criticism altogether: the knowledge problem. For the purposes of this argument one can suppose that the planning apparatus will be staffed by persons possessed of the moral stature and material requirements of a Mohandas Gandhi combined with the mental capacity and creative genius of a Leonardo da Vinci. The argument here is not that the worst will get on top, although I believe they will, but that even with the best on top they will not know about what is going on "at the bottom" in sufficient detail to be able to plan an economy effectively. The problem is not that people will be insufficiently motivated to do the right things but, more fundamentally, that they will not know what the right things to do *are*, even if they passionately wanted to do them.[7]

Whereas contemporary advocates of national economic planning have on occasion at least tried to grapple with the totalitarian problem, albeit perhaps unconvincingly, they appear to be almost completely innocent of even the existence of the knowledge problem, despite considerable efforts by some of the most famous critics of planning to underscore its nature and importance.[8] Of all the proponents of planning considered in this book, only one addresses himself to this issue and even he misconstrues the difficulty as a mere shortage of statistical data instead of as the more fundamental knowledge problem. Yet it is this largely ignored criticism of planning which shows most clearly why the failures of planning have not been due to insufficient adherence to its principles but that, on the contrary, the more consistently its principles have been pursued the more damaging have been the results.

This critique of national economic planning has important implications for the planning advocates' own diagnosis of contemporary problems. Part of this diagnosis—its focus on the problems arising from the conflict between the public and private spheres of social life—is valid, but the answer is not to extend the democratic public sphere at the expense of the competitive private sphere. The very competitiveness of the private sphere, which the original advocates of planning identified as the cause of most social problems, has been shown to be absolutely necessary for any technologically advanced economy. At the same time the extensions of the power of the government to the economic sphere have in practice not enhanced but rather drastically reduced its democratic features and increased the use of coercion in the necessarily competitive struggles among the members of society.

If the source of the pervasive problems of modern society is not that its competitiveness has been an obstacle to the extension of democracy, then the proper diagnosis of and cure for our social predicament will have to lead us in an altogether different ideological direction. This theme will be taken up in the last chapter of the book. Before turning to this critique of planning, however, it will be necessary to examine the nature of socioeconomic coordination, for it is on this that the knowledge problem hinges.

NOTES TO CHAPTER 1

1. For evidence of U.S. government involvement in these inhuman crimes see Noam Chomsky and Edward S. Herman (1979), although one can take issue with their exclusive focus on "right-wing" or American-sponsored oppression while ignoring that of left-wing or Soviet-sponsored regimes. For the crimes themselves see any publication of Amnesty International, an organization that does *not* confine its attention to the abuses of right-wing governments.

2. More will be said on this later, but perhaps an example will suffice for now to clarify the point. Michael Polanyi (1958a: 9–15) and Gerald Holton (1969: 133–97) have shown that even the most common textbook example of the supposed dependence of science upon conclusive experimentation, the articulation by Einstein in 1905 of the theory of relativity in order to account for the otherwise inexplicable results of the Michelson–Morley experiment that had been conducted eighteen years earlier, does not in fact bear out the thesis it was supposed to illustrate. Neither this nor any other controlled experiment played any role in Einstein's theoretical discovery. Indeed the original experiment (and thousands of replications of it by D. C. Miller from 1902 to 1926) actually did not give the results required by the theory of relativity. But this evidence was completely ignored by a scientific community that had already been convinced of the validity of Einstein's approach.

3. Michael Polanyi (1972: 49) has concluded from his studies of science that "exactitude is recognized then to be always a matter of degree and ceases to

be an all-surpassing ideal. The supremacy of the exact sciences is rejected and psychology, sociology, and the humanities are set free from the vain and misleading efforts of emulating mathematical physics."

Polanyi defines scientific value as the joint product of three virtues: accuracy, range of theory, and interest of subject matter. Sciences less accurate than physics may more than make up for it in other qualities. For example, "The glory of mathematical precision and elegance, in which physics far surpasses biology, is balanced in biology by the much greater interest of its subject matter" (Polanyi 1972: 50).

Many economists view science as nothing but measurement and presume that the exactitude of economic prediction to be its only standard. Milton Friedman's essay "The Methodology of Positive Economics" (1953) is far more representative of the profession's views than any of Friedman's other contributions. For some encouraging signs that some economists are beginning to free themselves from the serious limitations imposed by this view of method, see Caldwell (1982) and McCloskey (1983).

4. Revisionist historians such as Weinstein (1968), Kolko (1963), Horowitz (1971), and Domhoff (1970) have offered incisive criticisms of the actual political structure of modern American society (as opposed to the high school civics class version of it), of the way "our" government acts on behalf of a few powerful special interests rather than on behalf of the majority, and of the way a few wealthy bankers and corporate executives cynically manipulate supposedly democratic institutions to protect their own profits.

5. This idea is by no means unique to Marxism. A very similar conception is conveyed by many of the advocates of planning to be examined later on. Robert Reich (1983: 6) speaks of ending the "cleavage between the business and civic cultures"; Tom Hayden (1982: 43) urges people to integrate their "personal, economic and citizenship roles"; Amitai Etzioni (1983: xii) wants to go beyond the realm of individuals and of government to reach an integration of private and public spheres in "a third realm, the community." The same basic idea even lies behind neoconservative Irving Kristol's desire to allow "our private and public worlds" to achieve "a congenial relationship" (1978: 269).

6. For this interpretation of Marx's theory of central planning, see Reese (1980), Roberts and Stephenson (1973), and Lavoie (1985).

7. By "right things to do" I am referring only to means effective enough to achieve the ends sought by the planners themselves, which for the purpose of this argument can be assumed to have been somehow "democratically" determined. Ascertaining the *ends*, the consumption goods desired, is only half of the problem. The real difficulties arise from trying to put the *means* of production to their more effective uses in order to achieve these ends.

8. The knowledge problem was first systematically formulated by Ludwig von Mises over sixty years ago and was elaborated and extended by the most

famous critic of planning, F. A. Hayek, in repeated forays over the next several decades. Generally called the "calculation problem," this critique of planning has been misunderstood by nearly every economist who has tried to deal with it, and the one economist who had the *most* muddled interpretation, Oskar Lange, is the one widely thought by neoclassical economists to have supplied the conclusive answer to Mises's challenge. See Hoff ([1949] 1981) and Lavoie (1981; 1985). Although several advocates of planning have tried to respond to Hayek's famous statement of the totalitarian problem in *The Road to Serfdom* (1944), few have come to grips with his formulations of the knowledge problem.

2 COORDINATION IN SOCIETY
Tradition, Market, and Planning

Lamarckism, so far as we can judge, is false in the domain it has always occupied—as a biological theory of genetic inheritance. Yet, by analogy only, it is the mode of "inheritance" for another and very different kind of "evolution"—human cultural evolution . . .

Cultural evolution has progressed at rates that Darwinian processes cannot begin to approach. Darwinian evolution continues in *Homo sapiens*, but at rates so slow that it no longer has much impact on our history. This crux in the earth's history has been reached because Lamarckian processes have finally been unleashed upon it.

Stephen Jay Gould (1980: 83–84)

Man probably began with a superior capacity to learn what to do—or even more, what not to do—in different circumstances. And much if not most of what he learnt about what to do he probably learnt by learning the meaning of words. Rules for his conduct which made him adapt what he did to his environment were certainly more important to him than "knowledge" about how other things behaved. In other words: man has certainly more often learnt to do the right thing without comprehending why it was the right thing, and he still is often served better by custom than understanding. Other objects were primarily defined for him by the appropriate way of conduct towards them. It was a repertoire of learnt rules which told him what was the right and what was the wrong way of acting in different circumstances that gave him his increasing capacity to adapt to changing conditions—and particularly to cooperate with the other members of his group. Thus a tradition of rules of conduct existing apart from any one individual who had learnt them began to govern human life. It was when these learnt rules, involving classifications of different kinds of objects, began to include a sort of model of the environment that enabled man to predict and anticipate in action external events, that what we call reason appeared. There *was then probably much more "intelligence" incorporated in the system of rules of conduct than in man's thoughts about his surroundings.*

F. A. Hayek (1979: 157)

THE IMPORTANCE OF COORDINATING PROCESSES

Our species has survived and prospered by means of its unique adaptability, which in turn is made possible by its superior intellect. No other animal depends so heavily on its intellectual abilities, its capacity to understand and rationally alter its natural environment for its own purposes, its ability to *plan* and carry out production projects. (See Adler 1967.)

But the human mind works on an individual level, while economic survival is everywhere social. Rational thought processes, however much they depend on language and other cultural aids supplied by society, operate strictly within individual human brains. A conscious plan for a production project must necessarily reside in the mind of an individual person, yet, except in economics textbooks and other forms of fiction, such production is never found in isolation but is invariably a social phenomenon. In short, because *Homo sapiens* is both an intellectual and a social animal, some sort of knowledge dispersal process or telecommunications system, as Hayek calls it, a procedure for mutual adjustment and orientation, is required to achieve a degree of coordination of the various minds engaged in economic production.

Just as the human being as a biological individual is distinguished from other species by a powerful intellect, so is human society set apart from other animal societies by its greater ability to make effective use of individual minds. Not only is the human being more intelligent individually than, say, the termite or bee, but human society as a whole involves a far more powerful information-processing system than a termite colony or beehive.

These two levels, which could be called individual and social intelligence, are by no means the same. The overall intellectual capacity of several interacting intelligences may be quite different from that of its constituent parts, and it is not immediately evident in general whether the whole would be greater or less than the sum of its parts. Can the termite colony solve more complicated problems than the individual termite? This depends not only on the IQ, if you will, of each of the termites but also, and crucially, on the method of interaction among them. If this interaction process is very crude, it is conceivable that the individuals in a society would have to spend so much of their intellectual capacity on preserving the social structure that the society as a whole might be less effective as a problem solver than the isolated individual. Alternatively, it is just as conceivable that with a sophisticated enough process of interaction the society as a whole could be smarter, so to speak, than any single participant.

In fact, in the case of most social insects, it has been found that they generally interact in such a way that the intellectual capacity of the overall society far exceeds that of any of the participating individuals. The eminent sociobiologist Edward O. Wilson has documented in fascinating detail some of the highly complex activities of social insects in a manner that can illuminate this distinction between individual and social intelligence. Termite colonies have the remarkable ability to regulate precisely the temperature of their intricately constructed and often gigantic hills by sophisticated ventilation techniques that would surely perplex the cleverest single termite. Those bee, ant, and termite species that have evolved societies engage in activities as complicated as the allocation of work forces, the cultivation of crops, and the domestication of other insects.[1] But as Wilson (1971: 224) points out, these impressive feats are not attributable to any individual characteristics of the relevant species:

> The individual social insect, in comparison with the individual solitary insect, displays behavior patterns that are neither exceptionally ingenious nor exceptionally complex. The remarkable qualities of social life are mass phenomena that emerge from the meshing of these simple individual patterns by means of communication. In this principle lies the greatest challenge and opportunity of insect sociology.

This principle of "mass communication" will play a central role in my formulation of the knowledge problem. But my point here is that when we study a social system, we have to focus on the method of mutual coordination among the individuals, and not only on the intelligence of the average individual, in order to determine the system's social intelligence. Insect societies usually coordinate themselves by the use of chemical signals called *pheromones.* Honey bees have evolved a sophisticated sign language in the form of a dance that informs other bees of the distance and direction of flowers. It should not be surprising that we humans may have evolved our own sophisticated processes for social coordination and that our society may also exceed in complexity that which can be comprehended by any of its participants. In any case, an understanding of such processes must be at least as crucial and as great a challenge to sociologists as it has been to entomologists.

What makes this intellectual challenge all the more important in the case of human societies, of course, is the fact that we who are examining them also happen to be living in them, and our well-being—indeed our whole survival—is dependent above all else on the efficacy with which we solve the production problems of our modern, technologically advanced economy. All life, insect as well as human, faces the fundamental problem of scarcity. There is not enough of what we need for survival to go around unless we continually husband our resources and use them wisely. Biological evolution has forced plants and animals to cope relatively efficiently with scarcity in various specialized ways, in the multiplicity of environmental niches in which life can be found. Sociological evolution has produced ways by which the human species can use its remarkable intellectual skills to solve the problems of scarcity and carve out not just one specialized niche but thousands of diverse ones all over the world. The main factor in our relative ability to solve our scarcity problems is our social intelligence.

Each of the three human coordination processes to be discussed in this section—Tradition, Market, and Planning—can be judged according to its relative ability to use effectively the intellectual capacity of the individual minds it coordinates in order to solve problems of scarcity.[2] It may be misleading to speak of these three organizing principles as if they determine the choices of the human minds involved. To say that Tradition permits this or that form of behavior is not intended to imply that there is some disembodied entity called "Tradition" that acts in the world. And unlike much of neoclassical economics, by "Market" I will not mean a mysterious driving force like the notorious "Walrasian auctioneer." The terms "Tradition" and "Market" are meant to be shorthand for forms of social interaction undertaken in all cases by rational human minds. The coordinating process I will call "Planning" is not distinguished from the others by the presence of rational planning of some kind, which is found in all human societies, but by its intention of subsuming the whole of social production under a single rational plan.

Even in its "purest" form, each of these systems, Tradition, Market, and Planning, would necessarily be made up of a complex of elements that could be called traditional in the sense that they are passed on from generation to generation. A pure Market or Planning system, if it could ever exist, would possess very *different* "traditions" from those found in the prehistoric societies that could be called purely "Traditional." But no human society is conceivable that is dissociated from traditions altogether.

No respected social scientist today would deny the need for at least one of these three kinds of ordering processes nor has any coherent fourth been proposed that could take their place. And, of course, each broad category is capable of a myriad of variations. But most contemporary analysts believe that the ideal social system represents some kind of judicious mixture of them. In particular, all the prevalent theories of national economic planning are compromises aspiring not to supplant but to combine the market with planning. But for now I will use the term "Planning" strictly to signify that original engineering notion of comprehensive planning which aims at the complete replacement of Market and Tradition by a fundamentally different method of organization. Only after having elucidated the three basic principles in their pure form will it be possible to address the question of their compatibility.

This book will contend that a deeper understanding of the way each of these processes works would reveal that they, in fact, work according to such different principles that any attempt to conjoin two of them will necessarily result in their working against each other. They are in this sense incompatible. I do not mean to imply that these three organizing principles can never be found together. Indeed, of the three probably only Tradition has ever operated alone as the sole organizing principle of an economy. Every economy of the modern world contains elements of all three organizing principles. Moreover, it is undeniable that there are properly both traditional and planning elements involved in any working market system, such as "traditional" respect for property and the "planning" of a large corporation. Rather, what I mean is that *in its function as a process for social organization* each of these principles is logically irreconcilable with the others. Each in isolation represents a coherent socioeconomic ordering device that is capable of a certain degree of coordination or social intelligence, while any two in combination will necessarily clash with each other in such a way as to produce less coherence than is possible by one of them alone.

By this latter statement I do not mean to suggest that each of these three alone would work better than *any* combination of them. Rather, I am claiming that whichever of these three in its pure form can be shown to be capable of attaining a higher degree of social intelligence than the others would work better in this regard than any combination with those others.

Essentially the argument is that each—Tradition, Market, and Planning—has its own logic by which it generates social order through its selection of production methods. The organizing principle I am calling Tradition relies on either tacit or articulated rules or taboos to preserve productive techniques that were proven workable over the slow course of biological and cultural evolution. The Market involves a very different and much faster procedure for selecting alternative methods of production by means of economic competition for money profit. The Planning principle represents a bold idea, as yet never actually implemented, by which social production as a whole is to be democratically chosen and deliberately embarked upon, rather than left to emerge haphazardly as an unplanned outcome of biological, cultural, or economic competition.

TRADITION

Mankind arrived on the evolutionary scene already equipped with a set of production techniques supplied by habitual behavior that traces back to earlier primates. The oldest methods of production of our primate ancestors seem to have been various forms of hunting and gathering, organized in small, self-sufficient, and mobile bands, with a very rudimentary division of labor, a form of economy not drastically different (other than in the presence of food sharing) from that of modern baboons and chimpanzees. This hunter-gatherer economy constitutes the social environment in which the human race acquired—over some five million years—the basic genetic make-up that *does* sharply distinguish it from other primates, such as the physical equipment for thought, speech, and the upright walking that freed the use of the hands. Although this genetic equipment, especially the brain size, changed rapidly during the last half-million of those years, physical anthropologists agree that it cannot have altered much in the past ten thousand years. But during this period humanity's socioeconomic systems have changed and quite dramatically. Thus, it appears that something other than genetic change is involved in the emergence of human civilization.

During those early millions of years the human species gradually refined its tool-making abilities. The main tool evolved in this early period was not directly the physical brain or hands or the stone implements they produced but, more fundamentally, a new way of passing along habits to succeeding generations. Heretofore no animal had so refined the ability to pass along acquired characteristics that proved conducive to survival. Evolution, which had been strictly biological, or Mendelian, became cultural or Lamarckian. With the development of cultural tradition, even habits learned within the lifetime of one man or woman could be incorporated into traditions and physical artifacts and passed on to future generations, without waiting for the slow operation of purely biological evolution. Each generation could furthermore modify traditions passed on to it, and, in turn, pass these modifications on to the next generations, in an unending series of intergenerational changes.

One of the crucial ways in which we are different from other animals is in the length of time our offspring must be nurtured and trained. While all the higher animals engage in training and simple learning through imitation (playing, for kittens, is at least in part a method of training to become adult predators), humans must pass through an apprenticeship or enculturation in an intricate cultural environment involving such institutions as language, law, customs, production methods, religious ritual, and the like. Thus, while it is misleading to refer to the behavior of most animals as strictly determined by their genes—since some attributes can also be passed along by example to the young—it is absurd to speak of humans as so determined. For us, it is our upbringing that is the major influence on our character. As geneticist Theodosius Dobzhansky once put it, "In a sense human genes have surrendered their primacy in human evolution to an entirely new non-biological or superorganic agent, culture" (quoted in Wilson 1975: 550). Of course, biology still dictates the broad constraints over our physical and mental capacities, but within those overall limits the cultural domain rules.

The force of natural selection working through the mechanisms of differential reproduction remains operative as the basis of biological change. At this stage humans engage in life-or-death struggle with other animals, including other humans. Biological competition still occurs, but there is now a new kind of information bearer beyond DNA and a new source of change beyond the random and thus excruciatingly slow process of genetic mutation with natural selection. There is now the possibility of cultural "mutation" and the selection and preservation of acquired cultural and technological habits.

The fact that traditions can be lastingly revised without awaiting random gene mutation does not imply that the human species has at this stage become master of its own development. While cultural traditions are products of human minds, they are not in general deliberate constructs of rational design either. To take one of the most important examples of cultural tradition, nobody really invented language in the sense of conceiving the result in advance and then constructing it. Traditions are not rationally planned, but neither are they carried in our genes. Tool-making skills can be imparted to the young and preserved even though their rationale may not be understood and long before their biological advantage could become manifest. Much anthropological analysis has suffered by debating the question of whether human traits are genetic, and thus selected by evolution and transmitted biologically, or are cultural, and thus selected by conscious choice and transmitted verbally. In fact, some of the most important features of human societies represent neither genetic nor rational habits, but rather constitute traditions that are neither consciously understood nor genetically transferred. They make up what Hayek calls a "third source of human values."[3]

Thus, although early humans' mental superiority over other species was already a significant factor in their evolutionary struggle with the others, early humans cannot yet be said to have gained intellectual mastery over their own productive processes. Primitive peoples do not, in a sense, really know what they are doing or why. The particular form their overall methods of economic survival take is never deliberately chosen as such. Instead it gradually emerges in the interplay of choices by which those methods survive that seem to best fit the ecological niche in which the particular band happens to find itself.

The organizing principle of Tradition—sustained by social pressure on members of the band who break the (mostly implicit) cultural rules and occasionally revised when circumstances change—represents the basic prehistoric mechanism for the selection of methods of economic production. There is obviously great variety and apparent ingenuity in the economic processes with which hunting and gathering societies reproduce themselves. Still, there is little more reason to refer to these processes as "consciously designed" than there would be to call a complex ant colony an invention of some clever ant. Particular production processes are invented and occasionally passed along from generation to generation. Incremental changes are made and, where they prove successful, preserved. But the overall shape of the system of production is never chosen by anybody.

The highest productive achievement of Tradition was the adoption of agriculture, which required an evolved adaptation involving considerable changes in social rules. This, in turn, made human civilization possible. The very fact of settling down that accompanied this mode of production drastically altered our species' ability both to produce and to reproduce, for one of the serious disadvantages of the hunter-gatherer society seems to have been its inability to support population growth at anywhere near the rate that would be biologically possible. Although some anthropologists such as Richard Leakey wax eloquent about the carefree "abundant society" of hunter-gatherers, even Leakey agrees that some form of deliberate infanticide (usually female) or abortion was a regular feature of many of these societies. Infant mortality was so high in these societies that many communities were able to maximize the number of their adult offspring by devoting scarce resources only to the healthiest males and on fewer females. In either case, whether babies were killed deliberately or not, life was anything but rosy.[4] Agriculture made larger families possible and led to a rapidly improved economic ability to support the world's growing population.

When the human species first began the gradual adoption of agriculture and the domestication of animals, it was not because some farsighted social reformer sent around petitions that urged the abandonment of the hunting and gathering economy and urged the adoption of this new form of production with all its attendant benefits. Definite advantages accrued to those who learned to collect seeds systematically, to return to planting sites seasonally, and eventually to settle down permanently. Those bands which hit upon methods

for improving the "gathering" of plants by replanting seeds and cultivation and for improving the "hunting" of animals by gradual steps
in the direction of domestication and breeding found themselves
adopting the new economic system. Though relatively rapid by the
usual biological standards, and undoubtedly revolutionary in its consequences, the transition from primitive to agricultural economies
was quite slow by the standards of modern society. They took place
over the span of hundreds, perhaps thousands, of years. Both the
higher productivity and the definite reproductive advantages that
were made possible by the agricultural methods bestowed advantages
on those bands that began to practice such methods, resulting in an
eventual replacement of the improved form of production for the
old. Indeed, as noted archeologist Grahame Clark (1977: 41) put it,
the adoption of agriculture was "the platform on which civilizations
have had to build."

MARKET

If agriculture was the platform for building civilization, the market
was the brick and mortar. Every known prehistoric civilization from
the Sumerian to the Mayan shows ample evidence of regularized
trade relations, the use of money, and central marketplaces.[5] It even
seems likely that written language owes its origin to the emergence
of markets and the need for keeping accounting records.[6] And the
emergence of market relations was no more a social invention than
was the introduction of agriculture. Again, individual acts of trade,
which probably evolved out of the reciprocal gift-giving traditions of
primitive societies, bestowed biologically and culturally competitive
advantages on those who stumbled upon them, and hence they were
preserved. Nobody decides to begin to use a money; rather, through
mutually reinforcing incremental changes in traditional habits, a
money with its system of prices evolves.

Still it is cultural tradition with its largely tacit rules and habits
which constitutes human society's procedure for the selection of
production processes.[7] With agriculture, it had already become necessary for societies to adopt more systematic rules with respect to
property rights over land and domesticated animals. Now, with the
gradual emergence of exchange relations as an increasingly dominant
feature of society, these rules themselves begin to undergo modifi-

cation. Those cultures that refine their rules in such a way as to define and protect "private property" more effectively find that market relations are thereby enhanced.[8] The productivity of such societies spontaneously surges ahead of those that fail to adjust in this way, just as had happened with the emergence of agriculture.

At first market relations simply involve the trading of the products of traditional—now mostly agricultural—methods of production. But as the pervasiveness of money and prices increases, a deeper change in the economic structure of society begins to take shape. The mode in which the forces of natural selection operate undergoes a fundamental change that will prove to be of tremendous significance for human progress. Until this point, to the extent that any experimentation with production processes could occur at all, the cost of a persistent mistake might well be the gradual elimination in biological competition of the whole cultural group. With the development of a price system, a new production technique can be tried by an individual according to his anticipation of profit. If it proves to be a mistake, it results not in the decline of the whole community but merely economic loss to that individual. The society changes, in other words, from being one in which markets exist alongside traditional activities to one that is *driven* by the Market organizing principle.

Thus, if the emergence of Tradition marks a significant new way of *introducing* lasting modifications in productive techniques beyond those that can be channeled through genetic mutation, then the emergence of the Market signifies an equally important change in the way productive techniques are *selected*: by economic rather than biological competition.

As the modern work on the "rational peasant" shows, the member of a traditional society is typically a minimizer of risk.[9] In traditional societies it is quite rational to be reluctant to diverge from old and established methods. One of the chief advantages of the Market as a coordinating process relative to Tradition is that it facilitates a far more diverse and rapid experimentation with new productive techniques.

With technological experimentation now so much less costly, productive methods can change much more rapidly as guided by the attraction (or repulsion) of potential profit (or loss). The production methods of society are freed from the relatively rigid constraints imposed by the risk-averse adherents of traditional methods and now become increasingly dictated by the new standard of profitability. The refinement of a more complex division of labor, the extension of an increasingly complex capital structure, and the bringing of once separate and self-sufficient communities into contact and eventually economic interdependence with one another proceed at an unprecedented pace. The profit and loss calculations of entrepreneurs rather than the adherence to cultural tradition begin to assert themselves as the main procedure for the selection of production techniques.

This new market-oriented system evolving out of traditional society represents the first occasion of a clash between two basically different economic organizing processes. Market forces continually press for technological change, encouraging ever more efficient techniques to win out in economic competition, while the remnants of cultural tradition exert a pull on members of society to preserve techniques that had long proven successful in biological and cultural competition. Some societies resist the tremendous changes, but generally the higher productivity that accompanies the market system proves irresistible despite the havoc exchange relations wreak on many established traditions.

Traditional farmers, for example, taught to consider the land sacred, now find themselves selling or renting it for money. Indeed, virtually everything appears to be reduced to what Marxists call the "cash nexus," to the all-encompassing attribute of market valuation. While the advantages of this universalization of market relations are immense, the disadvantages should not be ignored. Many established traditional practices and ideas are utterly incompatible with the new, more productive form of economy and are swept aside by it.[10]

It is important to recognize that the market process itself depends on the preservation of many ingrained cultural and productive habits and itself only evolves by incremental adjustments to these traditional modes of behavior. The Market does not so much destroy tradition as mold it into new shapes and extend it to cover new areas of human interaction. Nonetheless, it can sensibly be said that as the basic process for selecting production techniques, Tradition has lost its former monopoly to such a degree that the most prevalent alternatives of the modern world are Planning and the Market.

One of the most significant changes in social relations that is necessitated by the transformation of society's organizing principle from Tradition to Market is in the manner and the complexity of interpersonal coordination. In a traditional economy, techniques of production change so slowly, usually over several generations, that there is no real problem in keeping up with the technological advancement. The only coordination that is required is the mutual adjustments of members of the small community in their implementation of the established traditional production techniques. And even there the coordination required is quite simple since the several members of the community are essentially engaged in the carrying out of a single "plan," although it may not be consciously thought of in these terms. They articulate to one another, both by spoken language and otherwise, their expected actions in order to deliberately coordinate them. The required coordination is the kind of face-to-face adjustment of members of a hunting team or the relatively simple allocation of labor time needed for the harvest.

The Market changes all that. The sheer number of persons whose productive activity has to be mutually coordinated grows until it includes most of the world's population. Simultaneously, the complexity and variability of this productive activity increases even more dramatically. Whereas it had been possible within traditional society to achieve a more or less complete coordination of actions of members of the community in their production activities according to one established technology, in the Market this becomes quite impossible. Instead, the most that the Market can achieve is a tendency for adjustment where at any moment thousands of parts of social production involving a variety of technologies are maladjusted but where definite coordinating forces are always operative. Rather than one simple unchanging plan within an isolated community, we have millions of complicated plans, all struggling with and adapting to one another in an unending flux of changing productive relationships.

The main procedure by which the Market achieves that degree of coordination of which it is capable is rivalrous competition in the pursuit of money profits. The contrary tugs and pulls of the various market participants bidding prices up or down constitute the driving force of mutual coordination. When a price is discovered to be too low (or too high), competitors in pursuit of profit will rush in to buy at the excessively low (or sell at the excessively high) price, this very response thus tending to drive up the low (and down the high) price. In this way the very discovery of a relatively uncoordinated situation, as revealed by prices so configured as to enable the discoverer to make pure profit by dealing at those prices, is itself the process by which the discoordination is removed. Competitive activity in the market system is clear evidence of the necessarily incomplete state of the system's coordination. It is also the system's method for achieving whatever degree of coordination it can.

It is the competitive quest for profit that directs productive activity in a Market, and it is the complex configuration of consumers' wants as registered in their expenditures which dictates where profits are to be made. Factors of production are not intrinsically valuable. They are valuable only because of their indirect ability to produce goods and services demanded by consumers. All "higher order" goods such as tools, machinery, labor hours, land, factories, raw materials, and the like receive imputed value first in accordance with their expected capacity to produce "lower order" goods that are less remote from the consumer, and ultimately from the relative allocation of the consumer's dollar to the various lowest order goods.[11] It is inherent in this system that those consumers who have more dollars will thereby command more influence, directly and indirectly, over the whole economy.

It should be noted that this "competitive" market process does not require that the rivals take any particular industrial or organizational form. The market process is certainly not presumed to be "competitive" in the neoclassical economist's sense; in this perfect competition model, there are so many firms in each industry that no competitor can substantially influence the outcome. Neither must it be thought composed of single, self-employed entrepreneurs. Its rivals will, on the contrary, often be firms—that is, individuals with a common goal combined in an organization. It may be composed of thousands of small rivals in a single industry or of an oligopoly of a few giants or even of a single corporation that is coextensive with an entire industry. What makes an industry competitive is the degree to which *entry* of new rivals into that industry is politically restricted or free. It is the threat of competition from other (perhaps only potential) firms or individuals that makes an industry competitive.

The extent of advantage that comes from rivalrous competition is not proportional to the number of competitors, as is often assumed by researchers in industrial organization. Cost advantages gained from larger scale production, purchasing, or sales will often spawn very large firms. Thus the relevant "rivals" upon whose contention the competitive process depends should not be thought of as individuals but rather as "islands of planning," whose size is itself a result of competitive forces.

Moreover, competition should not be thought to occur only within an industry. An industry can only be defined by cutting an arbitrary line through a continuum of similar firms producing comparable products. All contenders for profit in the market process compete for the consumer's direct or indirect expenditures of money.

Clearly whether one favors Tradition or Market, these first two principles of economic organization are, in the relevant sense, incompatible. Tradition resists the perpetual innovation of productive technique and seeks to preserve only that which has proven itself after many years of cultural evolution. As an organizing principle, the Market resists the traditional separation of mankind into isolated communities. It seeks to integrate all peoples into one world economy, in which productive techniques change at the breakneck pace dictated by economic competition. While, again, the Market itself relies on many of the evolved linguistic, legal, and cultural traditions that trace back to primitive societies (though they have been substantially altered), it does not permit Tradition to continue to dictate the methods of social production. It does not allow Tradition to act as the basic organizing principle of the economy. One cannot produce what one's ancestors did and simultaneously also produce what the consumers (directly or indirectly) currently make profitable in the market. If the Market is to be allowed to flourish and to work its logic on the economic processes of society, it must necessarily be allowed to replace the traditional modes of economic activity. Whether the fruits of technological progress made possible by the market system are worth its costs in the upheaval of long-standing cultural traditions may be debated. But that as systems Tradition and the Market are fundamentally divergent paths for society to take and that society cannot consistently embark upon both of these paths at once seems indisputable.

PLANNING

The idea of Planning as a third alternative economic system can be seen as a reflection of an understandable dissatisfaction with either Traditional or Market processes. Whereas Market as a process for coordinating economic activity may seem haphazard, replete with irrationalities, and dangerously conducive to divisive, antisocial attitudes, Tradition seems hopelessly primitive. The notion of comprehensive planning implicit in Marxism and in most of the classic social-ist literature was invented in order to restore what was seen as the social cohesiveness of the traditional economy while also retaining the advances in productive technology made possible by the Market system.

Comprehensive planning was supposed to achieve for the first time a stage of progress where humanity could actually "fashion its own history," and design its own paths for future development on a scien-tific basis. Such conscious, rational development was unthinkable within the confines of traditional society, because, as has been argued, traditional productive methods were not deliberately chosen but spontaneously emerged out of a gradual process of biological and cultural evolution. Primitive people are not yet intellectually ad-vanced or self-conscious enough to consider the idea of subsuming their productive efforts under a common plan for all of humanity. But the Market is also incompatible with this notion. The Market fundamentally depends on a rivalrous competition among its partici-pants in order to achieve whatever degree of plan coordination of which it is capable. While the Market has substituted the more rapid selection process of economic competition for the primitive selection process of biological competition, it is nevertheless still a competitive struggle rather than a series of deliberate scientific decisions that determines humanity's economic development.

Marx was quite willing to credit the Market with having intro-duced rational, scientific planning on a partial basis. However chaotic he thought competitive coordination processes between factories were, within a factory the productive activities were seen as deliber-ately coordinated with one another according to a plan conceived by the capitalist.[12] Indeed, the Market practically forces the factory owner to run the plant according to the latest advances of engineer-ing science.

This is not to say that the decisionmakers within one capitalist firm have really attained a fully detailed comprehension of all the causal forces they employ in the production process. Productive activity still amounts to incremental changes to habitual modes of behavior that producers pass along to successive "generations" of producers and alter in accordance with their reading of profit and loss indications, about the causes of which they have virtually no knowledge. Thus, just as we can argue that producers in traditional society do not really know what they are doing but, rather, do mostly what they have always done so long as it works, so can we argue that even in market society producers do not in a sense really know what they are doing.[13] Their knowledge is entirely dependent on the context of market relationships in which they are embedded. The vast majority of the variables that determine the causal processes that appear to be subsumed under any one producer's plan are in fact out of his or any single agent's control, and are continually being nudged this way and that by the rivalrous competition that takes place among capitalists. This is exactly one of the features Marx hated most about capitalism.

While the Market's unprecedented advances in productive technique were easy to admire, its essentially rivalrous form of organization was not. The loss of the sense of social cohesion that had existed in the traditional community renders the individual an alienated being, with no recognizable place in society, forever being jostled about by market forces over which he or she has no control. At least society ruled by Tradition seemed to have an overall purpose. It often had some sort of chieftain who could express such a "social will," and was coordinated in close-knit personal interaction in a way that made it possible for people actually to carry out communal goals together. The Market seems to abandon communal goals altogether and to work its own logic on social transformation without need or appeal to any communal will.

Not that the people who lived in the emerging Market systems haven't earnestly *tried* to retain an agency for the expression of the communal will. The agency to which people have turned for the articulation and execution of social goals is the state. I would agree, however, with Marx's view that government, at least in every historical case to date, cannot be said to constitute a genuine agent of rational Planning. It cannot design the course of its society's development, since it has always existed in combination with one or both of the other organizing processes, each of which has a powerful logic of its own. Is a production process to be selected because it conforms to established tradition, or because it appears profitable to some individual competitor, or because it has been deliberately chosen to conform to the (presumably democratically expressed) social will? Historically governments have not resolved this issue but have been only imperfect attempts to override the logic of Tradition or the Market.

Governments are vested with special coercive powers in the hope of placing themselves above the social order so that they can try to give to that order a measure of overall cohesiveness and guidance. But whatever a government within a Market system can be said to do, it cannot be called the Planning of the whole of social production. The selection of productive techniques is still the unplanned outcome of competition for profit among separately formulated plans, which include the particularly powerful and significant plans of the government. However, these separate plans are not *subsumed* under the one conscious will of government. Unless government plans come to dominate the market completely and replace its several competing plans with one comprehensive social plan, of which all productive activity becomes a part, there really is no Planning proper, but only governmental interference in an order that is fundamentally Market driven. Whether such government intervention would be preferable to a wholly Market-driven order is a separate question to which we will have occasion to return.

Whatever special powers such a government within a Market may have, it necessarily depends on the Market-generated environment in which it buys its material factors and labor services, and from which it must obtain credit. Thus, as perceptive Marxist critics of state capitalism have often charged, those who hold the purse strings in the Market, in particular those large industrialists and bankers who have privileged, state-protected, access to the cartelized credit markets, ultimately circumscribe the actions of governments. Indeed, the same can be said of the so-called socialist governments in Eastern Europe, who also must rely to a large extent on Western banks for credit.

The point is not to suggest that the world is run from the boardrooms of Chase Manhattan and Citibank, but simply to acknowledge that no government is isolated from the world's market institutions, or can survive without to some extent bending to their influence. In no developed country in the world can governmental leaders completely ignore or override the logic of the Market. Despite its system of central planning, the Soviet economy relies on prices, both internal and international, and measures of profitability to organize its economy (to the degree it ever *is* organized).[14] Production processes there as elsewhere are selected as a consequence of competitive struggles among separate producers. That these competitive struggles are often political rivalries rather than financial ones is significant but does not alter the fact that all these economies are fundamentally organized by Market-type forces that governments can drastically affect but cannot ignore.

The government, if it is powerful enough, can make itself a very influential consumer bidding against the other consumers and skewing profits toward the tastes of those who control governmental institutions. It might be thought that the government could in this way preserve the Market and yet genuinely control the economy by making itself the sole consumer, thereby dictating which factors are to receive imputed value, and thus which productive activities are to be undertaken by competing profit-seeking owners. But if such competitors are to attract labor services—the most important of all factors of production—they must be able to pay wages that the workers can use for something. If there is a labor market, there must also be a consumer market. Hence, so long as it refrains from taking over and planning in detail the whole of productive activity, government cannot deliberately direct the economy but can only exert an admittedly powerful influence into a market process that is under no single agent's control.[15]

Comprehensive planning, then, as Marx and his early followers conceived it, represents an attempt to institute Planning as an organizing principle in its purest form. It consistently entails the complete abolition of the Market as an organizing principle. Techniques of production are no longer to be selected by biological, cultural, or economic competition but instead are to be consciously, deliberately decided upon, carefully inserted into a single scientific plan, and then carried out by cooperating—rather than rivalrous—members of society. Institutions such as money, banks, stock markets, profit and loss accounting, advertising, and even prices would have no more place in the post-Market consciously directed society than they would have had in pre-Market traditional communities.

Although only a few of the contemporary advocates of planning would still view their goal as necessarily involving the complete abolition of the use of money, this was the serious aim of the classical Marxists.[16] While it is easy to sympathize with the modern planners' practical standpoint, which doubts that any advanced economy could possibly dispense with money, nevertheless the Marxists' aversion to money reflects a crucial insight on their part into the way a monetary system works, an insight from which most contemporary advocates of planning could learn. By its very nature money is an unplannable institution. The holding of money balances constitutes the temporary withholding of an unspecified demand, which can at any future time and on the whim of its possessor turn into a specific demand. If transactors were certain of the future direction and timing of their expenditures, they could hold interest-bearing assets that could come due at the desired times and places. The very use of money reflects a deep-seated uncertainty permeating the economy about its own future evolutionary direction. It is this same pervasive uncertainty about the future development of the economy that the idea of comprehensive planning aspires to eliminate.[17]

Thus, comprehensive planning represents nothing less than the ambitious aspiration of entirely replacing the competitive market system with a deliberate precoordination of all productive activity, incorporating it into a single hierarchical structure. Goals will be consciously broken down into distinct tasks for departments to carry out according to a single, chosen blueprint. How this plan is to be decided upon is another matter. We can suppose that free democratic referenda are held frequently to design the plans and that public-spirited officials eagerly try to carry them out. In any case it has to be acknowledged that this idea of Planning is a conceptually coherent alternative to the Market principle of social coordination which, even if rarely defended today, is at least a legitimate alternative that ought to be considered.

In fact at the time when this notion was first formulated, around the middle of the last century, the classical economists did not have a very convincing economic argument against it. All their analysis was directed at showing that government intervention into the Market will almost always bring about greater problems than it solves. Proponents of comprehensive planning might well be willing to accept this argument and insist that, so long as government exists within the Market, it is doomed to be a source of damaging shocks to what in their view is already a rather disorganized system, instead of a source of genuinely helpful guidance of the economy. It took practical (and catastrophic) experience with an attempt to implement comprehensive planning and two forceful theoretical critiques (the "knowledge problem" and the "totalitarian problem") by, among others, the twentieth-century Austrian economists Mises and Hayek, to dislodge this program from its dominance among planning proposals.[18]

THE CHOICES BEFORE US

Humankind's amazing development is primarily the result of gradual but ultimately radical revisions of the evolutionary process itself. Biological evolution works by means of genetic mutation and the reproductive transmission of those genes that survive the elimination process of natural selection. Our first major modification of evolution came with our development of the ability to adopt and retain beneficial characteristics without relying exclusively on slow genetic processes. This was accomplished mainly through the development of language and other cultural institutions. Effective habits could then be retained by cultural *Traditions* imparted to the young and need not be carried by genes. Our species' second major revision of its own evolutionary processes came with its adoption of economic as opposed to biological competition. Bad or ineffective practices could now be eliminated because they make, or are expected to make, monetary losses in the *Market.*

With these two fundamental modifications of evolutionary processes, *Homo sapiens* has substantially accelerated the rate of the species' own development and, in particular, its improvements in productive techniques. The material benefits resulting from the technological revolution and capital formation have in turn freed the human imagination from its exclusive concentration on mere biological survival, to devote itself to an unprecedented enrichment of its understanding of the natural environment and of the scientific laws that govern our technology.

We come into our own as genuinely rational beings, for the first time capable of applying the achievements of modern science to the planning of our own activities, of being not just animals subject to nature's laws but engineers consciously using natural law to achieve our own goals.

Yet there appears to be an inherent limit within the Market-organized society that prevents us from taking what would appear to be the *next* logical step in our natural progression toward rationality, self-consciousness, and the mastery of mind over matter. Though the human is necessarily a social being, even more so now under the world Market system than ever before, we conduct our rational plans for economic production in a sense individually. Economic production as a whole is not a single scientific plan but still an evolutionary outcome of an unplanned competitive clash among a multitude of separately conceived and mutually inconsistent plans. The first two advances humankind has achieved that raise us above simple biological evolution have not yet freed us from evolutionary processes themselves. They have only quickened the pace of such processes. The bold challenge Marx issued to social thinkers was to make us imagine a third stage of human development that would for the first time make the human race truly the master of its own destiny by means of *Planning.*

But of course to imagine such a stage is not to demonstrate its practicability. Despite the fact that the desire for comprehensive planning has been one of the major ideological forces of this century—and the professed aim of several governments for decades—no existing society has yet come close to this Marxist idea of a fundamental transcendence of evolutionary processes and a genuine dominance of mind over nature. The question arises: Is such a system even possible?

NOTES TO CHAPTER 2

1. As Lewis Thomas (1974: 12) puts it, with charming hyperbole:

    Ants are so much like human beings as to be an embarrassment. They farm fungi, raise aphids as livestock, launch armies into wars, use chemical sprays to alarm and confuse enemies, and capture slaves. The families of weaver ants engage in child labor, holding their larvae like shuttles to spin out the thread that sews the leaves together for their fungus gardens. They exchange information ceaselessly. They do everything but watch television.

2. Whenever the words tradition, market, and planning are capitalized, they are to be understood in this special sense, *as distinct principles for economic coordination.* Only in this restricted sense can it be said that Tradition, Market, and Planning are incompatible with one another.

    The next chapter will compare their strengths as social coordinating processes, but the aim of the remainder of this section will simply be to clarify the nature and origins of each of the three fundamental principles of economic coordination and to show how radically different they are from one another.

3. For example, much of the debate between sociobiologists and cultural anthropologists (see Caplan 1978) proceeds as if the only alternatives were unmalleable hereditary aspects of human nature and perfectly malleable, human-made, rational institutions. That a certain institution is too

complex to have been deliberately designed is not evidence that it must have been genetically conditioned. See the remarkable appendix to volume 3 of Hayek's *Law, Legislation and Liberty* (1979), which inspired much of this chapter's argument.

4. It was Marshall Sahlins (1972) who, in a fit of "dialectical" overreaction to anthropologists who exaggerated the harshness of preagricultural societies, chose to refer to the primitive economy as "the original affluent society." Basing his analysis largely on the seemingly undemanding conditions of the few remaining hunter-gatherer societies in modern times, especially the Kung San of northern Botswana, Sahlins points out that in several surviving primitive societies the average number of hours of labor required is surprisingly small (on the order of two hours per day). The argument can certainly be made that since populations were apt to be kept down (by occasional natural disasters) to a size that survived the very worst of times, life may have tended to be "easy" most of the time. Sahlins does not seem to have considered either the possibility (1) that surviving hunter-gatherer societies might in fact be highly unrepresentative of ancient ones and indeed might comprise those few cases where it was this unusual abundance that kept them from changing to agriculture, or (2) that hours of labor worked is not a very meaningful measure of the standard of living when, for instance, infanticide might be necessary. "Abundance" of other goods may have held, but there was a serious *shortage* of opportunities to bring children into the world. In any case Leakey (1978: 108) uncritically adopts Sahlins's terminology while at the same time conceding the "sad, but necessary" fact that abortion and infanticide are necessary methods of survival for these so-called affluent peoples. See also on this point Marvin Harris (1980: 67–68), who complains that the increase in productive capacity due to labor-saving capital goods has not resulted in "saving labor," in terms of reducing the number of hours worked per day, but has merely caused population growth; that is, it "has not been used to improve living standards but to produce additional children." The idea that the ability to raise several children to adulthood might be considered one of the most cherished parts of a person's standard of living does not seem to occur to these writers.

5. I use "money" in a broad sense to include regular media of exchange in which prices are enumerated, whether or not the institution has yet developed to the stage where only one such medium dominates the society. In many ancient communities the money doubled as one of the major factors of production. In ancient Greece, Rome, Mesopotamia, and Asia Minor, for example, payments were made and prices were reckoned in cattle. Carl Menger found that all of the following commodities were at some time and place once used for money: animal skins, precious metals, slaves, salt, wax, cod, tobacco, sugar, ivory, dates, tea bricks, glass beads, millet,

and "cocoa beans in small bags containing 8,000 to 24,000 beans." Clearly some of these commodities have proven less able than others to survive into modern times as the economy's medium of exchange, but in its day each served in the same economic function as dollars do for us today. (See Menger [1870] 1981: 262–271.)

6. Clark (1977: 91) points out that "much of the credit for the alphabet on which the literature of the western world has ever since been based must rest with the aesthetically unattractive businessmen of Phoenicia" who developed it for practical trading purposes.

7. Of course many important rules are explicitly articulated and passed along deliberately as part of the culturally enforced training of the young. Primitive peoples typically grow up consciously learning such things as kinship rules over who can marry whom or how to prepare for religious ceremonies. But much of the important transmission of cultural attributes in human society has been substantially unconscious. Typically transmitted by imitation and practice are skills involving tacit elements that neither teacher nor student are able to articulate. And even with respect to explicitly learned rules that serve definite social functions, generally the *reason* why they are necessary for the society is not understood. In either case there is a sense in which primitive people can be said to be only partly conscious of the rules they depend on for their survival. As I argue subsequently, however, the same can be said of modern man.

8. Hayek (1982) borrows the phrase "several property" from H. S. Maine, while Michael Polanyi (1951) uses the adjective "polycentric"; either term seems to be a more accurate designation for the alternative to common or state ownership than the more usual "private property." While rivalrous contention among owners rests on the existence of this kind of ownership, it is by no means necessary that the ownership be of any particular historically familiar form. It is only necessary that ownership be polycentric as opposed to centrally planned—that is, that it be divided among "several" different agents. Owners could be workers' councils, stockholders, wealthy capitalists, maverick entrepreneurs, or any combination of these or other as yet unimagined arrangements so long as their plans are separately devised, their person and property legally protected, and their projects permitted to strive in open competition for scarce resources.

9. See Barlett (1976), Chibnik (1980), and Gladwin (1979).

10. Indeed Karl Polanyi (1957) considers it one of the great advantages of modern government that it can slow down these drastic social transformations being caused by the rapid economic growth of the self-regulated market, and keep these changes from destroying culture altogether. While I disagree, I do find this the most plausible case for a useful role of government intervention into a market.

11. I use Menger's distinction between higher and lower orders of production, which has been extended in the capital theory of the Austrian school of economics.

12. Numerous passages in Marx's work suggest that he thought of an individual scientifically organized factory as a model in many respects of what the entire planned society was to be like. To take one of his more famous quotes, Marx chided his critics with the remark that "the enthusiastic apologists of the factory system have nothing more damning to urge against a general organization of the labour of society, than that it would turn all society into one immense factory" ([1867] 1967: 356). See the more extended discussion of these issues in Lavoie (1985: ch. 2), where I argue that the entire planning movement was originally inspired and long dominated by this extreme but usually only implicit conception of planning. Today the relatively few serious scholars in economics who continue to advocate comprehensive planning, are doing so from a self-consistent (but myopic) Marxist perspective. In addition, there are many neoclassical economists who spend their time devising abstract "planometric" planning models, some of which, were they thought to be practicable, would have to be described as a variety of computer-aided comprehensive planning. Many of the leading "planometricians," however, have admirably resisted the temptation to view these models as applicable to the real world. See Hurwicz (1973).

13. In neoclassical economics the assumption is typically made that at the producer's disposal is a complete set of recipes upon which to draw in order to respond to any conceivable configuration of prices. But this assumption precludes any need for experimentation with alternative methods of production, which is, in the real world, one of the producer's primary tasks.

14. See Nutter (1983), Michael Polanyi (1951), and Roberts (1971) for discussions of how the Soviet-type economy works.

15. Later chapters will go further to argue that such influence as a government can exert within a market will, except by accident, be discoordinating.

16. Roberts (1971) convincingly documents this point.

17. See Vorhies (1982), Roberts and Stephenson (1973), and Lavoie (1983) for sympathetic discussions of Marx's disequilibrium monetary theory.

18. The practical experience to which I refer is the "War Communism" period in the Soviet Union, when Lenin actually attempted to abolish the market and found the results so catastrophic that he eventually had to retreat completely from this policy. See Roberts (1971) and Richman (1981).

3 THE KNOWLEDGE PROBLEM

I am suggesting, in fact, that the co-ordinating functions of the market are but a special case of co-ordination by mutual adjustment. In the case of science, adjustment takes place by taking note of published results of other scientists; while in the case of the market, mutual adjustment is mediated by a system of prices broadcasting current exchange relations, which make supply meet demand.

Michael Polanyi (1962: 52)

The business man who forms an expectation is doing precisely what a scientist does when he formulates a working hypothesis. Both, business expectation and scientific hypothesis serve the same purpose; both reflect on attempt at cognition and orientation in an imperfectly known world, both embody imperfect knowledge to be tested and improved by later experience.

Ludwig Lachmann (1978: 23)

After all, what is Competition? Is it a thing which exists and is self-acting like the cholera? No, Competition is only the absence of constraint. In what concerns my own interest, I desire to choose for myself, not that another should choose for me, or in spite of me—that is all. And if any one pretends to substitute his judgment for mine in what concerns me, I should ask to substitute mine for his in what concerns him. What guarantee have we that things would go on better in this way? It is evident that Competition is Liberty. To take away the liberty of acting is to destroy the possibility, and consequently the power, of choosing, of judging, of comparing; it is to annihilate intelligence.

Frederic Bastiat ([1850] 1978: 328–29)

KNOWLEDGE VS. DATA:
THE NATURE OF THE PROBLEM

Each of the three kinds of coordinating processes discussed in the last chapter is intrinsically capable, within a given span of time, of attaining some degree of coordination, or in other words, each is capable of attaining a particular level of "social intelligence." The historical record strongly suggests that Tradition is a relatively crude ordering process, incapable of producing anything much more advanced than the agricultural peasant economy. The Market as a coordinating process has historically proven to be substantially more powerful, while the few serious attempts at Planning have been, for whatever reasons, thus far unsuccessful.

But how does the Market attain such a relatively high degree of social intelligence, and why can't Planning replicate this performance? In brief, the advanced technology that market organization based on private ownership of the means of production has made possible requires that the dispersed knowledge of thousands of individual minds be marshaled in a manner of which comprehensive planning is logically incapable.

Put another way, the evolution of markets has delivered us into a world too complex for any individual intelligence to comprehend in detail, thus necessitating our reliance on the greater social intelligence embodied in market processes. These market processes, if they are to generate and embody a high degree of social intelligence, require relatively free competition among (de facto) private owners of capital and other resources and the continuous (and nonegalitarian) ebb and flow of wealth caused by this competitive process. In short, it is impossible to achieve simultaneously advanced technological production and comprehensive planning. Moreover, this same argument provides a major component of the case against the contemporary, noncomprehensive proposals for planning that will be taken up in the next three chapters as well.

The knowledge problem is the contention that a central planning board, even if very well intentioned, would lack the knowledge to combine resources in a manner that is economic enough to sustain modern technology. The choices concerning which methods of production should be used—out of a virtually unlimited number of possible methods—could not be made intelligently enough by a comprehensive planning apparatus, and so must be left to emerge as an unplanned outcome of competition among separate owners.

It is often assumed that the choice of methods of production is only a technical matter that could be resolved by a committee of engineers, and thus one that has nothing to do with such legal matters as the kind of ownership of the means of production that happens to prevail. But as Ludwig von Mises, the first to clearly spell out the knowledge problem, pointed out, the mere technological knowledge that could be supplied by scientists and engineers would suffice as a basis for choosing methods of production only if one of two possibilities held true. Either each factor of production would have to be absolutely *specific* (that is, it could only be employed in one particular production process in one particular way), or they would all have to be perfectly substitutable for one another in definite ratios. In either case once the detailed information about the ends of consumers was ascertained, say, by permitting a free consumer goods market, or by allowing an elected government to express its consumption demands, the best method of production would already be implicit in the consumer goods price information. But of course "neither of these two conditions is present in the universe in which man acts."

If wood is nonspecific, let's say because it can be used for printing books or for building houses or for both in any possible combination, how are we to choose that combination which will best satisfy the demand for shelter and for reading? This is not an issue about which the engineer has any special expertise. It is not a question to which quantitative measurement of any physical dimension is relevant. It is a question of the relative *value* of wood in alternative uses.

Whether the ultimate "wants" in question are those of consumers or of a government, technology ignores the crucial economic problem: "to employ the available means in such a way that no want more urgently felt should remain unsatisfied because the means suitable for its attainment were employed—wasted—for the attainment of a want less urgently felt." Mises ([1949] 1966: 207) put the point concisely:

> For the solution of such problems technology and its methods of counting and measuring are unfit. Technology tells how a given end could be attained by the employment of various means which can be used together in various combinations, or how various available means could be employed for certain purposes. But it is at a loss to tell man which procedures he should choose out of the infinite variety of imaginable and possible modes of production.

The function that prices play in a market is a cognitive one. It is to reduce for each decisionmaker the otherwise overwhelming number of *technologically* feasible ways of producing things to the relatively much smaller number that appear *economic* —that is, appear to more than repay their costs. Without the guidance provided by price signals, each producer is likely to engage in a project which, were it the only goal of society, could probably be carried out (technological feasibility) but which, since it is not the only goal, finds itself running out of scarce resources used up by other producers (economic infeasibility). Price movements convey the more or less accurate knowledge of the relative scarcities, the values, of all the factors of production to those who calculate potential and actual profits with them.

Yet the only force that tends to pack this scarcity information into prices is the degree of the tug exerted on prices from various directions by multitudes of competitive bidders. Each is committing himself, and either his own wealth or that which it is his responsibility to manage, to his own assessment about where future profits are to be found. Hence comprehensive planning, because of inherent constraints of the individual human intellect, can at best achieve a level of social intelligence approximating that of a society guided by Tradition and so could only manage to sustain at bare subsistence levels a tiny fraction of the present world's population. This idea of planning may still be advocated, of course, but its appalling costs in human lives would render it undesirable to most of those who presently support it.

It might be objected that the limitation of the mental capacity of individual human minds could be overcome by modern (or perhaps future) computers. A vast network of computer terminals all tied in to a supercomputer at the Central Planning Bureau might be proposed as a replacement for the Market. Thus, it could be argued, human limitations are (or will someday become) irrelevant in the flowering of the computer age. "Planometrics," or as one critic has called it, "computopia," is the academic preoccupation of many East European economists who see in it the possibility of a more rationalized planning system than has ever been possible.

While I confess to being as romantic as anyone about the untold benefits that computers promise for future generations, it does not strike me as even a remote possibility that these machines could replace market institutions. Rather, we can expect them to facilitate market transactions increasingly and thereby improve the coordination of plans.

The reason is not only that computers are a long way from being intelligent enough to replace an individual human mind in the making of the sorts of skillful judgments that economic decisionmaking requires. More to the point, even if some supercomputers were invented that surpassed human mental powers in every respect, their "intellect" would be put to a far more effective use if organized competitively than if organized by a single plan. Minds, whether human or not, achieve a greater social intelligence when they are coordinated through the Market than is possible if all economic activity had to confine itself to what a single supercomputer could hierarchically organize. In any case few policymakers take this notion of computerized comprehensive planning very seriously.

But what about the less ambitious proposals for noncomprehensive planning which aim to combine the Market and Planning principles? Are they subject to this critique as well? I think so. A central theme pervading the current literature in support of national economic planning is that current policymaking suffers from a serious deficiency of detailed knowledge of what is really going on in today's increasingly complex economy. With this complaint I wholeheartedly agree. Public policy *is* being conducted in abysmal ignorance of its likely consequences, and this inadequate knowledge of how to achieve goals rationally *does* largely explain the policy failures that surround us. But it is on the question of how to circumvent this pervasive problem where I believe the advocates of noncomprehensive planning go wrong. Most proponents of planning would agree with Leontief's contention (1982b: 33) that the complexity of the modern economy makes necessary a vast national data-gathering effort, including the "monitoring in great detail" of "what is happening to the different parts of the U.S. economy." He echoes a thesis common to the whole national planning literature when he concludes a recent article with an urgent plea for more data collection: "[We] need to provide the foundation of factual analysis and economic projection that would make democratic national planning possible. Our political economy will continue to flail blindly unless we can *uncover its interacting empirical realities* and consider in what general directions it should move." (1982b: 34; emphasis added).

I shall argue to the contrary: The intricate complexity of our economy is such that removing our profound ignorance of its detailed workings is not just an ambitious and difficult task, as Leontief avers; it is a hopeless dream. The fundamental defect of virtually all proposals for planning—from Marx to Leontief—lies in what Michael Polanyi calls their "objectivist," or what F. A. Hayek calls their "rationalistic," concept of the nature of human knowledge.[1] This epistemological issue contains both the key to understanding most contemporary policy failures as well as the basic obstacle that stands in the way of all national planning proposals.[2]

A planning agency could, of course, collect mountains of data.[3] The question is whether the data that it is feasible to collect correspond to the knowledge that really guides economic decisions. The issue of the possibility of making policymakers more knowledgeable about the economy involves the question of obtaining that specific practical knowledge which is actually involved in the dynamics of changing productive techniques. The truly relevant "data" that a planning organization would need in order to "uncover" a modern economy's "interacting empirical realities," resides deeply embedded in and dispersed among the separate minds of millions of people. In the relevant sense of the term, *the data do not exist.* The knowledge relevant for economic decisionmaking exists in a dispersed form that cannot be fully extracted by any single agent in society. But such extraction is precisely what would be required if this knowledge were to be made usable for a single planning agency.

Thus the only way this decentralized knowledge can be used effectively is by relying on the competitive struggles among several different owners in a Market system. If true, this argument immediately disposes of the older extreme notion of comprehensive planning, which seeks to *replace* the Market with Planning. The Market is the source of that knowledge which rational activity requires; it is thus indispensable.

It might be objected that since most modern-day planners, including Leontief, advocate the retention and conscious use of market institutions rather than their abolition, the problem of knowledge relates only to the obsolete idea of comprehensive planning. However, the issue is more serious. The attempt to abolish the Market is absurd because it would leave economic decisionmakers in complete ignorance. The point is that even the more modest and popular attempts merely to guide or steer the Market toward particular outcomes are really blind and dangerous obstructions of the very source of that knowledge which is essential to rational economic decision-making.

Whether applied to comprehensive or noncomprehensive planning, the knowledge problem argument crucially depends on the view that knowledge is not the same as data, that is, given pieces of explicit information. If this conception of knowledge is valid, then what really is at stake in the knowledge problem goes far beyond the issue of merely gaining access to scattered bits of explicit information, and implies that the whole standard approach to economic planning has been based on a misconception of the real problem to be solved.[4]

In order to better understand the nature of knowledge in general, it will be helpful to refer to the example of the specific kind of knowledge with which the scientific community is concerned. If even scientific knowledge is found necessarily to contain certain non-objective elements, the kinds of knowledge practically relevant to economic decisionmaking can be shown even more dependent on such elements. In short, the whole case against planning that is being developed here is rooted in a critique of objectivist theories of knowledge.

The objectivist view attempts to treat knowledge as proven, unambiguously observable facts completely detached from the particular persons who articulate them, and therefore not requiring any support from judgments based on hunches, or mere beliefs, or appeals to authority. Knowledge is objective and quantitative and cumulative. It is completely "out there," as opposed to personally held convictions, which are subjective and which only occupy individual minds. Learning is depicted as the kind of process in which elementary bits of atomistic data are removed from the "unknown" pile and added to the "known" pile, reducing the size of the former and increasing that of the latter. General categories and abstractions are viewed as derived from such primary bits of data.

Furthermore, as knowledge grows, it is presumed to converge on an increasingly vivid truth while reducing the area of our ignorance to a smaller and smaller domain of reality. In the limit, objective knowledge can conceivably become complete, encompassing a fully predictive, deterministic model of the universe. In principle, then, if not in practice, we can one day come to know everything there is to know about everything. What distinguishes science from belief, in this view, is that while others argue about opinions, scientists accept only formally proven theories and empirically confirmed facts, and in their professional capacity they do not form mere opinions at all. Scientists are modest, disinterested, and self-critical servants of the truth.[5]

Although a flattering view for scientists to have of themselves, this idea of the nature of science and knowledge has been gradually eroded by the arguments of skeptics and is now all but abandoned partly as a result of the recent revolution within the philosophy of science that has come to be called the growth-of-knowledge literature.[6]

In the Polanyi/Hayek view, knowledge is justified as a kind of spontaneous outcome of the skilled performances of scientists interacting under certain special circumstances within a particular kind of community. Scientific knowledge is not seen as fundamentally different from practical know-how and its justification is not to be sought in sophisticated philosophical demonstrations of the logic of its methods. Rather, it is to be found in sociological investigations into the way the scientific community works and the values it imbues in its members. Knowledge is inextricably connected to the knowing subject and crucially dependent on the subject's values and beliefs rather than detached and "out there." The only difference between the statement "P is true" and the statement "I believe P" is one of emphasis, since all statements are really personal commitments. "Meaning" is not an attribute of articulated statements but rather of the relationship between a statement and a human being, whether its author or those who try to interpret it. Knowledge is qualitative as well as quantitative, and more integrative than cumulative. Learning is an enhancement of our interpretative powers and of our tacit understanding of an unfolding reality rather than the simple accumulation of data. General concepts or abstract wholes are not derived from elementary particulars but are primary and are akin to the basic perceptions of animals which precede and underlie the ability to ascertain particular facts.

Growing knowledge does constitute an ever-widening grasp of reality. But there is a sense in which we cannot say our ignorance is being reduced, for the more we know, the more new questions we are able to ask. Although reality is still understood as unitary, our increasing grasp of it continually takes on additional perspectives and discovers more aspects in such a way that the growth of knowledge is realized to be divergent. In this view it is impossible *in principle* ever to know everything about anything.[7] In particular, it may well be impossible that anyone could ever know the workings of an economy, or for that matter, a single human mind in that economy, in sufficient detail to predict its precise future development.[8]

A renowned physical chemist, Michael Polanyi has shown in painstaking detail that in virtually every aspect of a scientist's activity, from defining a problem to discovering a satisfactory solution, the scientist is called upon to make tacit judgments he or she cannot fully defend but which nevertheless work as indispensable aids in the effort to achieve knowledge. This tacit dimension plays an important role not only in the acquisition and use of specialized skills but also in the very act of articulation or the formulation and interpretation of a rigorous mathematical model. Thus knowledge, even knowledge of inanimate matter, necessarily carries with it an essentially personal component, and not as an unavoidable liability but as a skillful contribution to the social process of scientific discovery.

If even scientific knowledge contains personal elements, then the kind of knowledge relevant to economic decisionmaking can be shown to contain such elements to a much greater degree. Once the nature of technological and economic knowledge in society is properly understood it can be shown that it would be impossible *in principle* to obtain the sort of knowledge that is necessary for rational planning. The market can make effective use of personal economic knowledge in a way that comprehensive planning cannot.

The crux of this critique is the view that much of the knowledge practically necessary for economic production cannot be articulated. Stated more positively, there are in fact two kinds of legitimate knowledge—not only articulate but also what Polanyi calls "tacit" or "inarticulate" knowledge.

This idea of inarticulate knowledge may at first seem paradoxical. The point in a discussion when the speaker asserts that he really knows something, but just cannot express it, marks the end of the possibility of expanding knowledge in that discussion. The objectivist view of knowledge, taken consistently, would have to deny legitimacy to any knowledge claim that was rooted in tacit elements. Only a completely explicit statement, preferably a thoroughly formalized system on the model of Euclidean geometry, is deserving of the label "knowledge." However, some outstanding recent developments in fields as diverse as linguistics, ethology, physics, mathematics, psychology, and computer science have considerably weakened this objectivist view, which once seemed unchallengeable. They now make the achievement of such a complete articulation of all knowledge seem, for several reasons, far less likely than it may have appeared to the eighteenth-century philosophers who first clearly formulated it as an ideal.[9]

But this achievement is not only far more difficult than it had been thought to be; it is logically impossible. As Polanyi (1958b: 18) put it, "This exalted valuation of strictly formalized thought is self-contradictory" because it would, if taken seriously, undermine all knowledge, even the most fully articulated and carefully formulated ideas. If we demand of an idea that it be completely articulated before it be given the appellation "knowledge," then, Polanyi argues, we will find we know nothing at all. While there are some skepticist epistemologists who are completely content with that conclusion, many of us might prefer to use the word "knowledge" in a way that permits us to say, for example, that we at least know that one plus one equals two.

There are two related aspects of articulated knowledge that logically require us to admit that it rests on unarticulated foundations. (1) Even looking at the problem in a static way, the component parts of any statement, the words used, each require definition, which in turn entails the use of other, as yet undefined, words. If complete definition of all words is required before an initial statement such as "One plus one equals two" is accepted, this necessarily presents us with an infinite regress, or rather, circular reasoning in which some of the original words like "plus" or "two" reappear in subsequent definitions. (2) Looking at the problem dynamically, the very act of formulating any general statement necessarily requires using rules of proper statement formulation which are themselves inarticulate. For example we must select certain abstract qualities of the real situation to which attention is being directed. This implies, then, that nothing can be completely articulated, since the very process of articulation involves the abstraction from some real features of the entity or process that is being described.

It was the philosopher-mathematician Alfred North Whitehead ([1947] 1968: 95) who so concisely pointed out the first of these problems, the "static" limitation, when he noted that "there is not a sentence which adequately states its own meaning. There is always a background of presupposition which defies analysis by reason of its infinitude."

Whitehead illustrated this point by the example "One plus one equals two," showing that the unstated presuppositions of even so simple a statement as this are more numerous than can be articulated in a lifetime. He refers in this context to the background of common sense that we rely upon to express ourselves.

Thomas Sowell (1980: 335) was focusing on the other limitation, the "dynamic" one, of articulation when he pointed out:

> Because nothing can be literally exhaustively articulated, the process of articulating is necessarily to some extent also a process of abstraction. Some characteristics are defined, to the neglect of others which may be present but which are deemed less significant for the matter at issue.

There is what he calls a "purely judgmental decision" involved in such abstraction that cannot itself be reduced to explicit formal rules. The two problems could be summarized by Hayek's point that the very act of articulation requires that we focus our awareness on the ideas we are seeking to communicate clearly by employing unconscious rules of proper communication of which we must be largely unaware at the time (see Hayek [1962] 1967 and 1973). Thus, to engage in the process of articulation requires that we rely on unarticulated habits of thought—including habitually accepted definitions of words and rules of abstraction—in order to get our articulated point across.[10]

Polanyi and Hayek have usefully employed the example of a child's speech (as well as the intelligent behavior of animals) to illustrate their contention that our articulated knowledge must represent only a small part of what we know. That a child, who may not learn the rules of grammar for a decade, if ever, can nevertheless construct grammatically correct sentences is evidence of the kind of tacit knowledge that underlies all articulated knowledge. It is only because our minds are capable of operating according to effective rules of which we are unaware that we are able to learn to speak a language. The act of forming an explicit statement in a language requires our use of an extremely complicated system of rules, of conventional interpretations of words, of syntax, and of idioms, which could not be fully understood by anyone who had not already thoroughly mastered that language.

But this reliance upon implicit rules does not apply only to the remarkable phenomenon of a child's command of a language. Any time an adult formulates an explicit statement, he too must rely on rules and implicit meanings of which he himself is not consciously aware. Indeed, this phenomenon is far more comprehensive than the realm of language. It comprises everything we call skills. A skill is a learned rule of conduct which successfully guides the behavior of its possessor but which is rarely understood in a manner that can be made explicit. Gilbert Ryle (1945) made this point with his useful distinction between "knowing how" and "knowing that." One often knows how to do something without being able to explain how one does it. Polanyi gives the example of riding a bicycle without knowing the law of centrifugal force or the rule derived from it that if one turns the handlebars in the direction in which one starts to fall this force will keep the bicycle from falling. He refers to the apprenticeship of a scientist learning the skills of his teacher not by explicit instruction of methods but by the copying and refinement of good habits through practice.[11]

Articulation, then, is just one kind of skill that we learn without knowing precisely how we accomplish it. The very exercise of our ability to articulate ideas fundamentally relies on the use of implicit rules of which we are unaware. Polanyi argues that there are higher level orders that cannot be explained in terms of their constituent particulars, but whose grasp as a whole relies on these particulars as subsidiary clues.[12] Hayek refers in this respect to the intuitively understood "wholes" or overall patterns that guide the scientist's attention as he strives to extend his articulate command over his subject matter. In this view a crucial and primary part of knowing rests on an ability to perceive similarities between wholes from clues supplied by background subsidiaries. This kind of analogical skill underlies everything from sense perception to animal intelligence to scientific discoveries.

Hayek has elaborated the way the unarticulated components of our knowledge, the unconscious rules, guide virtually all our activity, from the way we speak to the way we conduct ourselves in society. Law, for example, was a necessary institution for the survival of primitive societies, yet it has only been (partly) articulated in modern times. Such unconscious rules more often work negatively than positively, guiding action away from inappropriate directions, for example when bad grammar "sounds wrong" to the child or when theft is punished in primitive communities unacquainted with the subtleties of the economic analysis of property rights.[13] Languages and societies that are insufficiently prohibitive of meaningless or antisocial actions do not survive in the evolutionary struggle.

Applied to scientific knowledge, the Polanyi/Hayek approach contends that the determining rationality of the scientific process resides not in any rationally articulated understanding achievable by an individual but in the particular kinds of social processes taking place in the scientific community as a whole and guided by tacit judgments of its skilled participants. It is through the tensions and pressures generated by struggles among scientists to persuade one another, as each is guided by his own inarticulate groping for truth, that the process succeeds in continually discovering new knowledge. Participants in this process contribute their own personal, professional judgment by committing themselves to the theory each senses holds promise. From the competitive rivalry among such judgments there emerges a gradual consensus in the scientific community as a whole.

Each judgment about the potential fruitfulness of a theory constitues an *expectation* about the unknowable future and therefore is not resolvable by any strict, logical procedures. Polanyi shows that this element of skillful foresight plays a role not only in the initial selection of research problems but, to varying degrees, in all aspects of scientific work. Even to hold that something is a fact is to maintain a particular set of expectations about the future: "To say that an object is real is to anticipate that it will manifest its existence indefinitely hereafter" (Polanyi 1972: 44–45).[14]

Scientific knowledge, then, is seen as an evolving outcome of the interplay of scientists who exercise their tacit skills in the pursuit of an improved personal understanding of the world. This discovery procedure can achieve progress only if the members of the scientific community, no matter what their paradigm, share certain essential values, among which must be the attainment of the greatest possible clarity and precision in their attempts to explain reality. Contrary to the popular view of the scientist as a disinterested and detached observer of facts, this approach requires of the scientist nothing short of impassioned commitment to his own conception of the truth and to the theoretical "spectacles" through which he perceives it. Justifiable scientific knowledge emerges only through the social process by which such personal commitments vie with one another, each relying on its tacit clues about the potential fruitfulness of intellectual paths that are not yet traversed.

One of the most vital values to which this social discovery process necessitates allegiance is that of complete freedom of thought. The moral issues of freedom and responsibility are inextricably connected to the epistemological issues of what and how we know anything about the world we live in. A substantial degree of opposition to the use of force in human relationships is not merely one particular moral position among others; it is a prerequisite for the growth of knowledge. Scientists must be free to maintain, reject, or invent paradigms or theories according to their own largely inarticulate judgments as to what they find intellectually convincing. They must be free to believe in ideas that they cannot *fully* defend. But at the same time this freedom does not say that anything goes; it is intimately bound up with the sense of responsibility the scientist feels toward the attainment of valid meaning, and it requires a willingness on the part of each scientist to submit to the authority of specialists in areas beyond his own expertise.

In particular, then, one of the chief aspirations of the older objectivist attempts to justify scientific knowledge must be abandoned: the exclusion from science of any appeals to authority. The popular idea of science has said that it constitutes a collection of observable facts that anybody can verify for himself, whereas in fact

> the acceptance of scientific statements by laymen is really based not on their own observations, but on the authority that laymen acknowledge scientists to have in their special fields; and this is true to nearly the same extent of scientists using results of sciences other than their own: they do not feel called upon, or even competent, to test these results themselves. (Polanyi and Prosch 1975: 184–85)

There is a network of overlapping specialities in the scientific community in which border contributions meet the pressure of criticism from related scholars, but in which no one scientist can possibly understand the whole. Thus, science does not reject all personal belief, or appeals to authority but, rather, constitutes a particular kind of believing based on a commitment to truth instead of blind faith, and uses a complex system of what Polanyi calls "mutual authority" instead of vesting authority with any particular agent or office (Polanyi and Prosch 1975: 182–97).

Those who try to ignore the fact that the purely objectivist foundations of science have been undermined will brand this new approach unscientific. But the choice is not between a rigorous, explicit, and logical foundation for science and an informal, tacit, and historical one, it is between the latter and the ultimate death of the scientific enterprise. For this great human achievement is doomed if scientists do not learn that the true basis of the successes of their efforts lies not in the formal logical structure of any particular theory or the proof provided by any given experiment, but in the kind of "republic" that the scientific community constitutes and the values it upholds.

The fates of science and of the human civilization that made science possible are intertwined because both depend upon the strong belief in values that cannot be established by the kinds of rigorous standards popularly demanded. Hayek (1973: 7) found this same impossible standard to be one of the central defects of the planning or "constructivist" mentality:

> The tendency of constructivism to represent those values which it cannot explain as determined by arbitrary human decisions, or acts of will, or mere emotions, rather than as the necessary conditions of facts which are taken for granted by its expounders, has done much to shake the foundations of civilization, and of science itself, which also rests on a system of values which cannot be scientifically proved.

THE PRINCIPLE OF "MASS COMMUNICATION"

The conclusion at which this discussion aims—namely that the social aspirations of advocates of comprehensive planning would more than exhaust the intellectual capacity of human minds—has a particularly troublesome obstacle to overcome. The most difficult thing to convince a person of is the existence of any sort of general and insurmountable limit to the powers of the mind, especially since the mind who tries to do the convincing is necessarily just as limited as the mind he is trying to persuade. It is exceedingly difficult for our intelligence to grapple with its own shortcomings, since to describe them *in detail* would require the spelling out of what we do not know, which, of course, is just what I am saying cannot be done.

Those who have embarked on this hazardous road of trying to convince human minds of their inherent limits have invariably been accused of obscurantism, of sabotaging the human species' greatest tool, and of resurrecting the mysticism of the prerational age that set dogmatic taboos on the activities of the mind. But is not the automatic denial that we can ever find such limits and describe them at least in general terms *itself* a form of obscurantism? If we agree, as most of us do in principle, that we are not omniscient, then is it not one of reason's most important tasks to clarify the nature—including the limits—of its own powers? If this tool is not perfect, then to try to outline in general terms what its imperfections are is not to sabotage it. On the contrary, to fail to recognize these limitations is to risk just such a sabotage.

Most advocates of national planning conceive of the knowledge problem in terms of a remediable deficiency of the data they think necessary to coordinate anything so complex as a modern economy. This very complexity of human society, which both planning advocates and opponents stress, makes it horrendously difficult to analyze in any satisfactory detail. Suppose, then, that we transplant this same sort of problem down to the less complicated level of the social insects—ants, termites, and bees—just so we can begin to grasp the general principles involved. While no human can claim to yet understand the detailed workings as a whole of his own society (whether, as Leontief believes, because of insufficient data or, as I am arguing, because of insurmountable limitations), many entomologists have been able to study entire insect societies in exhaustive detail, and, although much remains to be learned, they can now legitimately be said to have discovered the major organizing principles of these societies.[15]

While this analogy reaches below the level of the human economy to the lowly insect, a second analogy I will employ reaches above the human economic level to that higher realm of human achievement, science. All of these apparently disparate phenomena can be analyzed as special instances of what have been called "spontaneous orders." Hayek (1967: 96–105) and Polanyi (1951: 114–22) use this same phrase to represent that kind of ordered pattern which emerges without being the product of anyone's deliberate design but only as an unplanned outcome of the mutual adjustments of its parts. Such emergent orders are, in Hayek's (1967: 22–42) terminology, not necessarily complex, but in many cases can attain a degree of complexity that extends beyond that which is attainable to any of its constituent, mutually adjusting parts; or in the terminology I have employed, can achieve a social intelligence that is greater than the intelligence of any of its individuals.

Admittedly, any analogy is imperfect. Significant differences do exist among these three kinds of spontaneous orders.[16] But in these instances, to the extent that the market is unlike insect societies and science, I will contend that the argument is not impaired but strengthened.

The popular conception of an insect society is one of a centrally directed allocation of obedient insects to given tasks, in which no real knowledge problem seems to arise. Indeed many a polemical argument against comprehensive planning has employed the accusation that central planning would result in the reduction of a free society to the rigid military organization of an anthill.

In fact, however, modern research has shown that insect societies are neither rigidly structured nor centrally directed. This fact, when first realized, posed for biologists precisely the same kind of knowledge problem that has mystified many economists and sociologists. Edward O. Wilson (1971: 226) puts the issue clearly:

> The individual member of a large colony cannot possibly perceive the actions of more than a minute fraction of its nestmates; nor can it monitor the physiological condition of the colony as a whole. Yet somehow everything balances out, a fact that keeps drawing the mind back to Maeterlinck's poetic question about the termite colony: "What is it that governs here, that issues orders, foresees the future . . . ?"

But, as Wilson goes on to show, there is no need to postulate a central decisionmaker—perhaps some kind of master termite issuing decrees to his followers—in order to explain the remarkably well-ordered functioning of a termite colony. The complex activities achievable by these lowly insects are made possible by what Wilson calls "mass communication," which he defines as "the transfer among groups of information that a single individual could not pass to another."

Some of the many examples Wilson provides of such ordered behavior attained through mass communication are the complex flanking maneuvers of ant swarms, the regulation of numbers of workers pursuing odor trails, and the precise thermoregulation of nests. In these tasks the action of each individual is never strictly controlled by any mechanism but "results from the competing stimuli impinging on it, including those produced by other members of the colony." In other words we have a primitive form of mutual coordination in which the actions of each participant both contribute a kind of pressure to the actions of other participants while simultaneously being guided in its own actions by similar pressures contributed by others.

With this dual causation, the insect is not only guided by chemical signals (pheromones) contributed by others but also positively contributes similar signals of its own to the process. It is an essential feature of mass communication that "individual insects often seek the stimulus and are not always just passive recipients" (Wilson 1971: 226–28).

A pheromone is properly considered not a precise command but, rather, a partial signal. The particular chemical composition one termite passes into the mouth of another does not by itself result in any particular behavior, but instead it is the resultant chemical composition that emerges from hundreds of mouth-to-mouth signals that can be said to guide the activity of the recipients. Each participant has its own contribution to make to this composite signal, which essentially indicates which productive activity needs greater allocation of social resources. If, say, the chemical component secreted by defense workers falls off, this may mean that an invasion has killed off some of these workers. The termites' rapid response to this chemical signal is then to begin to withdraw workers from other tasks and allocate more to defense.

The main goal of the analyst of such mass communication phenomena should be to develop a compositive theory that builds up from our understanding of the simple behavior patterns of the individual insects into a coherent picture of their more complicated mutual interaction at the social level. Again, as Wilson argues, "The reconstruction of mass behavior from a knowledge of the behavior of single colony members is the central problem of insect sociology." That is, even though the individual insects do not themselves know how their actions contribute to an overall order, it is the aim of the scientist who investigates these orders to divulge "the principles of mass action by which insect colonies translate the numerous individual behavioral acts of its members into higher order effects" (Wilson 1971: 224).

The order that results from this mass communication can by no means be considered any kind of complete coordination and is only evident at a higher level—societywide. If one observes insects at the level of the individual, one finds what Marx calls an "anarchy of production," an ongoing rivalrous struggle among apparently uncoordinated insects, some feverishly attempting to achieve one purpose while others busily work at a contradictory goal. To take just one of several examples Wilson (1971: 224) cites, "Polistes colonies often build up brood cells while others are tearing them down, so that a greater effort in one direction or the other settles how many cells are to be constructed and where they are to be located." [17]

In other words the spontaneous order that emerges on the social level is the outcome of the rivalrous competition among individuals. It is a higher level order that evolves out of a furious turmoil of lower level disorder. "Although these various antagonistic actions seem chaotic when viewed at close range, their final result is almost invariably a well-constructed nest that closely conforms to the plan exhibited throughout the species" (Wilson 1971: 224–25). Of course Wilson is here using the word "plan" in an unusual sense. What he is really saying is that it is not anyone's deliberate plan that can be said to allocate, say, honeybees to a nest site, but instead it is the "competition" among bees that, depending on the relative intensity of signals supplied by different participants, results in an observable pattern of the swarm. Thus, even the marching patterns of army ants, which many people would presume represent some kind of rigidly controlled and centrally directed behavior, are treated by sociobiologists as a particularly striking example of how the "emergence of statistical order from competing elements" can occur.

How, then, does this "important first rule concerning mass action" in insect societies—that it is paradoxically the result of what Wilson (1971: 224–25) calls "conflicting actions of many workers"— relate to human activity in markets? Surely I am not suggesting that humans engage in such obviously contradictory activities as, for example, Wilson observes when some workers are scurrying one way in a tunnel with larvae while others are stupidly walking right by them carrying identical larvae the other way. We do not see humans in front of a building trying to put it together while others in back are obliviously tearing it down. Indeed the unique character of human beings, our ability not merely to *signal* each other with pheromones but to *talk* to each other, to consciously draw up blueprints and deliberately coordinate our activities with one another, would seem to be the main attribute distinguishing our societies from those of insects. [18]

However, the similarity between insects and man is greater in this respect than it may appear. Of course the contradictions among the far more complicated human plans are never so obvious as those of the insects carrying larvae in opposite directions appear to us. But we have the same general type of phenomenon when two capitalists embark on projects, however well designed in themselves, in direct competition with one another for the favor of a buyer, in a situation in which only one can ultimately succeed. The fact that the lowly ant seems hopelessly doltish to us should not detract from our recognition that in both human and insect societies a higher level of intelligence arises out of a competition among participants who are, relative to the intellectual achievements of the whole society, woefully ignorant.

The individual ant is capable of certain simple kinds of mental feats based on a combination of clues it can recognize both from the physical environment as well as from pheromones of other ants; its own behavior includes not only various physical actions but also the issuing of chemical signals that can be sensed by its fellows. The spontaneous result of the interplay among such relatively simple "minds" is a degree of social intelligence that far exceeds the capacity of an ant brain. Because we humans who observe this situation are so much more intelligent than ants, we have the ability to formulate problems that the ant brain cannot handle, to specify the exact limitations of the ant's intellectual powers, and to ridicule as obviously contradictory many of its primitive behaviors. Because we clearly do not possess any such superiority over the intellectual capacity of a human in modern society, we are unable to formulate precisely problems humans cannot handle or to specify in detail our mental limitations, and we are not likely to find our own mutually contradictory behavior so obviously ridiculous. But in fact I would argue that an individual human would be no more capable of subsuming the whole society's activities under his or her own mental control than would an individual ant be able to deliberately allocate its fellows to the construction and maintenance of an anthill. The human as an individual problem solver is clearly superior to any insect, but at the same time the complexity of the social problem to be solved is far greater for us than that of insect societies.

The human analogue of the insects' pheromone is the expenditure of money in market exchanges. Human mass communication takes place when an individual engages in the dual process of actively influencing others by secreting "money pheromones" in particular directions, thereby bidding up prices in those avenues, and of passively responding to the prices resulting from the money issuing from other individuals. Insects biologically read composite chemical signals according to genetically programmed procedures. Humans, on the other hand, rationally respond to constellations of price signals by conceiving of production plans that seem feasible (profitable) according to the prices of the inputs and outputs under consideration. But the added degree of rationality that humans impart to their individual activities should not deceive us into assuming that any single agent could rationally plan the overall result of a modern technologically advanced economy.

In a single firm's accounting statement itemizing the total costs of a project and comparing this total to the revenues received is contained a wealth of scarcity information that neither the accountant nor any other agent in the system could ever gather. Each price of purchased, rented, and hired factors reflects a complex tension among diverse plans that have tried to pull the relevant factor into alternative uses. The profit and loss calculus itself then determines whether the particular combination of inputs under consideration yields an output that is expected to pay its way in the market. The fact that all this scarcity information is expressed in quantitative form permits each decisionmaker to test extremely complex combinations of factors for their profitability while simultaneously relying on similar tests being conducted by rival decisionmakers.

In Polanyi's terminology we could say that those who use profit and loss accounting apply their *focal awareness* to devising or revising the particular combination of factors in their own production process while being guided in this skilled performance by the *subsidiary* clues that are contained in the prices of possible factors supplied by the market system. The ability to add up total costs as expressed in money units enables such decisionmakers to apply their tacit skills to increasingly complex projects, just as the ability to articulate permits people to extend their tacit powers of knowing far beyond those possible to animals.

Without the quantitative comparison of costs and benefits, Robinson Crusoe could still make rough (strictly ordinal rather than cardinal) comparisons between various courses of action: whether, for example, he should expend more labor hours on fishing by hand or on constructing a net. But Crusoe's "seat-of-the-pants" qualitative judgment can only encompass matters that lie directly within his purview. He must confine his cost/benefit judgment to the conditions of possible production processes that can be surveyed from beginning to end directly by him.

Not so for decisionmakers who act within the market system. Crusoe, when he returns to civilization, can now quantitatively weigh costs and benefits in terms of a common denominator—money—in such a way as to enable him to take account of conditions far beyond those of which he could himself be aware. Each input price of his own calculation represents the output price of the profit and loss calculation of another decisionmaker, who in turn relies on other input prices, in this way stretching a chain of information transmission throughout the stages of production.

As Hayek (1982) puts it, the price system represents a stage in sociological evolution comparable to the emergence in biological evolution of eyesight. It permits decisionmakers to take account of conditions beyond their immediate locality, indeed beyond what they can physically see, just as sight enables animals to take account of conditions they could not touch. Thus in the market system the focal decision about one's own production process is dramatically enhanced by the information supplied by others and imparted to the factor prices that serve as subsidiary clues to guide one's decisions.

Entrepreneurs in human society rely on such clues supplied by prices, which in turn result from independent decisions being made simultaneously by other entrepreneurs elsewhere in the system, in order to make choices about how to allocate scarce resources among competing ends. The clues are contained in the intricate and volatile constellation of relative prices, not only of the final consumer goods (toward which all productive activity is ultimately directed) but also of all of the various factors of production available. The crucial decisions being made throughout the economy about how to combine resources effectively are invariably keyed to the observed changes in relative prices and thus depend on the knowledge that is conveyed by them. At the same time, that knowledge is put into prices by the cumulative choices of market participants across the whole economy and the relative intensities of their multidirectional tugs.

Part of this relation between market choice and the price system has been accepted by the aforementioned planometric models of planning that have arisen within the field of comparative economic systems. It is now widely accepted (except by some stubbornly consistent Marxists) that intelligent production decisions must be based on price information and that any attempt to abolish prices is doomed. Just as an insect deprived of its ability to sense pheromones would be helpless to engage in complex social behavior, so a human, deprived of the opportunity to observe, respond to, and try to anticipate price changes, would be completely in the dark about how to make rational production plans effectively.

While modern planometric theorists have admitted that the "reading" of price signals is necessary, they have failed to recognize what kind of social arrangements are necessary for their "writing," that is, for the relevant information to get put into prices.[19] In fact it has been generally assumed that the ideal state of affairs (incorporated into abstract models misleadingly labeled "perfectly competitive") would be a situation in which all producers are pure "price takers" who have no influence whatsoever over prices but simply treat them as parametric signals to which they passively react. From this point of view, real-world markets can readily be shown to fall far short of the imagined ideal, since market participants regularly exert a substantial influence over prices. At the same time planning proposals can aspire to actually achieve the "perfection" that is evidently so lacking in the real world.

But this way of formulating the problem is fundamentally wrong. The fact that market participants exert influence over prices is no more a lamentable imperfection of the market's system of mass communication than an individual insect's exertion of influence over the composite chemical signals a colony relies on is an imperfection of their method of mutual coordination. For either of these processes to work, information not only has to be sifted out of pheromone or price signals but must also be injected into them. These signals carry only as much knowledge as has been imparted to them as an outcome of the rivalrous multidirectional tugging taking place among competing individuals. No single agent knows what the pheromone or the matrix of relative prices should be. But as an unplanned outcome of the contention among rivals, information gets packed into the signals in such a way as to lead to an effective coordination of the society as a whole.

It is important to recognize that the standard against which a society's organizing mechanism is being judged here is not the neoclassical welfare economist's Pareto-optimality conditions, which pertain to imaginary states of perfect competition, but rather the Austrian economist's conception of a politically unhampered market process. The prices that Mises, Hayek, and Kirzner describe as providing needed information to the human actors who employ them are *not* equilibrium prices, and the coordination they make possible is nowhere near the neoclassical economist's notion of general equilibrium where all plans mesh perfectly.

Like pheromones, prices are imperfect signals that guide a continuous coordinating process. For example, an economy with completely unhampered entry and exit is still deemed by neoclassicists to be suboptimal because in some industries large firms with high start-up costs have an "advantage" over new entrants, an advantage that should be counterbalanced by antitrust enforcement. Large economies of scale are thus seen as a source of market failure.

By the standards I am commending, however, no single agent in the economy, even those trained in neoclassical economics, is thought to possess sufficient knowledge to decide whether or not the size or number of firms in an industry is "optimal." Thus, government interference into the market process in order to shrink or break up "excessively large" firms (or for that matter to enlarge "excessively small" ones to take advantage of economies of scale), with the purpose of deliberately making the economy more competitive, is ill conceived. A truly competitive industry is one in which the firms are the size and number dictated by the competitive process itself.

When the neoclassical welfare economist labels a situation a "market failure" in the provision of certain goods, he has to admit that he is suspending judgment on whether government provision of the good would improve circumstances. But if the government cannot be shown to do better, the "failure" is no failure at all. The point of the Austrian view, by contrast, is that no single agent can be trusted to be able to identify consistently particular instances of real market failure—that is, instances where government planning is known to be able to do better.

Many advocates of planning have been willing to concede the necessity for *some* competitive markets as a method for imparting information to prices. But they have argued that the material factors of production need not be separately owned in order to set the prices of those factors. The means of production could all be commonly owned, it is argued, and at most only the final output (the consumer goods) and the primary inputs (raw materials and labor) would need to be the objects of free exchange among separate competing bidders. Once prices have been generated in these limited markets, all the other prices of the various factors of production can simply be computed from them. In the equilibrium theory of economic textbooks, when certain data are said to be given, the values of all intermediate factors get imputed from the relative values of the final consumer goods, as determined by the expenditure of incomes from wages and from selling or renting raw materials. Thus, it is argued, markets in the factors of production are superfluous and can be replaced by economists, no doubt armed with computers, instructed to derive factor prices from consumer goods prices.

But it is not only in one's capacity as a consumer that one imparts information to the price system; it is in *all* market-related decisions. To make all material factors of production common property, as is the traditional goal of comprehensive planning, *would be to deprive the economy of its main source of economic knowledge.* It is primarily the rivalrous competition among separate owners of factors of production, trying in their diverse and often mutually incompatible ways to employ them in what they believe to be the most profitable avenues for investment, which generates information-laden prices. Factor prices in the real world cannot be derived from consumer goods prices since, unlike in the textbooks, the set of specific production methods from which the choices are to be made are not given but are exactly what is at issue.

Once again such production methods, as Mises has argued, can only be derived from consumer goods prices under the highly unrealistic assumptions that factors are perfect substitutes for one another or that they are perfectly specific. Since neither condition holds in the real world, no producer can know in advance of his participation in the competitive struggle with others whether his own production technique is economically appropriate.

Another way to put this point is to say that when a rival outbids me for a factor of production (say, by pushing its price so high that I can no longer afford to use this factor in my own project), he is not only hurting me by frustrating my purpose. He is also *informing* me. He is telling me that this factor has more highly valued uses than the one to which I would have put it. When the bidding of thousands of participants instead of just two is involved, the informing process is still going on, but it is now the scattered bits of knowledge from all the participants that combine to produce a price that is informative, in turn, to each of them. It is only by being informed in this way — by the contrary tugging of all of one's rivals — that any one producer can be said to know what he is doing.

Or, in the terms of the last chapter, it could be said that the Market exhibits a social intelligence greater than the individual intelligence of its contentious participants. The question at hand is whether Planning can exhibit a comparable social intelligence.

To be sure, a planning office can marshal, in some manner, the abilities of thousands of minds more effectively than any termite could organize his comrades. A human planning agency must be hierarchically organized or it will display the very lack of control that constituted its raison d'être. Whether this agency is directed by an individual or a committee, it will be limited by the individual or organizational intelligence of that director. But in a spontaneous order there is no such limitation.[20]

This same limitation pertains to a profit-making corporation. Its effective size is also limited by the organizational capacity of its director. A large private corporation can admittedly often look deceptively like a small planning agency. It might even be argued that a planning agency could engage in internal accounting procedures in the same way that a large corporation like IBM does. But in a market order, much of the necessary information available internally to an organization is supplied to it by the external competitive order, by the organization's freely competing rivals. A comprehensive planning agency, on the other hand, *has* no rivals, while a noncomprehensive planning agency's rivals are at an inherent disadvantage that may keep them from supplying such information. The planning agency may be preventing the discovery process from operating by "rigging the game" for the industries it favors.

The principle the sociobiologists call "mass communication" reveals how partial, localized knowledge on the part of a termite in one part of a colony can be merged together with similar bits of knowledge of all the other termites in such a way that the system's overall allocation of resources is informed by more knowledge than any one participant to the process can possess. It seems to me that the very same kind of mass communication is the principle that operates in market systems. In either case, the resulting order of the system is necessarily an imperfect one since it only comes about as a result of the conflicting tugs and pulls of chemical or price signals. Yet despite its close-range chaos, the overall system exhibits a degree of coordination that far surpasses what has ever been consciously undertaken by any one member of insect or human societies.

SCIENTIFIC AND MARKET DISCOVERY PROCEDURES

It might still be objected that one attribute of humankind which I have stressed and which is denied to insects might make us capable of overcoming this kind of reliance upon disorderly competitive struggle as the method of roughly coordinating social activity. This is the human ability to articulate knowledge of productive techniques and thereby to refine our understanding of the production processes in which we are engaged. The ant has to be unconscious of the reasons for his actions, but we human beings are increasingly aware of how the world works and can apparently explain to others what we know. What is manifestly unavailable to insects, the capacity to accumulate clear scientific knowledge of their own activities, is just as clearly an option for humans. And it may appear that this makes it possible for us to attain a degree of deliberate self-control over our whole society's activities heretofore denied to both insects and people. What has always been widely dispersed, localized knowledge, can perhaps be rendered global and universally accessible by means of extensive data gathering and the ongoing accumulation of scientific knowledge. It might be argued that in spite of the similarities I have been describing between human and insect societies, an effort at information collection such as that proposed by Leontief might make it possible for us, for the first time, to rise above the crude coordination processes of insect societies and truly come to control our own development. In other words, can most of what has been said up until now be accepted, and yet the further claim be made that individuals, instead of bidding against one another, can articulate their local knowledge and expectations to a central authority who could then coordinate their actions with one another?[21]

This is where the discussion of the contemporary work in the philosophy of science and the difference between knowledge and data comes to bear on the issue of planning. The general conception of the nature of knowledge that emerges from that analysis suggests that articulated knowledge is only the visible tip of the iceberg, representing only what we are able to *say* about what we know, which never comes close to encompassing our full understanding. While our ability to articulate ideas is the main intellectual advantage we have over other animals, this ability is itself rooted in tacit mental operations of which we are largely unaware. Articulation is an indispensable tool we use for the advancement of our mostly tacit understanding of the world.

Now the knowledge of insects, of course, is entirely tacit and hence it is blatantly obvious that they are unable to explain what they know to an "insect planning authority" in order to deliberately organize themselves. But the intelligence of humans, though immensely strengthened by articulation, nonetheless contains a large component of tacit understanding by individuals who know more than they can say. If this is also true with respect to the sorts of knowledge relevant to our economic activities, then no comprehensive planning agency could obtain the sort of knowledge necessary for economic planning, for it would lie buried deep in the minds of millions of persons.

Is it legitimate, then, for us to extrapolate from the fact that scientific knowledge rests on tacit or personal components to the contention that the kinds of information relevant to economic decisionmaking also rest on such inarticulate foundations? In other words, having seen that (with respect to the first extended analogy) the crucial difference between human economy and that of insects is the human ability to articulate (at least part of) our understanding of the world, we are now led to consider the second analogy: Is our economic knowledge similar, in the relevant respects, to scientific knowledge?

Even if it is accepted that science involves all the subtleties of interpretation that make complete objective articulation impossible, it could still be argued that the kinds of information needed for economic decisionmaking are less problematic, and are mere matters of indisputable fact like how many plastics factories there are in California.[22] After all, it might be argued, the typical business manager does not have to speculate about alternative scientific theories but simply relies on the current state of technology. He or she just applies scientific discoveries to the mundane problems of social production.

There is no doubt that business entrepreneurs or managers solve *different* sorts of problems than scientists do, but this only means that it requires different skills. Entrepreneurship certainly involves as much skill, tacit judgment, and imagination as scientific research. Much laboratory work is exasperatingly laborious, while there is nothing dull about the challenge of keeping a business in the black in a competitive industry.

But all of this is really beside the point. Like individual scientists, individual businesspersons know very little *compared* to the knowledge contained in the entire community in which they operate; each crucially depends on interaction with rivals in order to be tacitly and explicitly informed by their contrary tugs. Hence the point is not to compare the individual intelligence of businesspersons to that of scientists. It is that the intelligence of each of them is meager in comparison with the social intelligence embodied in the overall community in which each participates.

There is, in fact, a fundamental difference between the kind of specific, detailed knowledge of the particular circumstances of time and place relevant to economic activity and the general knowledge of interest to the scientist (Hayek 1948: 80). While this difference might make economic decisions *more* dependent on the kinds of rivalrous mutual adjustment processes I have been describing, it certainly does not make them less so. A good case can be made for the position that the complexity of the overall social problem of applying scarce resources to the millions of competing ends in the economy is greater than the complexity of the overall sum of scientific knowledge. If competitive discovery processes are necessary to science in part because it is complex and ever-changing, those processes must be equally necessary to the economy, whose intricate details are undergoing such turbulent change as to make science look almost simple and static by comparison.

The quantities and qualities of the myriad of resources available for economic production, indeed of even notions of what constitutes a resource, are continually changing as an inherent by-product of production processes. Specific techniques of production alter much more rapidly than do scientific theories of technology. The crisscrossing lines of interdependence among economic choices are far more intricate than those of scientific choice. Although it is quite likely that pathbreaking developments in genetics will have little or no impact on particle physics, it is hard to think of an instance of any major change in one sector of an economy that will not have significant rippling effects throughout the system.[23]

In other words the very features of the scientific enterprise that make it impossible for science ever to be fully articulated by an individual scientist are even more pervasive in the economic realm and hence make it impossible to obtain comprehensive, fully articulated knowledge of an economy. In particular, the two kinds of limitations to scientific articulation which I have called the "static" and "dynamic" limitations have counterparts in the case of market processes.

With respect to the first, the static limitation to articulation, one can argue that just as an articulated statement only carries meaning to other people because of a shared definitional background in un-articulated assumptions about the use of language, so too do articu-lated prices only carry meaning to those who calculate with them because of a shared background in unarticulated assumptions about the characteristics of the priced goods and services. Just as articu-lated statements in science constitute an indispensable aid to our advancement of a largely inarticulate understanding of the world, so too do articulated prices provide an indispensable service to our largely inarticulate production activities. But neither articulated statements nor posted prices have any meaning when divorced from their inarticulate foundations.

The articulate information supplied by prices is only informative because they are juxtaposed against a wide background of inarticulate knowledge gleaned from a vast experience of habitual productive activity. A price is not just a number. It is an indicator of the relative scarcity of some particular good or service of whose unspecified qualities and attributes we are often only subsidiarily aware. Yet were these qualities of a good to change in the slightest respect, this could change incremental decisions about the uses of the good just as significantly as a price change could. As Sowell (1980: 180–81) reminds us, what we mean by an apartment or a can of peas is not generally clear even to ourselves; but if any of the unspecified fea-tures of either were to change, we would substantially alter our demand for it.

There has been a great deal of attention in recent years to Hayek's conception of the price system as a means of transmitting informa-tion. As interpreted through orthodox economists' analytical lenses, the idea is rendered as the claim that a market economy is "informa-tionally efficient" in that prices contain all the information needed for decisionmaking. In the literature on planometrics, this view has led to the calculation of the number of prices and quantities of goods that have to be communicated back and forth between plant mana-gers and the central planning board during the planning process. The confident conclusion is that the number of numbers to be passed around is small enough to be manageable.

Now it is true that one of Hayek's main points was that prices act as a summary of detailed changes that allow decisionmakers to re-spond to fluctuations in relative scarcities without knowing the causes of such changes. But Hayek was not contending that prices as numbers are the only pieces of information that the market requires. On the contrary, it is only because of the underlying tacit meaning attached to the priced goods and services that prices themselves communicate any knowledge at all.

This is not to say that the relative significance of the tacit parts of these two kinds of knowledge—scientific and economic—are the same. But it seems that, if anything, we might expect economic information to have an even larger tacit component. The primary aim of the scientific enterprise, after all, is to advance our explicit knowledge of the world, to widen the scope, precision, and clarity of our articulation. The driving force of market activity is the competitive groping for pure profit opportunities in which the "articulation" of information from which the more promising paths for investment can be discovered via the constellation of relative prices is but a by-product (although of course an important one) of profit-seeking behavior.

Capitalists, unlike scientists, are not deliberately trying to improve the informational content of the articulation that results from their respective activities. For markets, it is only as an unplanned result of their competitive bids tugging in various directions that such an improvement in price information emerges. With scientific activity the central aim is to validate and improve upon the existing structure of articulated knowledge. To use Polanyi's phrase again, scientists are "focally aware" of the extent to which their knowledge is well articulated whereas capitalists and entrepreneurs are only "subsidiarily aware" of their articulation of price information while focusing their awareness instead on the profit implications they believe are suggested by relative prices. Thus the relative importance of the tacit component of *market* knowledge is apt to be at least as great as that of *scientific* knowledge simply because it is one of the main purposes of the latter and not of the former to make the articulation as thorough as possible even if it is never complete.

Two other features that distinguish economic information from scientific knowledge, both of which relate to the relatively greater significance of time in the market process, can also be shown to accentuate the limitations to full articulation that apply in the case of the market. First, market activity is oriented toward future and hence more uncertain circumstances to a greater extent than most scientific work. The scientist primarily aims to improve the current state of articulated knowledge, while the businessperson produces mainly to satisfy future consumer demand. In both cases the decision is bound to carry with it a certain tacit element, a kind of educated hunch about either future scientific tests and theories or future conditions of supply and demand. But the extent to which the entrepreneurs' activity is based on subtle clues, subjective expectations, and tacit judgments seems at least as great as that involved in most scientific activity.

The other time-related aspect of market information that differentiates it from scientific knowledge is the fact that it tends to be of only fleeting interest or validity, whereas scientific knowledge is intended to be universally true and inherently interesting. A fall today in the price of oil may be of tremendous importance for a while, but were it to rise tomorrow this would instantly make the old price obsolete and of interest only to a few scattered economic historians. In other words price information represents knowledge about a continually and rapidly changing structure of economic relationships, while scientific knowledge represents a gradually changing knowledge of universal laws that are believed to be permanent. Thus it is to be expected that it would be easier to formulate scientific articulation into relatively comprehensive form than it would be to get any relevant economic information into this form before it becomes obsolete.

Not only is economic information of limited temporal usefulness, it is equally confined in its spatial usefulness. The relative scarcity of coal in Ethiopia today may have little to do with its availability in Mexico and is likely to be of little immediate interest to most Mexican businessmen. But clearly a new scientific contribution that happened to be made by an Ethiopian scientist will be of relevance to scientists in that field all over the world. Again we have every reason to believe that the tacit elements, this time relating to local circumstances, will be at least as significant a part of the intellectual apparatus of businessmen as will be the corresponding tacit elements in the case of scientific knowledge.

Thus in all these respects it appears that the static kind of limitation to articulation, which indicates that a scientific statement can never be completely articulated because of the implicit reliance on the tacit meaning of the words used, presents just as strong a corresponding limitation to the articulation of market information. If even scientific knowledge—which is intended to be as fully articulated as possible, primarily oriented toward the current state of science and presumed to be universally valid independent of time and place—if even such knowledge necessarily contains a tacit component, then we should certainly expect economic information to be at least as dependent on tacit knowing. Market participants do not deliberately aim at improving the articulation of price information, their actions are largely oriented toward the uncertain future, and the information they use is normally of only temporary and local significance. All these features suggest that the economic information is likely to be at least as deeply imbued with subjective or personal elements as the modern philosophy of science has shown scientific knowledge to be.

There is also a counterpart in the market context to the second or dynamic limitation to articulation. Just as the process of constructing or using a formal system or scientific statement involves a creative imagination that necessarily lies outside of the framework of the formal system itself, so does the construction or use of a configuration of prices rest on knowledge that is not contained in that set of prices. Just as the acceptance or rejection of a scientific theory rests on the personal commitments of members of the scientific community to truth, so does the "survival" of a posted price or a particular production project rest on the personal commitments of market participants to profit.

The extent to which a scientist is willing to adhere to a theory, or an entrepreneur to a production project, depends on his or her whole set of personally held and inarticulate beliefs about other theories or other production projects with which the presently contemplated theory or project must be complementary. Entrepreneurs' subjective expectations about the future course of demand and supply for all the related goods and services determine their decisions. Yet, like the ideas of scientists about what constitutes good science, these expectations are inarticulate. Profit and truth are not so much seen as imagined, not so much grasped as pursued.[24]

The role controversy plays in ferreting out less defensible beliefs in science has its counterpart in the role rivalrous competition and the calculation of profit and loss play in eliminating less economically viable methods of production. It is the challenge of fellow scientists or of competing producers that applies the pressure that keeps each of these social processes going.

Thus market participants are not and could not be price takers any more than scientists could be theory takers. In both cases a background of unquestioned prices or theories is relied upon subsidiarily by the entrepreneur or scientist, but the focus of the activity is on disagreeing with certain market prices or scientific theories. Entrepreneurs (or scientists) actively disagree with existing prices (or theories) and commit themselves to their own projects (or ideas) by bidding prices up or down (or by criticizing or elaborating existing theories). It is only through the intricate pressures being exerted by this rivalrous struggle of competition (or criticism) that new workable productive (or acceptable scientific) discoveries are made and that unworkable (or unacceptable) ones are discarded.

As Polanyi points out, there can be no pure statement P independent of the person of a scientist willing to commit himself to the proposition "P is true." The enterprise of science can only progress so long as scientists are free to attach or withdraw their commitment to propositions on the basis of the rivalrous process of criticism taking place in the scientific community. Hence, "to say that 'P is true' is to underwrite a commitment or to sign an acceptance, in a sense akin to the commercial meaning of such acts" (Polanyi 1958a: 254). Scientists can be said to "invest" intellectual resources on behalf of theories in which they believe truth to be forthcoming in much the same way that capitalists invest in productive projects in which they believe profit to be forthcoming.

Without the pressure that such personal commitments impart to science and to the market, each would lose what Sowell (1980: 102–3) calls its "determining rationality." It is precisely because the scientist has his reputation (and self-esteem)—and the capitalist his wealth—*at stake* that he is impelled to make his commitments for or against any particular direction of scientific or productive activity. Thus both the property rights that permit separate owners to use their resources as they see fit and the intellectual freedom that permits scientists to adhere to the theories of their choice play the same roles. To the extent that either form of personal commitment is undermined—when scientific reputation or economic wealth depends on loyalty to a party line rather than to a personal devotion to truth or a pursuit of anticipated profit opportunities—each of these great achievements of civilization, science and our advanced economy, is to that degree sabotaged.[25]

Coercion obstructs the flow of knowledge in the market process for the same reason it obstructs it in the scientific community. The spontaneous transmittal of scattered information that is continually being accomplished by the various tugs of market rivals is distorted when some of the participants gain the coercive advantage. As Thomas Sowell (1980: 172) points out, when the effects of government policies such as wage and price controls are examined, "The element of force is crucial to the distortion" that they cause.

> The knowledge transmitted by voluntarily chosen prices conveys the terms on which various forms of mutual cooperation are available. The knowledge transmitted under government price constraints reflects the desire to escape punishment, and the knowledge conveyed by such prices does not reflect the full array of options actually available to the economy.

Managers of different "departments" within a planned economy would be expected in practice to *contend* with one another, although they would have to do so without claiming a firm title to property over the resources each controls. But, the objection could be raised, the scientist is in the same circumstances, unable, except to the very limited extent protected by patent or copyright laws, to hold any clearcut property rights over his "products." Yet with rivalry but *without* property rights and a price system, this process works to generate the scientific discovery procedure. Why, then, can the market-science analogy not be turned into a planning-science analogy that answers the critique heretofore presented of central planning? Could not a new procedure of interdepartmental rivalry take the place of the scientific and market rivalries that enable these processes to generate and disperse knowledge?

This line of argument for planning has a serious shortcoming: No advocate of planning has yet indicated a workable *medium*, analogous to the insects' pheromones or the scientists' journals or the market's money prices, through which the interdepartmental rivalry could generate a level of social intelligence that exceeds the individual intelligence of its participants. If, on the other hand, the advocate of planning answers that he will borrow the procedures of science for the needed interdepartmental rivalry, he faces the difficulty that most of the knowledge needed for the working of our economy has never been and is unlikely ever to be articulated. The first part of this chapter argued, in fact, that the task of allocating resources efficiently is not the kind of project that can be subsumed under the conscious direction of articulate discourse. On the other hand, if he answers that he would model his interdepartmental rivalry after the procedures of the market, he will have to face the difficulty that his departments and managers would seem indistinguishable from the firms and capitalists of the market system.

These diverse spontaneous orders, from primitive insect societies to such complex institutions as markets and science, all exhibit as a basic organizing principle a competitive process of discovery whereby each participant both actively contributes and passively responds to signals. Whether these are crude chemical compositions with which termites communicate or complicated price configurations or articulated theories with which entrepreneurs and scientists communicate, the same principle is at work. In all these processes the very contentiousness or "rivalrousness" of separate, independent, self-motivated agents each guided by his own personal, largely tacit, perspective is what determines the degree of higher level order or of social intelligence that emerges.

Comprehensive planning, the classic doctrine of planning advocates, seeks to achieve economic coordination without relying on the contention of separate decisionmakers with one another; it thereby deprives itself of access to one of the most important sources of knowledge exhibited by these kinds of orders. Just as in biological competition, there is the "information bearer" function of DNA, so in the society of Tradition, this function is further served by such developments as language and culturally acquired techniques and habits. In the society of Market, profit and loss signals are added to this array. In the society of Planning, there is no new information bearer and those of the Market are discarded. It is this lack that gives the knowledge problem argument its force.

The description of the knowledge problem as a full critique of national economic planning is not yet complete. The three varieties of noncomprehensive planning to be taken up in the next chapters can be understood as representing three ways of attempting to resolve the knowledge problem by reducing the comprehensiveness of the planners' task. One tries to rely on an aggregated rather than a detailed use of knowledge in the planning process. A second aims at decentralizing the decisionmaking in the planning system as compared with the hierarchically organized procedures of comprehensive planning. The third proposes that the planning agency focus attention on propping up only certain "structural" sectors, rather than reach for so comprehensive a grasp over the whole economy. We must next consider whether any of these attempts are able to solve the knowledge problem.

NOTES TO CHAPTER 3

1. I hasten to add that Polanyi and Hayek do not contest the fact that in some sense what distinguishes the scientist from quacks has to do with the scientist's objectivity and rationality. The problem these two writers are concerned with lies in the question of just what is involved in this objectivity or rationality. They both are painfully conscious of having to give up two perfectly good words to their opponents. See Hayek (1967: 82–95) and Polanyi (1958a: 403). The word "positivist" is often used to denote this objectivist epistemology but that word is sometimes taken to mean only the particular school of logical positivism, which is a much narrower category than the position I am criticizing here. (Incidentally, this objectivism has nothing to do with the epistemology of Ayn Rand. Although the style of presentation of her position is diametrically opposed to that of Polanyi and Hayek, the content of her position is not nearly as different as it may appear.)

2. It may seem odd to find so much discussion of the philosophy of knowledge in a book on economic planning. But it has been shown (Gray 1984) that Hayek's theory of knowledge is the foundation of all of his work, including his critique of central planning. The first of this chapter's epigraphs reveals Polanyi's view of the close relation between epistemological and economic issues. I should point out, however, that it is quite possible for someone to reject much of this epistemology, which has substantial implications for all the sciences, and still agree with most of the basic critique of economic planning elaborated in this book. Thus I have relegated my more detailed discussion of these issues to the appendix.

3. It should also be admitted that individual projects of government-financed data gathering or forecasting may, in many instances, be found to be superior to any done within the private sector. The crop forecasts of the U.S. Department of Agriculture, or the money supply statistics of the Federal Reserve Bank may well be the best available sources of these kinds of information. Similarly impressive individual accomplishments can be cited in any area that has received large investments of government research monies. But we must bear in mind that the forgone uses of the massive funds that have been spent by these tax-supported research institutions are unknowable, and in most cases could probably have produced more useful knowledge or other kinds of products that would have been deemed more valuable.

4. Elsewhere I have discussed the history of the classic debate in which the knowledge problem was first formulated. Oskar Lange is generally thought to have won this "calculation debate" with his claim that the equations of Walras and Barone supplied the definitive answer to Mises's challenge. I have argued (1981, 1985) that this was a gross misrepresentation of the nature of the challenge being made, since Mises never tried to deny any of the formal deductive logic of general equilibrium analysis. To Mises's challenge that planners would lack the knowledge to run a technologically advanced economy Lange offered the answer: Under the assumption that all "data are given," as he liked to put it, there is no problem. "The administrators of a socialist economy will have exactly the same knowledge, or lack of knowledge, of the production functions as the capitalist entrepreneurs have" (Lange [1938] 1964: 61). But the point is that persons embroiled in a competitive process can, by virtue of their very rivalry with one another, impart information to the system of relative prices that in the absence of competition they would have no way of obtaining.

    I should point out that one of the several purposes of the discussion of epistemology in this chapter and the appendix is to provide a justification for the *kind* of demonstration I am trying to make. One of the most serious misinterpretations of earlier attempts to explain the knowledge problem, especially the attempt of Ludwig von Mises, was the notion that he was supplying some sort of rigorous formal proof of the impossibility of a planned economy, the reaction to which was that on the strictly formal level of economic analysis the knowledge problem does not exist. I argue, on the contrary, that nothing of importance concerning the viability of planning can be settled by means of such formal proofs. The argument does not pose as any sort of rigorous proof but is simply an attempt to persuade the reader that planning is not a very plausible way of running an economy. The main tools of this argument are not formalistic and mathematical but descriptive and analogical. To many economists this form of argument already condemns it as unscientific. It is partly in order to anticipate and counter this charge that I embark on this epistemological reconstruction.

5. I have of course packed many different epistemological positions into this one view of knowledge and it is quite possible for someone to hold only a subset of these positions, but space will not permit dealing with all the different permutations. The package as a whole seems to capture an overall attitude that has dominated much of philosophy at least since Descartes and that underlies the arguments for national economic planning.

6. The appendix will discuss this important revolution, which was ignited by Thomas S. Kuhn and try to relate it directly to Michael Polanyi's notion of "personal knowledge." Polanyi was not himself an active participant in the philosophical revolution with which I am concerned here, and

neither was Hayek, even though I will be using their work as well as Kuhn's to present what I believe is the most promising alternative to this objectivism. Hayek's and Polanyi's ideas are broadly consistent with the main elements of Kuhn's growth-of-knowledge perspective. In fact Kuhn has explicitly credited Polanyi with having influenced his ideas concerning the important role of paradigms in the scientific community:

> Mr. Polanyi himself has provided the most extensive and developed discussion I know of the aspect of science which led me to my apparently strange usage [of paradigm]. Mr. Polanyi repeatedly emphasizes the indispensable role played in research by what he calls the "tacit component" of scientific knowledge. This is the inarticulate and perhaps inarticulable part of what the scientist brings to his research problem: it is the part learned not by precept but principally by example and practice. (Crombie 1963: 392)

7. Students of philosophy will recognize many of these points as having been made by several important philosophers prior to Kuhn, Polanyi, and Hayek, including Locke, Hume, and Kant. In particular, the work of the later Ludwig Wittgenstein on the idea that the meaning of a language is culturally embedded has been cited by Thomas Kuhn as an influence on his thought, and it has been shown that Wittgenstein's work borrows much from the continental tradition of phenomenology that stems from the work of Edmund Husserl and even from some of the work of the existentialists. See for example Helmut Kuhn (1968), C. Daly (1968), Gier (1981), Gelwick (1977), and Barrett (1979) for some of these fascinating connections. Incidentally, the last of these studies explicitly draws the implication from this epistemology that comprehensive planning would be an impossibility (p. 114).

8. Indeed, it can be argued that the objectivist view of knowledge is primarily responsible not only for the fallacies of all varieties of planning, but also more generally for the lag of social sciences behind the natural sciences. While it was possible for the natural sciences to achieve success in spite of their commitment to this faulty theory of knowledge, the social sciences have been positively crippled by it. Ignoring the personal element necessarily involved even in the study of the contents of test tubes may have little impact on the progress of chemistry, but ignoring this personal element in the study of persons or of interactions among them has proved a positive hindrance to such fields as psychology and economics.

Polanyi (1958a: 347-380) has shown the reason the objectivist view of knowledge is more damaging to social sciences: "Facts about living things are more highly personal than the facts of the inanimate world. Moreover as we ascend to higher manifestations of life, we have to exercise ever more personal faculties—involving a more far-reaching participation of the knower—in order to understand life." (p. 347)

Polanyi's philosophy of science contains a kind of methodological dualism by degree. There is no sharp dividing line between natural and social sciences but, rather, a single spectrum in which all knowing requires *some* personal participation on the part of the knower; the social sciences, however, require more than, say, the study of insects, which in turn requires more than physics. See also Polanyi (1958b: 71–102). This issue bears on the argument of the latter part of this chapter that the personal component of socioeconomic knowledge is greater than that of the natural sciences. Axel Leijonhufvud (1981: 307) makes a very similar point when he contends that "the degree" to which subtle problems of interpretation "force themselves on the average practitioner and shape the collective style of the pursuit of knowledge in economics will pose problems for the extension of natural science-based Growth of Knowledge theories to the field."

9. For linguistics see Chomsky (1963), Hattiangati (1973), and Campbell (1982), and for the study of animal behavior see Thorpe (1963). The emergence of modern physics and especially quantum mechanics is often cited as having set in motion a serious retreat from the rigid deterministic model of Newtonian physics, which inspired the quest for certain, objective knowledge. On mathematics see Lakatos (1978) and the excellent survey of the "loss of certainty" that has taken place in the history of mathematics in Kline (1980). On psychology see much of the work of the gestalt school and modern, antibehaviorist cognitive psychology, such as Piaget (1971), Lackner and Garrett (1973), and Rosch (1977). For a nontechnical summary of much of this work, see Hunt (1982). And see Dreyfus (1979) for a fascinating if perhaps overpolemical study of the developments in the field of artificial intelligence, where the serious difficulties encountered are largely attributed to their lack of a notion of tacit knowledge.

10. One implication of this theory of knowledge is that it is *logically impossible* for a mind to understand itself in detail, because the individual mind is itself a spontaneous order of propensities and practical habits, none of which controls the outcome completely. Hayek ([1952] 1963) has argued this in more detail and with reference to the neurological functioning of the brain, and has concluded (1967: 73) that "the brain of an organism which acts as the directing centre for that organism is itself in turn a polycentric order, that is, that its actions are determined by the relation and mutual adjustment to each other of the elements of which it consists." The emerging consensus among cognitive scientists seems to agree with this view of the mind as itself, in an important sense, unplanned.

11. Or as Kuhn concisely puts it, "Knowledge of nature can be tacitly embodied in whole experiences without intervening abstraction of criteria or generalizations. Those experiences are presented to us during education and professional imitation by a generation which already knows what they are exemplars of" ([1962] 1970: 275). See also Kuhn (1977: 305–18).

12. One example from physics that Polanyi uses is in the study of the molecular motion of gas; he argues that "to specify the randomness of a gaseous molecular aggregate in terms of its mechanical particulars . . . is logically impossible (1958a: 391).

13. Hayek ([1962] 1967: 56–57): "Like scientific laws, the rules which guide an individual's act are better seen as determining what he will not do rather than what he will do."

14. See Polanyi (1972: 44–45). See the appendix for an elaboration of this point. The scientists' "hunches" about the potential fruitfulness of various avenues for future research, Polanyi insists, "are conjectural and may prove false, but they are not therefore mere guesses like betting on a throw of dice. For the capacity for making discoveries is not a kind of gambler's luck. It depends on natural ability, fostered by training and guided by intellectual effort. It is akin to artistic achievement and like it is unspecifiable, but far from accidental or arbitrary" (1958a, p. 106). Polanyi does not, however, equate the sort of meanings involved in the sciences, and the standards appropriate to them, with those of the arts. While the former is focusing on the nature of reality itself, the latter examines our emotional responses to reality. See Polanyi and Prosch (1975).

15. Many biologists and social scientists have fruitfully employed this type of analogy between animal and human societies, and I claim no originality for my use of this heuristic device. I will be trying only to draw out certain features of insect societies which I think are particularly important for understanding markets, not trying to supply an adequate description of the nature of insect societies.

16. For example, the previous chapter has just stressed the importance of humans' cultural transmission of effective habits and their economic selection of profitable methods of production as two particularly significant distinguishing characteristics of human as compared with other animal societies.

17. See also Thomas (1974: 12–13): "It is only when you watch the dense mass of thousands of ants, crowded together around the hill, blackening the ground, that you begin to see the whole beast, and now you observe it thinking, planning, calculating."

18. See, for example, Marx ([1867] 1967: 178): "What distinguishes the worst architect from the best of bees is this, that the architect raises his structure in imagination before he erects it in reality." Hayek (1967: 73) makes the same point: "The unique attribute of the brain is that it can produce a representative model on which the alternative actions and their consequences can be tried out beforehand."

19. This critique of neoclassical price theory has been one of the main themes of Kirzner's work (1973, 1979). Some important advancements within neoclassical economics are beginning to get away from this perfect competition approach; see, for example, Nelson and Winter (1982).

20.   "Organizational intelligence" may be differentiated from social intelli-
       gence in that it must resolve somehow—usually by an individual director—
       its internal conflicts. A society's social intelligence need not resolve such
       conflicts. On the limits to the organizational capacity of hierarchical orga-
       nizations, see Roberts (1971: ch. 3) and Polanyi (1951: 111–37).

21.   This has been proposed by Hurwicz (1973: 5) in an attempt to answer
       Hayek's critique of planning (1935, 1948). Some of what follows is taken
       from an article in which I criticize this approach.

22.   The first part of the next chapter will take up the issue of how detailed
       the collected information must be in order to guide an economy rationally.
       There it will be argued that knowing such things as how many factories
       there are in a given industry is useless unless you also know exactly how
       each factory is organized internally.

23.   For a lucid discussion of the complex network of continually changing
       and interrelated plans that can be called the capital structure, see Lach-
       mann (1978).

24.   Of course the point here is not to equate these two pursuits, of truth and
       of profits, as intrinsically or equally admirable, but rather to suggest that
       each form of personal commitment is a necessary component of social-
       evolutionary processes the results of which most of us cherish.

25.   Polanyi was drawn to the study of the sociology of science by his obser-
       vation of the crippling of science, especially but not only biology, under
       Stalinist-type regimes. It appears that even the most totalitarian system
       is forced to permit a substantial degree of freedom to its scientists if it
       expects the scientific discovery process to work. For an interesting ac-
       count of the delicate relationship between the scientific community and
       the political rulers in the post-Stalinist Soviet Union, see Parry (1966).

4 LEONTIEF AND THE CRITIQUE OF AGGREGATIVE PLANNING

At first sight, this looks exactly like a true plan, namely like a comprehensive purpose elaborated in detail through successive stages; the kind of plan, in fact, which can be carried out only by appropriate central direction.

But in reality such an alleged plan is but a meaningless summary of an aggregate of plans, dressed up as a single plan. It is as if the manager of a team of chess-players were to find out from each individual player what his next move was going to be and would then sum up the result by saying: "The plan of my team is to advance 45 pawns by one place, move 20 bishops by an average of three places, 15 castles by an average of four places, etc." He could pretend to have a plan for his team, but actually he would be only announcing a nonsensical summary of an aggregate of plans.

Michael Polanyi (1951: 134)

There can be no systematic thought on anything without a measure of abstraction. Thus, at some stage, we have to abstract from these individual differences. We may, then, speak of consumption patterns and the composition of the gross domestic product. We have no right to assume that these aggregates can, over time, lead a life of their own. All the time they will be shaped and re-shaped by forces emanating from the microsphere, forces that ultimately stem from human choice and decision.

Ludwig Lachmann (1973: 53)

[If] one starts unsystematically to interfere with the spontaneous order there is no practicable halting point and . . . it is therefore necessary to choose between alternative systems. [Interventionists] are pleased to think that by proceeding experimentally and therefore "scientifically" they will succeed in fitting together in piecemeal fashion a desirable order by choosing for each particular desired result what science shows them to be the most appropriate means of achieving it. This "realistic" view which has now dominated politics for so long has hardly produced the results which its advocates desired. Instead of having achieved greater mastery over our fate we find ourselves in fact more frequently committed to a path which we have not deliberately chosen, and faced with "inevitable necessities" of further action which, though never intended, are the result of what we have done.

F. A. Hayek (1973: 58–59)

THE CRITIQUE OF AGGREGATIVE DATA GATHERING

The proper response to my argument against the comprehensive form of planning would seem to be to relax its stringent requirement of controlling the details of economic activity. Surely it should be possible merely to attain control over broad aggregates, to guide the economy's general directions rather than each of its intricate parts. It would seem that the very factor which made the knowledge problem such an overwhelming difficulty for comprehensive planning—its detail—is easy to relinquish. Indeed virtually all modern advocates of planning would argue that if we simply lower our ambitions to the steering of the economy's "broad paths of development," as Wassily Leontief would say, instead of its precise evolution, then the difficulties elaborated in the previous chapter completely disappear.

Such an apparently plausible retreat to noncomprehensive or aggregative planning is fundamentally illusory, however. Once control over detail is abandoned so must be control as such, except in the sense that the basic legal "rules of the game" within which economic choices are made can and should be decided upon. That is, some sort of well-defined system of rights which tells people what kinds of actions they are entitled to take with respect to one another is necessary. But insofar as anything that can sensibly be called "national economic planning" is concerned, aggregative planning is more akin to throwing a wrench into a complex piece of machinery than it is to controlling anything.

Essentially, the problem with noncomprehensive planning is a direct corollary of the critique of comprehensive planning. The latter is impossible, because no single agency could attain a level of individual intelligence that could rival the social intelligence that emerges from the competitive process. While noncomprehensive planning is not an impossibility (indeed the world has seen little else this century) it does represent an attempt to interfere with the competitive process in order to steer it onto desired paths of development. But the same lack of knowledge on the part of any single person or organization which makes it impossible for comprehensive planning to replace the market also makes it irrational for a noncomprehensive planning agency to try merely to "guide" the market. If the guiding agency is less knowledgeable than the system it is trying to guide—and even worse, if its actions necessarily result in further undesired consequences in the working of that system—then what is going on is not planning at all but, rather, blind interference by some agents with the plans of others.

A comprehensive planning agency, if it could exist in a modern economy, would be distinguished from planning of the more mundane and partial variety (as it is done, for example, by businessmen) in that it would be able to plot all the consequences of its own actions. In that case unintended consequences could be dispensed with and humanity could truly become master of its own future development. But if this ambitious goal proves unattainable, as most advocates of planning now admit it is, then what can be said in this regard of noncomprehensive planning? How does it differ from the partial planning of the individual firm? Surely neither can pretend to be able to anticipate the remote consequences (both in time and place) of the limited variables it controls. In each case the attempt by any one decisionmaker to solve one problem may unintentionally lead to the creation of new problems for other decisionmakers.

The primary characteristic that distinguishes the noncomprehensive planning done by a government from the familiar planning the rest of us engage in during our daily lives would seem to be that the former has the advantage of being able to employ coercion to help achieve its purposes. The rest of us have to persuade others, for example by offering them something valuable in exchange, in order to get them to cooperate with us so that we can achieve our goals. This coercive advantage does not guarantee, however, that the goals promoted by the government planners will be accomplished. By definition, noncomprehensive planning seeks to control only part of the economic system and hence those parts which it does not control are free to react in their own ways and at their own initiative to government policies. These reactions and the consequences they engender cannot be fully anticipated by noncomprehensive planners, and thus may cause undesirable and unplanned results to follow in the wake of their policies.

All proponents of noncomprehensive planning ought to address themselves to this issue. They ought to explain why any one agency in society should have this coercive advantage over others in the economy. In particular, in light of the knowledge problem, why should we expect noncomprehensive planners to be any better informed about the remote consequences of their coercion-backed plans than the rest of us are about the consequences of our persuasion-backed plans?

What makes Leontief outstanding among the advocates of national economic planning is that (1) he is the only one of them to refrain, for the most part, from advocating any specific policies, which he says cannot be rationally discussed in the absence of better procedures for data collection; and (2) he is the only one to concentrate on this fundamental problem of trying to drastically improve the status of the information relevant to policymaking. Leontief seems to address the existence of the knowledge problem as the chief obstacle to rational policymaking as it is conducted now, and to attempt to resolve this problem by proposing specific data-gathering methods that he thinks will adequately inform policymakers. In contrast, the other proponents of planning are all too ready to support their favored policies without first suggesting how to improve the information we have about the likely results of such policies.

Wassily Leontief, distinguished Nobel Prize winner in economics and inventor of the input-output method of statistical organization, is undoubtedly the nation's leading academic advocate of planning.[1] He has supported every flicker of interest in the national economic planning idea that he has been able to discern in this country, and he promotes the idea all over the world. He served with then United Automobile Workers president Leonard Woodcock as co-chairman of the Initiative Committee for National Economic Planning; he helped to create and then actively promoted the two major planning bills of recent years (Humphrey-Javits and Humphrey-Hawkins);[2] he has participated in major planning-related projects for the United Nations; and he has seen his input-output method implemented as a basis for planning in dozens of countries including France, Japan, the USSR, and several developing countries. In short if we are to end up with some sort of national economic plan in this country, Leontief's ideas will almost certainly have been among the chief influences in its design.

This is not to say that any planning agency and its periodic plans would take exactly the form Leontief wants. He is sophisticated enough in the ways of politics to recognize that "the final version of the national economic plan will be an end product of the typically American political logrolling and legislative wrangles" (Leontief 1977a: 155). But he does not at all consider this a liability. He believes that, supplied by the planning agency with "nontechnical descriptions of feasible alternatives among which a practical choice can actually be made" (1981: 6–7), the logrolling and wrangling will be conducted on a far higher level than they are now.

Indeed in this respect Leontief differentiates himself from most of the other planning advocates. For him the issue is neither which interest group runs the planning agency nor what goals it pursues, but simply the need for rationalizing the policymaking process as such. He frankly admits what the advocates of economic democracy, for example, would strenuously resist conceding, that there is "no reason to assume that the introduction of national economic planning would require or could bring about a marked shift in the overall national balance of economic and political power. The wealthy with the support of their retainers can be expected to continue to rule the roost" (1977a: 158). Although his own political sentiments favor a substantial redistribution of wealth, Leontief insists that planning is a general *method* for improving the process of policy formation and implementation and should not be advocated mainly or solely as a vehicle for any one particular set of policy goals, whether his or any other economist's: "In choosing between the alternative combination of ultimate social and economic attainments, professional economists cannot claim and should not legitimately expect to be given a greater voice than anyone else" (1981: 6).

Thus Leontief makes his pitch for planning strictly in the guise of a scientist, as an economist who explains to political decisionmakers what are the possible future paths of the economy. He does not try to influence the choice, except to try to ensure that it is rational. Throughout the political battles that will inevitably be fought over these paths, and at each new stage of compromise between factions, the task of the planning agency will be to make sure that "through all its transformation from the first to the last, the overall plan retains its integrity: Do not allocate more than you can produce, but also see to it that nothing is left over" (1977a: 155).

Surely this sounds like a purpose anyone could agree with. Leontief is saying that policymakers should know what they are doing, that they should figure out whether whatever they advocate is at least achievable. The planning agency, staffed with disinterested professional economists, will simply draw up a set of alternative scenarios from which other, presumably interested, parties can choose. Politics can thereby rid itself of its ridiculous contests among fantasies such as those embodied in Ronald Reagan's popular 1980 and 1984 campaign promises to simultaneously balance the budget, cut taxes, and increase military spending.[3] Now the facts about what can and what cannot be achieved will be firmly established by the planning agency first, and the competition will have to be among feasible policies instead of fantasies. "Adversary policy debate could and should continue, but *adversary fact finding would have become impossible* and policies that tend to cancel out or contradict each other would at least be shown up for what they are" (1977a: 157, emphasis added).

All of this assumes, however, that the relevant facts can be ascertained in the absence of the sort of rivalrous discovery process depicted in the previous chapter. It assumes that a single agency would be able to establish objectively what future paths the economy can traverse. Leontief believes this can be accomplished by means of the input–output data-collection method to be examined below. I will argue on the contrary that competition among persons who hold different expectational scenarios, which Leontief condemns as "adversary fact finding," is among the most important and indispensable functions of the competitive process. Vera Lutz (1969: 149) made this point succinctly when she wrote:

> The "logic of the market economy" pre-supposes that different operators, having different expectations, different judgements and access to partly different information, make their forecasts and take their decisions independently of one another. It implies that competition in prediction is an integral part of competition in the wider sense and a part which cannot be eliminated without eliminating the whole.

In any case Leontief does make a respectable attempt to circumvent the central issue of this book, the knowledge problem, even if his success in resolving it can be seriously questioned. As for the secondary issue, the totalitarian problem—that national economic planning is apt to lead to an undesirable concentration of power—he has virtually nothing to say at all. In response to radical economists who accuse him of putting terrific power in the hands of the powerful, Leontief's (1976: 13-14) answer is

> I think transferring real power from one strata [sic] to another is an incredibly difficult process. I think if planning is introduced, the power structure will remain the same and planning will be done by the same people who are now running the country. Essentially they are doing it anyway, so to my radical friends my answer is, "Look, since it is being done, why shouldn't it be done more efficiently?"

Leaving aside for now the question of whether the efficient exercise of power is, as he seems to think, an uncontroversial goal everybody including radicals should share,[4] there is a deceptive plausibility to Leontief's argument. First of all, we must admit that the government's left hand ought at least to know what its right hand is doing. If the government is to protect us from pollution, for example, surely we can at least advocate that it do so consistently. Unless one stands unalterably opposed to the government's activity in these areas, there is nothing very contentious in the proposal that the Department of Energy coordinate its policies with the Environmental Protection Agency. It is hard to imagine anyone positively advocating that these policies should clash with one another as they often do now.

But if this is accepted, Leontief continues, what if these two departments of government are mutually coordinated, but their policies clash with decisions of the airlines, car manufacturers, and railroad and highway builders, all of whom can seriously affect the environment? Should not these decisions then also be coordinated? What is the point of consistent governmental policy if it is nullified by contradictory private sector activity? The consistent advocacy of any purposive government policy, Leontief (1977a: 157-58) argues, should lead all the way to national economic planning.

Of course it is desirable that private and public sector activities be coordinated with one another. But it is not immediately evident why the best way to accomplish that end is planning, which would imply a drastically increased role for governmental control over nongovernmental institutions. If the government has been unable even to coordinate its own institutions, perhaps the best way to improve coordination is to reduce and simplify the role of government in society, not to expand and complicate it. Leontief's argument jumps from the uncontroversial statement that government should put its own house in order to the more contentious claim that government should intervene into the market to try to put all our houses in order.[5]

Leontief has a point, however, when he stresses that if planning is to be rational it cannot be a hodgepodge of decentralized plans all jumbled together at the national level, but will have to be centrally coordinated. He dismisses the economic democracy notions of localized planning with the remark, "You cannot do national planning by town meetings" (1976: 15). Such decentralists, he says, fail to realize how technically complicated the task of coordinating a nation's economy is. Only a large, centralized, well-financed data-gathering agency could possibly take on the extremely difficult task required.[6] "Without a comprehensive, internally consistent plan there can be, in this sense, no planning" (1977a: 150). Of course, much of the data collection itself will be decentralized, but for it to be meaningful the standards for data will have to be uniform, and its coordination will have to be done by a single agency since "incompatible data are useless data" (1977a: 31–32).

Leontief further shows how the traditional use of monetary and fiscal policies is grossly inadequate to the complicated task of planning a modern economy. The problem, he says, is not so much that these tools are inherently inadequate, as it is that the government currently does not have a clear view of where it wants to go, and so is using these tools blindly and inconsistently. But if formulating a coherent plan to give policy its needed sense of direction is the primary goal, simply publishing such a plan or "map" is not sufficient. Making up a feasible plan is a necessary first step "but the preparation of a script is not enough; the play has to be staged and acted out" (1977a: 150).[7]

Against the argument that planning requires predicting the uncertain future and trying to shape it to one grand design, Leontief (1977a: 151) insists that "a plan is not a forecast. The whole idea of planning assumes the possibility of choice among alternative feasible scenarios. Feasibility is the key word." In other words, he is not trying to confine policy choice to a single master plan, but to a selected subset of all imaginable plans that are achievable. In fact he says the planning agency "should be able to develop as many plans as there are different views regarding what direction the economy and our government should move (1976: 15).[8]

The fundamental problem of our modern policies, which Leontief sees quite clearly, is that ad hoc and tentative measures to tinker with our complex economy are being used without any awareness of their intricate train of consequences rippling through interdependent sectors of the economy.

> The effects of any major policy cannot be assessed without also taking account of the mostly unintended indirect effects of other policies applying to other problems. . . . Thus it is not surprising that actions intended to solve one particular problem create new problems elsewhere. If policy makers act in ignorance of such indirect interrelationships, measures taken by one government or corporate office will tend to cancel out the effects of actions taken by another. . . . As things stand, one group of policy makers often becomes aware that it works at cross purposes with another group; but neither one possesses sufficient knowledge about the combined effect of each other's policies. (1982b: 31–32)

In other words, current policymaking is plagued by the knowledge problem, in which uncoordinated plans clash with and cancel out one another. In such a situation, no overall rational planning is possible, and as Leontief points out, none would be possible so long as government lacks comprehensive and detailed information about how the economy is working, including the ability

> to anticipate potential trouble spots, the parts of the economy where, to name only a few examples, energy shortages, technological unemployment, population movements, or sudden needs for long-term credits may arise. . . . This would, in fact, be the only means by which the government and the electorate would be enabled to make informed choices among different policies. (1982b: 33)

What is entailed in the task of obtaining such intricate knowledge of what Leontief calls the "interacting empirical realities" of a modern economy? He does not agree with the Marxist view that only the total comprehensive control of all details of the whole production process by a single administrative agency can accomplish this goal.

Like most modern planners, Leontief explicitly denies that private ownership and the price mechanism would have to be abolished in order to achieve the comprehensive knowledge of the economy's workings that he says is needed. He contends that the market system is a marvelous system of automatic coordination which is indispensable but simply does not always work right, and so needs to be subsumed under and guided by a planning agency. "In a planned economy," he adds, "the price mechanism will be an effective but humble servant of the society not, as it frequently is, an overbearing and all too often fumbling master" (1977a: 156).

Generally speaking, this mixed-economy view—that planning and market institutions are compatible and that the latter ought to be controlled by the former—is the mainstream perspective on this issue. Establishment Keynesians (and indeed most modern economists) view the application of fiscal and monetary measures in this light as attempts to steer a market system through macroeconomic policy without seeking comprehensive control of its every detail. Modern economics is vested with the task of determining which macro tool to apply in any given situation in order to guide the market.

But Leontief offers some rather convincing arguments against trying to control a complex modern economy according to the dictates of this mainstream economics. In fact his critique goes to the heart of orthodox neoclassical economics, charging that it has split into two equally irrelevant branches: an increasingly abstract and formal theory, and a body of empirical work that is more notable for its sophisticated econometric massaging of already existing and highly aggregated data than for any substantive addition to our factual knowledge. From the practical standpoint of, say, the day-to-day operation of a steel plant, the exquisite mathematical models that reside and prosper in the academic journals are quite useless: "Page after page of professional economic journals are filled with mathematical formulas leading the reader from sets of more or less plausible but entirely arbitrary assumptions to precisely stated but irrelevant theoretical conclusions" (1982a: 104).

Leontief's point is not that any use of mathematics is inappropriate in this science but that economics is coming to look like, and conform exclusively to the standards of, pure mathematics. Problems are taken up not for their possible relevance to, say, the seriously crippled economy we actually live in, but simply for the exercise of mathematical and econometric tricks. As with pure mathematics, many of these problems have an intrinsic fascination all their own, but this development has been most tragic to the extent that it has squeezed out of the journals virtually all work relating directly to actual economic problems.

The irrelevance to the real world of purely theoretical work, such as the rarified "existence proofs" of general equilibrium analysis, is neither surprising nor especially controversial. But Leontief goes on to point out the irrelevance of the supposedly empirical part of modern economics as well. The chief reason for this, he demonstrates, is the way economists so readily resort to aggregation.

> The primary information, however detailed, is packaged in a relatively small number of bundles labeled "Capital," "Labor," "Raw Materials," "Intermediate Goods," "General Price Level," and so on. These bundles are then usually fitted into a "model," that is, a small system of equations describing the entire economy in terms of a small number of corresponding "aggregative" variables. (1982a: 104)

After listing as an example a production function model in which a half-dozen equations are supposed to describe an economy's production of some sort of undifferentiated steel, Leontief observes, "To ask a manager of a steel plant or a metallurgical expert for information on the magnitude of the six parameters appearing in these six equations would make no sense" (1982a: 104).

This, I think, is the precisely appropriate standard to use in judging the relevance of economic theories: Are they built up from those microeconomic elements that would be understandable to the real individual decisionmakers whose cumulative choices actually keep an economy running? The economic system is quite oblivious to whatever magnitude macroeconomists measure "Capital" to be and would hardly notice if this quantity, which somehow manages to add together completely heterogeneous things, were, say, to double overnight. The money value of the capital goods owned by an individual firm can be added together to give a meaningful number only because these goods are all part of a single plan. But once attempts are made to aggregate capital goods across an entire economy the numbers that result from the arithmetic lose their significance because they add up components of mutually incompatible plans. As Ludwig Lachmann (1978: 2) once put it, "We cannot add beer barrels to blast furnaces nor trucks to yards of telephone wire" in any meaningful way. The widespread use of money prices as the common denominator by which such aggregation is performed would only be legitimate in an equilibrium context in which all plans are perfectly coordinated with one another.[9]

In the real world, of course, one firm's truck may be used as a competitive substitute for another firm's telephone wire, in such a way as to make the future value of one dependent on the loss of value of the other. Rivalrous competition means that one agent's plan can succeed only at the expense of some other, incompatible plan. In such circumstances (which *always* exist in the real, disequilibrium world) adding together the values of the capital used by rivalrous firms has about as much meaning as adding the value of a bridge to the value of the bomb being built to blow it up.[10]

The very process of aggregating, even if not carried to the extreme of adding up an economy's capital, necessarily involves the loss of information.[11] As Leontief puts it, "The difference between copper and nickel vanishes as soon as both are treated as 'nonferrous metals' and both become indistinguishable from steel as soon as the qualifying specification 'nonferrous' has been dropped too" (1977a: 36).

In other words more aggregated categories such as "metals" have secured a somewhat dubious degree of "comparability . . . at the cost of analytical sharpness in the description" (1977a: 36). When such loss of sharpness in description is carried to the extremes common in most of modern empirical research, the results are models that operate in terms of constructs of the analyst's mind that are practically meaningless, having nothing to do with the disaggregated reality they purport to describe.

When such meaningless aggregates are then plugged into computer forecasting models in order to extrapolate their trends and predict when recessions will occur and end, and when it is this kind of soothsaying that guides our leaders' economic policies, the profession moves from the "irrelevant" category to the "dangerous." Armed only with these aggregative models of the economy, it is hardly surprising that government policy has been completely impotent in the face of the severe and worsening problems of the contemporary world. With so little direct contact with the actual disaggregated data of the decisionmakers, it is little wonder that the injection of government policies into the market will bear more resemblance to the bludgeoning than the guidance of an intricate mechanism. One does not have to be particularly skeptical to doubt that the salvation of our economy will ever come so long as economic policy prescription is so remote from the specific details of the economy its users are trying to understand and direct. As Leontief has written,

> Can one seriously believe that a significant contribution to the solution of our economic problems will be madé by efforts to increase the reliability of econometric forecasts through tinkering with already highly sophisticated statistical procedures, or by making marginal improvements in the accuracy of aggregate price and other indices that would identify the day and hour when recession ends and recovery begins? I doubt this can be done and so, I believe, does much of the informed public. (1982b: 31)

LEONTIEF'S ALTERNATIVE: THE INPUT–OUTPUT METHOD

What does Leontief offer instead of this naïve faith in aggregative modeling techniques? His central contribution has been the famous input–output method whose purported advantage is its avoidance of the very aggregation that had served to separate mainstream economists from the decentralized information relevant, for example, to the manager of a steel plant.

The basic idea of input–output tables is to show the interrelations between relatively disaggregated sectors in the form of a matrix in which the "horizontal rows of figures show how the output of each sector of the economy is distributed among the others" while "the vertical columns show how each sector obtains from the others its needed inputs of goods and services" (1966: 15). In this way the output of each sector is shown to be an input in some other.

What is compelling about this approach is that it is, in principle, microscopic rather than macroscopic. That is, it directs attention to the complex details of interdependence of the structure of production rather than to some single-dimensional measure of the size of the nation's wealth or capital stock. Causal change is presumably to be depicted as a series of the economy's actual detailed decisions rather than as a direct relationship between aggregates constructed by model builders.

> Economists have generally based their analyses on relatively simple data — such quantities as the gross national product, the interest rate, price and wage

levels. But in the real world, things are not so simple. Between a shift in wages and the ultimate working out of its impact upon prices there is a complex series of transactions in which actual goods and services are exchanged among real people. These intervening steps are scarcely suggested by the classical formulation of the relationship between the two variables. . . . (1966: 14–15)

Here [with input-output] we have our bridge between theory and facts in economics. It is a bridge in a very literal sense. Action at a distance does not happen in economics any more than it does in physics. The effect of an event at any one point is transmitted to the rest of the economy step by step via the chain of transactions that link the whole system together. (1966: 24)

Thus the essential advantage about which this technique can boast as contrasted with standard approaches to empirical work is that it claims to be able to bring us down to the level of these individual transactions and their involved structure of interdependence with one another. Since it is only on this detailed level where human choices about concrete uses of factors of production are made, this appears to represent a fundamental improvement over the empirical work of orthodox economics. Unlike those models, "the input-output table . . . reveals the fabric of our economy, woven together by the flow of trade which ultimately links each branch and industry to all others" (1966: 15).

However, this apparently qualitative advantage, which Leontief implicitly claims for his method in these passages, and upon which his entire critique of aggregative empirical work is based, turns out to be illusory. In fact, the input-output method resorts in practice to some rather drastic aggregation of its own, which serves to nullify any advantage it might seem to have over other empirical methods as an instrument of planning. All the same reasons that make Leontief so suspicious of government policies guided only by aggregative models should leave him profoundly dubious of policies guided by his own method as well.

Leontief does admit in some places that in practice the input-output method never reaches all the way down to those individual transactions that really drive the economy: "The number of goods and services that more and more detailed observation of various processes of production and consumption would permit us to distinguish is much greater than even an input-output matrix containing many thousands of rows and columns can possibly hold" (1977a: 48).

The national input-output tables that have been produced so far are more on the order of at most a few dozens of rows and columns. Thus it appears that his argument in practice is not against aggregation as such but only against excessive aggregation. In fact Leontief's method rests on precisely the kind of extrapolation of statistical trends among aggregates which mainstream economists use; his aggregates are merely smaller.

> It is true, of course, that the individual transactions, like individual atoms and molecules, are far too numerous for observation and description in detail. But it is possible, as with physical particles, to reduce them to some kind of order by classifying and aggregating them into groups. This is the procedure employed by input-output analysis in improving the grasp of economic theory upon the facts with which it is concerned in every real situation. (1966: 15)

But on what basis can it be argued that Leontief's smaller aggregates offer us a substantially better "grasp of economic theory upon the facts" of the real world than the larger aggregates he ridicules? What is there about the smallness per se of an aggregate that makes it preferable? And if somehow smallness is to be the standard, why stop at the level of sectors and why even stop at the level of those individual transactions that Leontief rightly says are the real stuff of the economy? Why not argue for reducing individual choices to the even smaller level of atomic particles?[12]

The peculiar references to physics in the preceding quotations may suggest that Leontief has misunderstood the nature of the difficulty involved in aggregation. The reason that the details of actual transactions are far more valuable than gross aggregates is not just that they are smaller, and has little to do with the physicists' aversion to explanations in terms of action at a distance. Details about concrete individual transactions are more valuable than gross aggregates because only such details are meaningful to the human minds whose interaction drives the economic process. Understanding how an economy works involves paying attention to the circumstances, meaning, and consequences of the individual human actions that make up an economic order. The irrelevance of aggregates is simply a consequence of the fact that quantities like "Capital" have no meaning to human actors like that manager of a steel plant Leontief refers to, and play no role in their choices. It by no means follows from this argument that a slightly smaller aggregate, say, "Electrical Machinery" should be any better.

Like so many of the modern economists he criticizes, Leontief has failed to realize the important difference between what constitutes a satisfactory explanation in physics and what can do so in economics. Although physicists lack any direct knowledge of how a molecule works but can observe that, on average, groups of them behave in predictable ways, they can indeed employ aggregative methods to some advantage. But economists know a bit about how human beings work, since they are human, and find that statistical aggregates of human actions or of their artifacts show little of the neat regularity found, for example, in the study of gaseous molecules. A mere extrapolation from statistical patterns may very well suffice as a physical explanation, but it will in most cases be entirely unreliable and unsatisfactory as an economic explanation. Instead, what the economist can do satisfactorily is explain overall social patterns by making them intelligible in terms of the purposes of the individuals involved. Here, taking advantage of what each human being knows about purposive behavior, economists have proven able to elaborate an illuminating "logic of choice" that can explain a great variety of economic phenomena.[13]

In complex phenomena such as life and human economies it is nearly always impossible to build precise, deterministic models of the workings of the entities under scientific study. The most that can be expected in such studies is what Hayek calls "explanations of the principle" as are exemplified in the modern theory of evolution in biology and in the principle of purposefulness in economics. Specific biological events, such as the emergence of mammals, can be explained by the principle of evolution (for example, why certain working characteristics survive and reproduce themselves), in much the same way as specific historical events, such as the emergence of money, can be explained by the principle of purposefulness (why certain characteristics of goods made them more likely to evolve into money). In both cases there are emergent characteristics that result from the particular evolutionary forces in question and in both cases these emergent properties exhibit a certain degree of order that cannot be called "designed." The sciences of biology and economics have been able to provide some of their most valuable contributions to knowledge in the explanation of such orders. Neither discipline, however, has proven particularly adept at precise quantitative predictions.

What is properly involved in economics is the building of a conceptual framework for historical interpretation capable of making certain kinds of outcomes understandable in terms of the purposes that led to them. For example, such interpretative frameworks for studying economic growth as Marx's and Böhm-Bawerk's were intended as theoretical "spectacles" through which the technological and economic progress in the emerging capitalist economy could be rendered intelligible. They were explanations of principles and were never intended or expected to be predictive models in the tradition of Newtonian mechanics.[14]

Leontief (1977a: 70–71) somewhat ambitiously believes that his input-output method's "dynamic inverse" is a historic advance over these famous economists' theories, for the same reason that I would consider it a retrogression: "While these great economists had to content themselves with verbal description and deductive reasoning, we can measure and we can compute. Therein lies the real difference between the past and the present state of economics."

But the accumulation of numbers cannot be called "measurement" unless some constant unit is postulated in which measurement can be made, the adding up of which captures some meaningful aspect of reality. Yet the clearest and most widely agreed upon fact of economic circumstances is that no such unit of measurement exists. Nobody needs to be told today that the value of money is highly variable, and economists agree that there is no single way to construct an indexing method that can measure changes in the value of money. (See Mises [1912] 1980: 215–23 and Jones 1934.)

The only economic numbers that are meaningful to the real decisionmakers whose interaction drives the economy are money prices and the accounting exercises that are carried out in terms of them, and even there they cannot properly be called a measure of anything. As Mises ([1949] 1966: 349) put this point:

> Cost accounting is . . . not an arithmetical process which can be established and examined by an indifferent umpire. It does not operate with uniquely determined magnitudes which can be found out in an objective way. Its essential items are the result of an understanding of future conditions, necessarily always colored by the entrepreneur's opinion about the future state of the market.

Prices of specific goods and services carry meaning with them because of the largely inarticulate attributes these goods and services are presumed to have. Only particular goods and services enter into transactions and thus only their particular prices have meaning. Arbitrary bundles of goods whose prices we can sum under some general category of our own invention cannot be said to mean much of anything, if they do not carry any meaning to the transactors themselves. Leontief would presumably argue that because his electrical machinery category, for example, is *closer* to the meaningful level of individual transactions, it is therefore *more* meaningful than the orthodox economist's capital. But the meaning of the concept "closeness" is itself questionable in this context. Concrete economic decisions are never made in terms of the quantity of electrical machinery; they are made in terms of specific pieces of such machinery at particular times and places destined for particular uses. Computing a total sum of a nation's electrical machinery involves exactly the same questionable procedures as adding up a nation's capital. The result in either case is an arbitrary construct of the analyst, not a concrete element in the causal functioning of the economy.[15]

While Leontief (1977a: 49) has admitted that "even a most detailed input-output table" can only "be said to present the actual economic system . . . in an aggregated . . . form," his work is infused with statements suggesting that it is in fact the concrete details of individual transactions, and thus the fundamental causal elements of economic change, that input-output tables depict. He asserts, for example, that "the full interdependence between the 18 metalworking industries engaged in the manufacture of raw and finished metal products can be brought out" through the use of input-output tables (p. 44). He claims to be seeking "concrete rather than purely symbolic description of alternative methods of production and the realistic delineation of alternative paths of technological change" (p. 152). He comments (1977b: 2) on the model he helped to construct for the United Nations (*The Future of the World Economy*) that "despite its global scope, the model displays an unusual degree of detail" and "permits a detailed analysis of prospective changes in technology, cost of production and relative prices."

In fact, this unusual degree of detail amounts to the breakdown of regions into such localities as "North America" and "Eastern Europe" and reduces products to such categories as "textiles" and "communication." Examples of the "relative prices" that can be extracted from such a model would be the relative price of "metal products" in terms of "services," or "transport" in terms of "industrial chemicals." Would it be unfair to ask to what possible uses the manager of a steel plant might be able to put such relative prices?

Leontief (1977a: 134) believes that his world input–output model, which includes a total of only forty-five productive sectors, can "provide a framework for assembling and organizing the mass of factual data needed to describe the world economy. Such a system is essential for a concrete understanding of the structure of the world economy as well as for a systematic mapping of the alternative paths along which it could move in the future."

Of course including much more detail than these forty-five sectors when dealing with the world's economy would have been prohibitively expensive. What about the more modest applications of the input–output technique to a single nation's economy? After all, it is only national and not world economic planning that is at issue here. Is it not possible on a smaller scale to empirically capture the particular level at which the causal movement of the economy is discernible? Apparently not. Even though hundreds of distinct sectors of national input–output tables are being compiled, the categories are invariably aggregated constructs, constructs in terms of which no transaction is ever carried out. After referring to the most detailed form of input–output data gathering (which is not used nationally but only within certain industries and localities), Leontief (1977a: 152) hastens to add, lest he be misunderstood to be an advocate of comprehensive planning, that he would never think of including such extreme detail as this in a national economic plan.

But if the planners cannot obtain such detailed knowledge and are forced to formulate their plans in terms of broad aggregates, then they are in the same position as Michael Polanyi's chess captain who wants to control the general direction of his team even though he lacks the knowledge his individual players possess. The planner would be trying to push their actions in general directions, analogous to the chess captain commanding his players to move, say, more of their castles toward the left, even though the captain may not know where all the castles are much less how they fit into any particular plans of the players. Making such planning directives more vague and general, rather than detailed, does not in the least answer the challenge posed by the knowledge problem. If the planners do not know the details, then they do not know what they need to know to justify the imposition of their choices over those who they are trying to direct.[16]

Even though keeping track of the input-output interrelations among hundreds of sectors is unusually detailed for economists, it is still so far removed from the concrete decisionmaking that moves the economy as to render this information, although perhaps of interest to many economic historians, utterly useless for uncovering the interacting empirical realities that Leontief rightly says we need to know for planning. Nobody in the real economy weighs the value of aggregated constructs of particular goods. They directly assess individual goods in particular combinations and thus it is only on this particular level that the causal movement of economic phenomena can be adequately explained. Changes in an aggregate, whether as large as "GNP" or as small as "electronic components and accessories," are purely accidental by-products of individual human actions which are actually undertaken with respect to particular goods.

THE LEAP FROM DATA GATHERING TO PLANNING

So far the problem with Leontief's proposal for planning has been presented as if it were merely a practical difficulty involved in the limited extent to which input-output data can be disaggregated. It may appear that if, so far, Leontief has been unable to afford the costs of getting as detailed as his method promises, then perhaps the solution is for the government to invest far more substantial funds in data collection until Leontief's tables *are* complete. In terms of neo-classical economics, one might argue that there are potential economies of scale in the production of information which cannot be exploited by the relatively small firms in the private sector but which can be exploited by government.[17] Even so, in light of the knowledge problem, one might question whether anyone could ever know when such a massive investment of government funds toward data gathering was appropriate and when it was not. It might be supposed, then, that there is nothing more to be said on the matter.

But to leave the discussion at this point would be misleading, because the really essential problem of planning is not merely this *practical* difficulty of collecting data that is sufficiently detailed, a problem that we could perhaps imagine being overcome one day by some sort of technological revolution in information-handling systems. The central problem is rather that the knowledge that is truly relevant for economic decisionmaking is inherently uncollectible.

To bring this point home we can assume that a super Data-Gathering Agency has received such funding as to enable it to actually disaggregate the data it assembles into input-output tables right down to the level of the particular concrete goods and services that enter into the transactions of individuals. That is, let us presume that the input-output tables are constructed with as many rows and columns as there are goods and services that are separately priced in the whole U.S. economy. Indeed, let us further suppose that all these data are collected and updated so quickly as to actually keep track of the ongoing development of the economy, transaction by transaction.[18] Even if we grant him these highly implausible assumptions, Leontief has provided us with no argument that would logically permit us to proceed from the possession of this super input-output table to the presumption that we could use it to plan the economy.

The reason lies in the problem of inarticulate knowledge. Any data that can be gathered by a single agency, whether in the input-output form or in more traditional statistics, and whether aggregated or not, must perforce be made up of articulated specifics. But only a tiny fraction of the actual knowledge that guides decisionmakers in the economy can ever be put into explicit form. The entrepreneur who decides to engage in a transaction, say, to buy a particular tool, has far more going on in his mind than he ever has to, or could, articulate to anyone. He views this particular tool as an integral part of a *plan* that in turn fits into a general expectational scenario he has about how he intends to implement that plan through time.

It might be thought that the advocate of planning could simply respond that he doesn't care what options decentralized decisionmakers would have considered or chosen, since he has no intention of imitating them, and therefore can safely dispense with these difficulties of tacit, contextual knowledge. To take this position, however, would be to abandon all reliance on the market process, the distinguishing attribute of noncomprehensive planning. He would thus push the issue back to the arguments of the previous chapter. Either the central planning office will have to replace the market process altogether, or it is going to have to use the decentralized knowledge that is actually relevant to market participants in order to guide the market intelligently. But if this relevant decentralized knowledge is, as the chess analogy suggests, not merely objective data about transactions but inherently contextual and tacit in nature, then the "data-collection" task turns out to be not just difficult but completely unmanageable.

Thus even if the national planning agency could monitor each transaction in detail, it would still lack information about how each decisionmaker perceives this transaction *in the context of his own plans.* Yet without this context the transactions themselves are meaningless by-products of choices, and hence knowledge of them is insufficient for the purpose of rationally controlling the causal sequence of events of a modern economy.

In the passages subsequent to those excerpted in this chapter's first epigraph Michael Polanyi (1951: 135) proceeds to ask why it is not possible to conduct a hundred games of a chess team by central direction, making one person responsible for all bishop moves, another in charge of castles, of knights, and so on.

> The answer is that the moving of any particular castle or bishop constitutes "a move in chess" only in the context of the moves (and possible moves) of the other pieces in the same game. It ceases to be "a move in chess" and is consequently meaningless in the context of the moves of all castles, or of all bishops, in a hundred different games. Such a context is a senseless collocation, falsely described as a purpose.

Similarly it can be argued that the detailed economic transactions of our society constitute economic transactions only in the context of related transactions (and possible transactions) involved in the particular production plan. The only context in which such an action can be explained meaningfully is that of the particular choice being made at its time and in its circumstances as perceived by the chooser.[19] Whether the context is a chess game and its particular configuration of pieces or an economic choice and its particular configuration of relative prices, specific institutions, and productive relations, it is that context which renders the respective action intelligible. But clearly then no attempt to get at what Leontief calls the economy's interacting empirical realities, and especially no attempt to control the future direction of these causal forces, can afford to drop that context.

It is not enough for the chess team captain to monitor each move of each of his teammates in order for him to guide their moves. If the captain is to be a true planner, he must be able to place himself intellectually in the exact choice context of each player, view the full expectational scenario of each player's individual and unarticulated strategy or plan, and from this standpoint dictate or encourage the moves that conform more closely to his own purposes. Anything short of such full contextual knowledge would be insufficient to justify his presumption of superior knowledge, which he would need to override his players' own decisions. The attainment of such full contextual knowledge would require of the captain an individual intelligence that equals the combined intelligence of all of his players. This hardly appears to be an effective way to marshal intellectual resources.[20]

To return for a moment to the problem of aggregation, it should be clear that this difficulty of dropping the choice context is necessarily greater where aggregates instead of specific transactions are involved. It makes no more sense to plan the total quantity of sheet metal an economy should produce than it would for the chess team captain to plan to have his team move twenty bishops by an average of three squares. The reason both of these plans are nonsensical is that they treat aggregate summaries of detailed decisions apart from the context of the decisions themselves.

Indeed, this chess analogy breaks down precisely on the point that was a central theme of the last chapter: the difference between individual and social intelligence. Chess team players are only rivals of single opposing players and need not coordinate their activities with one another. Each game can be viewed in isolation and thus the combined intelligence of all the players on one team is only a function of their average intelligence. But in the case of insect societies, human economies, or scientific communities, the overall intelligence of the system is greatly enhanced by the process of mass communication, the method of mutual adjustment of each participant to the signals supplied by his fellows. In other words, whereas for the chess team captain to plan his teammates' moves he need only know all of their strategies in each of their specific contexts, for the economic planner to direct the economy would require that he know all the decision-makers' strategies and also that he know something none of them know: how their rivalrous multidirectional pulling and tugging will affect one another's choices.

Thus it is far less plausible that a single agent in an economy could attain the relevant contextual knowledge necessary for socioeconomic decisionmaking than it would be for a particularly accomplished chess captain to attain such knowledge for playing chess. In addition, in any chess game the possible outcomes can be listed, at least in principle (if not in practice because of their sheer quantity), whereas economic outcomes can be, and often are, complete surprises.

How, then, does Leontief propose to get from his massive data gathering to the actual steering of the economy? What arguments are we given to suggest that the planning agency will know enough to intervene intelligently into the sequence of market transactions to guide them toward socially desirable goals? Here, in stark contrast to the extensive arguments Leontief supplied in critique of aggregative methods, we find no substantive case whatever. Instead, we are treated to a series of superficial analogies between, on the one hand, running the economy and on the other, driving a car, operating a computer, choosing a dish in a restaurant, designing a flood control system, and steering a sailboat. Since in each case a spontaneous order of plans is being compared to a single plan, the basic issues involved in the knowledge problem, as well as the distinction between individual and social intelligence, are entirely avoided.

When Leontief (1977a: 157) tells us we already possess all the governmental tools we need for achieving any plan we want, he likens the economy to an automobile already equipped with accelerating, braking, and steering devices:

> The real trouble is that, at present, not only does the government not know what road it wants to follow, it does not even have a map. To make things worse, one member of the crew in charge presses down the accelerator, another pumps the brakes, a third turns the wheel, and a fourth sounds the horn. Is that the way to reach one's destination safely?

Of course, if the economy were simply one person's plan, as with the driving of a car, we could demand consistency in the person's actions. But the economy is unavoidably the outcome of millions of plans whose complete consistency *cannot* be achieved, and indeed whose very complexity is a resultant of knowledge generated by the clash of the inconsistent plans in market competition. The interventionist policies to which we are treated by various governmental agencies are, to be sure, irrational, but not because the government so far has lacked a sufficiently detailed map. More fundamentally, the difficulty is that no such map can ever be drawn up and the economy is already *steering itself* by the market's discovery processes. All that the "crew in charge" can really do is obstruct these processes.

We are told that the economy is like a "gigantic computing machine capable of solving its own problems automatically" but which, like any computer, can break down and cannot operate unattended. To keep this "semiautomatic engine" running, "we must not only understand the general principles on which it operates, but also be acquainted with the details of its actual design" (Leontief 1977a: 33). However, what essentially distinguishes the economy from a computer is precisely the fact that the economy has never been and could never be designed at all. Understanding the general principles on which it operates is the best that economic science can hope to achieve. Pretending we can treat an economy like any of the millions of particular problems of human design (such as operating a computer) of which it consists is to miss the point. Of course we have seen our modern economies break down, but the only recourse we have is to learn enough about the general principles of their functioning to devise an institutional framework within which they can achieve greater stability. To pretend that we could "fix" the economy by referring to its wiring diagram the way computer engineers solve problems is, again, to use a misleading analogy and to beg the question of the knowledge problem. The point is that human minds have deliberately designed the computer. Naturally they can repair it by reference to the details of its actual design. But the question is, What scientific justification do we have for treating the economy in this manner?

A closer analogy for Leontief to have used than that between the planner and the computer repairperson might be that between the planner and the brain surgeon.[21] Both are intervening in complex orders that they never designed and about which their knowledge can only be on the level of general principles of operation. But perhaps to use this analogy would be to come too close to suggesting the plausibility of the *opposite* policy position from that intended. Surely no brain surgeon aims at *running* the whole process, of dictating, for example, which neuron paths to activate and which to phase out, the way a Reconstruction Finance Corporation bureaucrat might dictate which firms or industries to subsidize. Given the enormity of our ignorance in these two areas, it makes sense for us to adopt a general perspective of "hands off" or laissez-faire unless severe catastrophe (death or economic ruin) is otherwise imminent. And in those rare cases when an interventionist policy *is* recommended, the policy itself, it seems, tends in both cases to be more a matter of quickly getting something that has been obstructing the (mental or market processes) out of the way, and then getting those hands off again, rather than continually shaping the way these processes work. The most we can do is to promote conditions in which the complex processes are best able to function. Even this analogy cannot be asked to carry the weight of the argument, however. Intervention into economies may be either more or less hazardous than brain surgery.

But the advantage of the computer analogy for Leontief's argument lies not only in the fact that we necessarily know more about a computer's "details of design" than we do about our economies or our brains. If someone intervenes into the working of a computer in ignorance, it can be repaired or replaced; a healthy economy and a healthy human brain cannot.

More recently Leontief has made a different argument relating to computers, which illustrates his failure to grasp the true nature of human knowledge and therefore of the knowledge problem. He contends that the introduction of "smart machines" is causing technological unemployment. Earlier technological innovations improved our economic circumstances by doing our physical work and leaving for us the mental tasks for which the human species is particularly well suited. Computers, on the other hand, are a threat because they do our mental work for us, leaving us, presumably, with nothing to do. While Leontief does not propose that we become Luddites with respect to computer automation, he does suggest that this technological unemployment is one of the reasons why we need a planning agency to help the economy adjust to the information age. (See Silk's discussion [1983: D2] of this point.)

But all of this fundamentally misconceives the nature of computers. As any programmer will agree, the computer is *not* a smart machine. It "knows" only what it is explicitly told by its programmer, who in fact is the one who does all the real mental work. Just like earlier technological innovations, computers relieve people of the boring, tedious, repetitive tasks that can be performed without recourse to human imagination and creativity. Just as earlier technological revolutions did not destroy jobs but shifted them (from blacksmiths to auto mechanics, for example), the information revolution is changing the nature of employment (from filing clerks to COBOL programmers). It makes it increasingly possible for us to do what the human species is uniquely equipped to do, that is to use our minds.

It is highly significant that Leontief mistakes computers for intelligent minds. If one's view of knowledge is restricted to explicit numerical data and if one supposes mental processes to be no more than mechanical data processing, it is not surprising that one may feel a threat at being replaced by smart machines. What Leontief fails to realize is that the intellectual processes of the mind and the market processes of human societies are both undesigned and complex spontaneous orders, while the operation of the computer is a designed and relatively simple product of human minds.[22]

Similarly, Leontief's analogy between planning and restaurant menus misses the point. His statement (1977a: 153) that rational decisionmakers need to see the alternative scenarios his data-gathering agency would supply before making decisions for the same reason that a restaurant-goer would want to see the menu completely assumes away all the pertinent issues. The government can no more choose the future shape of its economy than can a single termite decide the shape of its hill or a single scientist the shape of future scientific knowledge. We are dealing with complex orders that emerge from individual action and mutual adjustment, not with simple rational choice.

The analogy between the tasks facing an economic planner and that confronting a hydraulic engineer, Leontief (1977a: 156) says, is "more than superficial": "Dams, dikes, and occasional locks have to be placed so we can take advantage of the natural flow propelled by gravity (the profit motive) but at the same time permit us to eliminate floods and devastating droughts." This analogy, as well as the one he tries to draw between the market system and a sailboat, reveals the nature of Leontief's misunderstanding of the way the market system works. In both cases he wants to treat the profit motive as a driving force that lacks any steering mechanism: "Under our system of free enterprise the profit motive is the wind that keeps the vessel moving. But to keep it on a chosen course we have to use a rudder" (Leontief 1973: 101–104).

However, the profit motive cannot be viewed as merely a wind or current, a driving force that keeps the economy moving or flowing. Inextricably bound up with its operation is its function as the economy's rudder, or as its dikes and locks, as well.

When the government tries to steer a market system, it is not simply providing direction to an otherwise drifting economy; it is necessarily pulling against the directions already indicated by the principle of profitability under some agreed-upon rules of social cooperation. It is not providing guidance to a rudderless ship of state. It is instead struggling to gain control of a rudder that would in its absence steer the economy toward a relatively well-coordinated outcome, even though the government has no scientific grounds for its pretense that it *knows how* to steer the economy toward some alternative, equally coordinated, outcome. By blindly interfering with its rudder, the government will misdirect the ship and possibly damage or destroy its rudder. But it lacks the knowledge to replace the rudder already supplied by the profit motive.

NOTES TO CHAPTER 4

1.   Silk (1976) entitled a chapter of his book *The Economists* "Wassily Leontief: Apostle of Planning."

2.   These were, respectively, the Balanced Growth and Economic Planning Act of 1975 and the Full Employment and Balanced Growth Act of 1976, the latter of which, in a gutted version, even passed Congress in 1978.

3.   Unfortunately, the only one of these three contradictory promises he has delivered on was definitely the least popular and on any radical view the least desirable of the three—increased military spending. This example, used by Leontief and typical of his writings, is, however, highly misleading. National planning faces basic difficulties in the problem of *knowing how* to achieve the goals desired; the fact that the federal budget is rarely balanced, however, is not because people do not know how to achieve this goal but simply because too few people really want to. There is rather more involved in trying to direct a vast modern economy than there is in balancing the revenues and expenditures of the government.

4.   In the final chapter I take the position that we should resist attempts to make active governmental policy as we know it more effective, and instead should reduce government, if we still want to call it that, to the function of protecting the rights of individuals from violation by anyone, including itself.

5.   Vera Lutz (1969: 17) has concisely identified four distinct meanings of "economic planning" in the literature, which range from a view so extreme that few advocate it anymore to one so tame that no one would oppose it:

   a. a system of *integral* planning from the centre, implying that all economic operations are centrally "guided," "coordinated," or "directed" by a "National Plan;"

   b. a system of *partial* planning from the centre, entailing measures of government intervention for purposes of modifying specific aspects of the pattern of production, consumption, or distribution;

c. the government's programme for the public sector of the economy, or . . . the "Plan of the State" as distinct from the "National Plan" of which it would constitute only a part . . . ;

d. to denote that every economy is "planned" in the sense that the various economic agents . . . almost all engage individually in some sort of forward planning or "programming" of their activities.

I have been calling Lutz's "integral" and "partial" planning "comprehensive" and "noncomprehensive," but have not considered her other two to be varieties of planning at all. Leontief's contention that government should put its own house in order corresponds with Lutz's third sense of the word "planning," but that it should try to put all our houses in order corresponds to her second sense of the word.

6. Leontief (1982b: 33) says that we should set up "a strong, autonomous research organization that would be analogous to the Congressional Research Service, but much larger; its task would be to provide all agencies of government with the information needed to work out a systematic, coordinated approach to the main problems of national and local economic policy." When he warns that "the future of such a complex phenomenon as the world economy is particularly difficult to anticipate or even to visualize" (1977b: 13), one gets the impression that he thinks the difficulty he is stressing is surmountable so long as the research organization is large enough. For an explicit attempt to indicate just how overwhelmingly complex the task of national economic planning is, see Clarkson (1976).

7. However, Leontief does sometimes advocate mere "Indicative Planning" on the model of the French experience, in which the plan would have no teeth but would somehow be self-fulfilling. For a thorough refutation of this idea see Lutz (1969: 99), who concludes from a close empirical study of French planning that

> individual branches . . . had *large* recourse to those "adjustments" or deviations from the Plan which the "flexibility" of indicative planning left them free to make. These adjustments were too many and too big for us to be able to conclude that the coherent system of forecasts, or "image of a coherent future" furnished by the Plan to economic operators was an effective guide to their actions.

8. I assume that Leontief does not really mean what he says here. Surely even he would not want most of our economy's productive effort to be devoted to the formulation of millions of "alternative scenarios."

9. In fact, since in the wholly imaginary world of equilibrium there would be no need for money, the common denominator for aggregation would have to be prices in terms of a *numeraire* rather than money prices.

10. I owe this illustration to Israel Kirzner.

11. This is a misleading way of putting it, however, since it suggests that information is lost by degrees as one goes from totally disaggregated individual transactions to totally aggregated GNP concepts. I will argue, on the con-

trary, that one loses all the information relevant to planning as soon as one leaves the level of the individual transactions.

12.   This attempt at a reductio ad absurdum of the argument against aggregation was proposed by Nozick (1977).

13.   This general logic of choice or science of action should not be confused with what is sometimes called the "pure logic of choice" that pervades modern microeconomics. The latter is a much narrower notion of maximization of some given end within given constraints, whereas the former encorporates the creation or selection of the ends-means framework itself. See Kirzner (1973) and Mises ([1949] 1966).

14.   For a justification of the method of "explanations of the principles" see Hayek (1978: 35-49; 1967: 3-21). Marx may be accused of such Newtonian thinking; however, he did not view his analysis of capitalism as a predictive and deterministic model. Rather, he saw it more as a Darwinian explanation of the principles of capitalist evolution.

15.   It might be objected that since there is a genuine demand in the private sector for the forecasting of hundreds of aggregated categories such as "electrical machinery" by large econometric modeling firms such as DRI or Chase Econometrics, such categories should be considered scientifically meaningful. There are several reasons, however, why this fact cannot serve as an effective response to the argument of the text:

First, forecasters and their techniques have to compete with one another for customers, whereas Leontief wants to give one data-gathering agency the special privilege of massive government financing. It is not clear why people should not pay for their own data gathering.

Second, even the defenders of these models, such as Bails and Peppers (1982: 68), refer to their methods as "guessing techniques" rather than genuine science, and their forecasts have often been embarrassingly bad. Bails and Peppers (1982: 86) admit, for example, that "no well-known or established forecasting group accurately projected, with even the crudest degree of precision, the economy's path from the peak in November 1973 to the trough in March 1975." As such, these econometric methods hardly appear appropriate as a basis for national policy.

Of course, there is nothing wrong with the voluntary collection of data where those who want such information are willing to pay for it. But the fact that some aggregated data is voluntarily paid for in the market neither proves that it is genuinely meaningful and worth the money—after all, astrological forecasting, like econometrics, is a thriving business—nor that it could remotely serve the purposes of planning.

16.   This argument applies quite generally to planning advocates, and indeed others are, if anything, guiltier than Leontief of trying to plan by pushing in vague or aggregate directions instead of specific and detailed ones. See for example Etzioni's (1983: 312-16) discussion of what he calls the

"semi-targeted" approach, in order to contrast it to more detailed planning proposals (including some economic democracy advocates), which he calls "targeted," and to laissez-faire (including Reaganite supply siders), which he calls "non-targeted." He points out quite correctly that "we do not have the analytical capacity to determine who will be a winner, who a loser" and thus "we would misidentify industries and sink vast amounts of public resources in tomorrow's Edsels" (p. 316). But he fails to see that under his own scheme the planners would, for the same reason, be likely to misidentify categories of industries.

17.   The best attempt I have found in the literature to articulate this line of argument for government data gathering was by Saul Estrin and Peter Holmes in their book on French planning. They argue (1983: 39) that "if there are economies of scale in the gathering and processing of information" then "a centralized agency could pool information across a broader range of possibilities than any individual." Their argument represents a "classic welfare economics case for government intervention in the supply of information because of the externality, public good, and monopolistic properties of the commodity" (p. 40). Unfortunately like all such welfare economics arguments, it fails to explain how government can correct this "market failure."

18.   It now takes several years to compile a single national input–output table. Leontief (1977a: 151) has suggested five-year plans that "should be revised each year," but it may be that such revisions would have to be made several times an hour in order for the plan to really keep track of the transactions that drive the economic process.

19.   The classic statement of this radically subjectivist theory of cost is Buchanan's *Cost and Choice* (1969).

20.   There is an important body of work in sociology on the interpretation of human action, stemming from Wilhelm Dilthey and Max Weber, which has stressed this point that social science must always refer to the subjective meaning of action. In fact, this very chess game example was used as an illustration by one contributor to this interpretive tradition, Robert Park (1931: 1073–75), who similarly concluded that "the moves and tactics of every individual player as well as the general plan and purpose of the game become intelligible only when one understands what each player is trying to achieve."

21.   Leontief used this analogy between economic planning and medical surgery in a debate at New York University where his colleague Israel Kirzner responded that perhaps what the "patient" needs is not more surgery but a breath of fresh air.

22.   Some would view developments over the last twenty years in the field of artificial intelligence as representing a counterargument to this statement that computers are fundamentally different from human minds. However,

Dreyfus (1979) has used these very developments to show that, while the amazing things computers can do are very important and useful, they do not remotely approximate true human intelligence. Though lightning-fast calculators, and capable of voluminous, if sometimes slow, memory retrieval, computers have yet to challenge chess masters or even speak a language with the skills of a six-year-old. One need not necessarily agree with Dreyfus's conclusion that computers will never attain human intelligence, to recognize that what intelligence requires is much more involved than the running of a preprogrammed algorithm in a machine. As one of the most articulate defenders of artificial intelligence, Douglas R. Hofstadter (1979: 676), admits, "One must run on faith at this point, for there is so far to go!"

5 PLANNING FROM THE BOTTOM UP?
The Myth of Economic Democracy

Just as corporate planners like Felix Rohatyn contemplate the use of a re-designed Reconstruction Finance Corporation to shore up faltering banks and corporations in the distressed Northeast and industrial Midwest, planners on the democratic left could direct capital toward defense contractors who agree to convert their facilities to the making of buses and subway cars, developers who are willing to construct housing for low and moderate income families, medical entrepreneurs whose Health Maintenance Organizations serve inner city and distressed rural constituencies, and local groups who engage in energy production from renewable sources.

Robert Lekachman (1982: 195)

A rationalization of our economy is likely. . . . Will this rationalization occur from the top down via corporate and government planning and attempt to preserve and extend old privileges and institutions? Or will it be from the bottom up, through citizens' initiatives leading to a safer energy and economic future?

Tom Hayden (1982: 6–7)

The delegation of particular powers to separate agencies creates a new obstacle to the achievement of a single co-ordinated plan. Even if, by this expedient, a democracy should succeed in planning every sector of economic activity, it would still have to face the problem of integrating these separate plans into a unitary whole. Many separate plans do not make a planned whole — in fact, as the planners ought to be the first to admit, this may be worse than no plan.

F. A. Hayek (1944: 67)

"DEMOCRATIC" PLANNING AS THE ALTERNATIVE TO PLANNING BY THE CORPORATIONS

There is no single intellectual leader of the economic democracy movement who could serve as a convenient object of criticism the way Wassily Leontief served in the last chapter. Differences among individual advocates of this idea range from the subtle to the profound.[1] But among the predominant voices for national economic planning in contemporary America there can be discerned a particular "package" of ideas which, while it may not prove self-consistent, is quite consistently advocated by most of the leading leftist intellectuals in this country. The basic message of this movement is that a "democratic" form of planning ought to be advocated as the only feasible alternative to fascism or corporate planning.

The criteria I have used for selecting the representative articles and books at which this critique will be directed involve a combination of prominence and clarity of exposition. I have included four articles by John Buell, Tom DeLuca, Gar Alperovitz, Jeff Faux, and James Crotty and Raford Boddy from *The Progressive*,[2] and one by Michael Harrington from *Dissent*,[3] two leading leftist magazines promoting economic democracy; a pamphlet titled "An Economic Recovery Program" written by Woodrow Ginsburg (1982) from Americans for Democratic Action, one of the leading lobbies that promotes this idea; articles by Robert Heilbroner[4] and Robert Lekachman,[5] two of the more prominent academic members of Leontief's Initiative Committee for National Planning; and four books, by Tom Hayden, Lekachman, Barry Bluestone and Bennett Harrison, and Martin Carnoy and Derek Shearer, which have been highly praised in these circles for setting out the main goals of the movement.[6]

Of these, the book by Martin Carnoy and Derek Shearer titled *Economic Democracy: The Challenge of the 1980s* could be called paradigmatic of this literature. The editors of *Social Policy* were so impressed with Carnoy and Shearer's book that they devoted a special lead editorial[7] to a rousing review of it, which concludes:

> This is a book to discuss. For a long time now, leftists and liberals involved in improving actual conditions in this country have longed to go beyond saying what's wrong and naming the enemy. We've talked about a dearth of action-generating theory, and we've been accused of not offering workable

alternatives. Here is a genuine point of departure from which to answer both complaints—the challenge of the 1980s. If not now, when? (Greer and Reissman 1981)

The central idea associated with the phrase "economic democracy" is the pleasant-sounding notion that democracy, which has heretofore been restricted to the political sphere, should be extended into the economic sphere. As Hayden (1982: 46) explains, "To intensify the democratic process means allowing people to make direct input into decisions that affect their lives. The trend should be towards a fuller, more inclusive democracy in which all institutions are made accessible and accountable." Carnoy and Shearer (1980: 3) define economic democracy as "the transfer of economic decision making from the few to the many" and, inexplicably, assert that the "very same" arguments that have supported political democracy "also provide the rationale for" economic democracy. Alperovitz and Faux (1977: 6) conclude their article with this challenge: "The major decisions in our economy are now or will soon become explicitly political; democracy, therefore, cannot stand still. If it is to survive, it must be extended to the economy." For Bluestone and Harrison (1982: 245) the "principle of economic democracy" involves the need "to radically *transform the nature of active popular participation in the day-to-day running of the basic institutions of the economy and the society* (emphasis in the original).

For these writers the "extension of democracy" seems to mean finding an alternative both to the centralized Communist party control of the Soviet-type economy and to the centralized corporate control that typifies, or will soon typify, the American economy.[8] They are more likely than other planning advocates to call their ideas "socialist" and "radical," but they view their socialism as having nothing to do with the Soviet model. Workers' control of the means of production appears to represent the long-range goal of these democratic socialists, but not much is said about what this entails concretely; neither is it ever explained why workers' control over their workplace should require, or even be consistent with, national economic planning.

In fact, one of the leading theoreticians of workers' control, Jaroslav Vanek (1971: 11) has argued that "the labor-managed economy must always be a *market economy*" and that economic planning may only use "indirect policy instruments, discussion, improved information, or moral suasion" but should never issue direct orders to firms.

If workers find it to their advantage to form self-managed firms and can compete with any other voluntary institutions then there is no reason why they should not do so, and indeed they have occasionally done so. But the planning advocates who talk about economic democracy are not content with merely letting workers' control emerge wherever it is chosen voluntarily. Rather they insist on governmental "encouragement of employee ownership and participation in management." As Alperovitz and Faux (1977: 6) put it, "Worker participation . . . should be systematically expanded and supported through research experimentation, financial incentives, and, above all, through a national moral commitment," while Carnoy and Shearer (1980: 191) say they "see the government . . . as the primary source of financing and technical assistance for the worker control movement." And Bluestone and Harrison (1982: 253) agree that, without government aid, worker-owned enterprises "are almost impossible to get off the ground."

This call for coercive governmental control over the organizational form of firms fundamentally changes the nature of economic democracy from increasing the control and participation in the workplace by workers who want to attain it, to forcing workers—who may not want to take on the risk, expense, and responsibility involved in managing a firm—to do so anyway. After all, there are potentially several advantages to workers who choose to specialize in earning wage-income in order to be insulated from the vicissitudes of market competition. There is often an advantage in allowing someone else to be the boss and thereby reducing one's concerns to the fulfillment of a wage contract, letting the management fret about the firm's profit and loss statements. While there is nothing inherently wrong with workers' control, or ownership, or participation (for many small firms in particular, those organizational forms may prove more efficient), there is also nothing inherently wrong with a voluntary separation of the ownership, management, and employee functions.

Indeed, one gets the impression that the emphasis in this literature on increasing the worker's control over his own job is intended more to harm the corporations than to help the worker. Whether the democratic consciousness of the workers is sufficiently raised yet for them to favor this policy or not, these writers believe that reducing corporate control over the economy and turning workers into risk-bearing entrepreneurs will be good for them.

This complaint that "the corporations" are currently "in charge" of our economy is so popular among these writers that it can be argued that it constitutes the basic distinguishing attitude of advocates of this type of planning. For example, Harrington (1982: 407) complains that, despite the progress he says was achieved by the welfare state, "basic economic decisions were still made in corporate boardrooms" and "the private sector remained in charge of the allocation of most resources." Later on he tells us that "investment in this society is controlled, not by the poor, the workers, or even the middle class, but by the corporate rich" (p. 413), and that "corporations and the corporate rich are in charge of the critical investment decisions that determine the economic course of the society" (p. 416). Similarly, Ginsburg (1982: 17) insists that corporate power must be "curbed" because at present "a few firms control more than two-thirds of our industrial production and markets." Tom Hayden (1982: 175–205) spends the better part of his book assailing corporate power, while Carnoy and Shearer (1980: 87) lament the fact that "the top wealth holders in the United States maintain . . . substantial control over the economic life of the country" in such a way as to skew investment toward "the needs and priorities of the large corporations." Buell and DeLuca (1977: 4) charge that "In our capitalist economy, the most fundamental decisions—how much we produce, what we produce, how much we consume, what we consume— are made for us by an elite which is always guided by its quest for profits, power and privilege." Bluestone and Harrison (1982: 119) drag out dubious concentration ratios to show "which companies may have the greatest opportunity for directly controlling their own prices and output." The corporation is thus painted as the chief villain in the modern economy.

The basic argument, in a nutshell, is that the ideal state of free or perfect competition is not approximated by real capitalist institutions and that the corporations, not the anonymous forces of supply and demand, fix prices. Sometimes this allegation of corporate control reaches the tone of conspiracy theory, such as when it is suggested that the corporations actually engineer recessions or intentionally devise routinized, boring jobs as ways of keeping the workers in their place.

A quick survey will show that this summary of their views is accurate. Ginsburg (1982: 17) ridicules those corporate leaders who "mouth the values of a competitive free market as though supply and demand determine prices and resource allocation." Hayden (1982: 50) declares that the free-market prescription does not work because "it is based on a model of competition which has long since been replaced by a structure of corporate oligopoly and government income-maintenance programs" which "make the free market model obsolete." Lekachman (1982: 197) contends that "the operation of free markets guided by invisible hands" has been "inoperative within the lifetime of the oldest inhabitant" of this country. Carnoy and Shearer (1980: 200) echo the point that unlike the imaginary agents of economic theory, actual decisionmakers exercise a considerable measure of what they call "market power." Buell (1982: 22) blames inflation on the excessive market power of corporations: "Where a business controls a large portion of the market, it can push prices up even when demand is decreasing." Harrington (1982: 408) employs John Hicks's notion of fix price markets to suggest that corporations are "insulated from the forces of supply and demand" and contends that the "increased control corporations can exert over prices . . . subverts the very market mechanism."

Suggestions that recessions are deliberately engineered and that work is intentionally made boring are scattered throughout this literature. Crotty and Boddy (1975: 4) assert that "it has . . . become possible for a U.S. recession, needed for domestic purposes, to be turned into a weapon" and that "maximizing the threat of world recession may, therefore, be attractive to those concerned with the maintenance of the American empire." Buell and DeLuca (1977: 1) remark that "an increase in unemployment must be encouraged from time to time to 'discipline' the labor force and diminish its demands." Lekachman (1982: 200) contends that "unemployment . . . is privately welcomed by conservative politicians and corporate employers." Bluestone and Harrison (1982: 207–8) suggest that "Capital" deliberately disciplines the workers by fomenting recession. Buell and DeLuca (1977: 2) assert that "the actual skills required for most jobs have been reduced to limit the worker's knowledge and diminish the worker's opportunity to market his or her talents." Carnoy and Shearer (1980: 201) and Bluestone and Harrison (1982: 294) refer approvingly to Harry Braverman's thesis that "modern management practices . . . are based fundamentally on the removal of technical knowledge from workers, so that such knowledge becomes the province of the corporation and its technical elite." Buell (1982: 22) contends that "when work is organized to maximize corporate profits, blue-collar labor tends to become monotonous, demeaning, and even dangerous."

Unfortunately these arguments about corporate power do not distinguish between two very different aspects of the modern economy which they seem to dislike. First there is the undeniable (but not undesirable) fact that the organization of industry does not conform even remotely to the perfectly competitive ideal of the economics textbooks, according to which there is virtually an infinite number of homogeneous competitors, none of whom have any influence over prices. Second, there is the fact that we do not live in a freely competitive environment, but rather one in which corporations, unions, and others use government institutions to enhance their power and protect their profits and privilege from potential competitors.

Whereas the second of these complaints is a legitimate one, it is likely to be worsened in a regime in which a single national planning office is given greater governmental power. For example when Buell and DeLuca (1977: 3) point out that "money endows capitalists with disproportionate power within the political process—power to buy elections, to hire lobbyists, to shape legislation, and to impede the effects of laws through the courts," one would be hard pressed to deny their argument. But of course the question is whether to try to alleviate this problem by continually evening out wealth holdings so that nobody ever has any disproportionate power, or by taking away the ability of government to bestow privilege on anyone. In other words, is the real problem the unequal wealth or the fact that this wealth can be abused by bribing political dispensers of privilege? Similar comments apply to Carnoy and Shearer's (1980: 21) complaint that "the corporate sector converts economic power into political power" and to Bluestone and Harrison's (1982: 203–4) statement that "where government is an important actor in the economy, the political stake is *particularly* important since influence over public power is critical in securing profitable public sector contracts, special tax advantages, and government subsidies." The point is that investing special powers with a national planning agency will not necessarily change this state of affairs and could very well worsen it, while reducing the number of benefits the government has to offer would definitely weaken the ability of anyone to convert economic power into political power.[9]

On the other hand the first complaint, that the real world is unlike perfect competition, relies on the mistaken assumption that the forces of supply and demand only work under the unrealistic conditions of this model, whereas I have argued (in Chapter 3) that the "price-taker" assumptions of this model would in fact, if they ever obtained anywhere, *preclude* the forces of supply and demand from working at all.[10] Rivals in a market exert influence over price, and it is only by such influence that price signals contain the knowledge decisionmakers need to plan rationally. Far from being an imperfection, this influence over price is the sine´qua non of the law of supply and demand.

But there is a big difference between admitting that corporate rivals exert influence over prices and asserting that they thereby fix or control prices, or that corporations are "in charge." Indeed, except where control over the reins of government has legally protected them from their competitors (in which case we are back at the second complaint), corporate leaders are no more in charge of our economy than anybody else. They vie with one another for the favor of consumer dollars. Who wins control over investment funds depends on the outcome of their competitive struggle with one another, a struggle that no one agent controls. To say that there are less than an infinite number of competitors is not to say that there is no competition, and to argue that each rival exerts *some* influence over prices is not to argue that any one rival firm can fix its prices at will.

In fact, these statements about how the corporations join together in controlling our economy are inconsistent with one of the main propositions put forward by these planning advocates—that our present economy is "out of control" like Leontief's metaphorical car with many drivers.[11] They cannot have it both ways. Since one of their main arguments for planning involves the view that competition is an unplanned and unruly clash of purposes[12] whereas planning can bring things under control, perhaps we should not take them seriously when they exaggerate the extent to which the corporations are in charge.

So if the real problem with the corporations is not so much that they control *everything* as that they exert *unwanted influence* over the economy, what in particular do they do that these planning advocates dislike? The usual objection is made to what are considered unproductive commercial acts of various kinds,[13] including advertising, mergers,[14] speculation, purely financial transactions, profiteering, and excessive debts.[15] One of the recurrent themes in this literature (and one that differentiates it from most of the writings urging reindustrialization) is the argument that we do not have a capital shortage problem but only a problem of how our existing capital supply gets used, whether for productive or for supposedly unproductive purposes.[16] The implication is that, if we would just stop siphoning investment monies into all these so-called purely financial transactions, there would be plenty of capital available for expanding the economy.

Yet this diagnosis is hard to reconcile with the facts. Why is it that investment funds which for centuries have been used for financial transactions are only recently drying up? Might it have something to do with the fact that government indebtedness has grown alarmingly and is increasingly crowding out private investment?[17] Moreover, most of the "purely commercial investments" that these writers condemn as "unproductive" are in fact absolutely essential to the working of our economy and are not substitutes for the sort of productive investments they desire, but rather are complements to them. Bluestone and Harrison (1982: 124) make the statement that "if the capital that went into acquiring existing companies had been spent instead on new plants and equipment, national investment in 1968 would have been 46 percent higher than it was."

Unfortunately, this ignores the fact that the acquired companies thereby gained access to the full amount of investable funds allegedly lost to the acquisition process. When financial resources merely change hands, there is no net loss to the investing community's supply of investable funds. Mergers very often increase efficiency and, as we shall see in the next chapter, many other proponents of planning want to *promote* mergers. Advertising serves not only to inform potential buyers but also to grab attention, to alert people to the existence of products. Presumably even in a democratically planned society someone will have to alert potential buyers to the availability of goods. As for speculation, we must, in any case, commit ourselves to our own expectations of the uncertain future. All planning could do is reduce the divergence of speculative actions, and thus *increase the risk of error*; it cannot dispense with speculation.

Perhaps the tendencies of our recent economy to which these writers really object are the consequences of our high taxes and severe inflation: the flight of investment funds into inflation hedges like land or precious metals and various tax dodges. To the extent that it is these tendencies that are at issue, of course, the evident solution is to reduce the burdens of inflation and taxes. But as we shall soon see, the policies these writers favor are likely to worsen these burdens, not lighten them.

Actually it appears that one of the things the corporations do that most irritates advocates of economic democracy is to cater to the demands of consumers. Despite all the rhetoric against the corporate elite and in favor of democratized, decentralized control over our own lives, and so on, most of these writers reveal a deeply ingrained bias against the actual tastes of the consuming public.[18] As such this form of planning comes to represent a thinly disguised attempt to impose a whole set of particular values on the American people.[19]

Not only are the ends of capitalist production, the final consumer goods, condemned by these writers, but so also are the means, the technologies used to produce those consumer goods. Economic democracy advocates are generally in favor of "soft," "alternative," "small," "high," or "appropriate" technologies. Carnoy and Shearer (1980: 195–232) spend a whole chapter of their book describing what they call "A Democratic Technology." Nowhere do any of these authors consider the question of whether a democratic planning office can ever obtain the knowledge to decide what is the best sort of technology for society to use. It is one thing for the legal system to define whatever constraints on technology are necessary to preserve our rights to clean air and water. It is another matter altogether for us to rely on government to specify positively whether, say, to invest in passive solar or hydroelectric power. It is only in the rivalrous process of competition among specific technologies that their relative advantages can be rationally weighed. Governmental interference with this competitive discovery process will only obstruct its ability to generate and disperse knowledge and will give unearned advantages to some of the rivals, at the expense of others. Indeed, this is exactly what has happened.[20] Economic democracy offers us the absurd spectacle of radical ideologists making politicized decisions for us about which technology our society should adopt.

This question of encouraging approved technologies also recalls the issue of aggregation. "Solar power" is an aggregate construct intended to treat as one all the various specific firms that use the sun in different ways as an energy source. There is no way to give subsidies to solar power as such, but someone must decide which specific firms to favor with special advantages. Indeed, many sincere proponents of solar energy argue that government funding of certain extremely large and costly solar projects has already been quite damaging to the technology by making it appear less cost effective than it is capable of being.

But the most distinctive attitude of advocates of economic democracy that sets them apart from advocates of the other major types of planning is their insistence that the planning they advocate must be decentralized, or "from the bottom up," rather than centralized, or "from the top down." Since this idea of decentralized planning appears to be a contradiction in terms, it must be clarified that these writers do believe there will have to be one central office that will have to oversee and coordinate the plans of other levels and branches of government. But it is generally supposed that most initiative for socioeconomic change will come from local, democratic, workers', or community-based institutions.

Now it might well appear that this decentralized approach to planning is able to circumvent the knowledge problem. After all, it could be argued that social results under decentralized planning would not be decided by any one agent but would be the outcome of the tugs and pulls among rival programs initiated by local, state, and federal governments. To their credit most of these authors are often skeptical about whether our current policymakers, especially on the federal level, know what they are doing. Is it not possible that by decentralizing, that is, allowing rivalry among local planners, the attempts to plan from the bottom up can deflect the argument presented in Chapter 3 against planning from the top down? [21]

I think not. One must distinguish between the political rivalry that is entailed in decentralized planning and the market rivalry that drives the discovery process of the price system. What makes market rivalry effective as a mechanism for conveying knowledge is the fact that entrepreneurs' tacit views about which technologies are more likely to be effective are directly reflected in their voluntary actions, and in particular in the relative intensities of the bidding pressure they impart to prices. In contrast, when several monopolized institutions vie with one another for political power, the success of one rival will tend to reflect directly only that institution's perceptiveness of the workings of the political structure, *not its understanding of the workings of productive relations in the economy itself.* Struggle for the command over political institutions, which the modern public choice economists call rent seeking, will tend to supersede struggle for the command of direct sources of money profits from mutual gains of trade.[22]

Whereas market rivalry can take advantage of tacit knowledge and can anonymously convey information through the tugs and pulls of the price system, rivalry among separate, decentralized political institutions involves the direct and explicit struggle for special privilege. While the defeat of one market rival by another supplies a useful signal to the other participants of the price system, the defeat of a political rival by another only transfers the control over—and disposal of the fruits of—the apparatus of coercion. A market participant succeeds over the long run by satisfying the desires of others better than rivals do. Success among political rivals tends to depend more on the ability to intimidate or deceive others.

Thus it can be argued not only that political rivalry is unable to generate the sort of social intelligence to which the other kind of rivalry leads, but worse, that it actively hinders this knowledge dispersal process. If this is true, then the result of decentralized planning would be and can only be the injection of a substantial dose of socially unnecessary chaos into the market system. Each of the various policies of economic democracy to be discussed in this chapter will be criticized on the grounds that undesirable and unpredictable consequences will invariably flow from these measures.

In short, even taken singly, each of the policies proposed by these writers will be shown to be subject to the knowledge problem, and thus would lead to undesirable consequences, a problem that can only be compounded where there is a flurry of mutually contradictory policies emanating from all levels of government, instead of just one central policymaker. And it is difficult not to notice that such uncoordinated, decentralized planning represents little more than an extension and acceleration of the very same clash of mutually contradictory policies we have been suffering under for years.

One of the rare comments in this sample of literature even to address the question of the knowledge problem is by Lekachman (1978: 159): "The case for planning does not demand that the planners be wiser or more altruistic than chairmen of the board." But we have seen that this is the wrong comparison to make. The real issue is whether the planners can comprehend as much information in their individual intelligences as can be contained in the social intelligence that results from the competitive tugs and pulls of market participants, not whether some people are individually more intelligent than any others.

Since these particular writers focus on democratic processes, they may be expected to be more concerned with the political issues of planning than with economic issues like the knowledge problem. Yet even on the totalitarian problem, the issue of finding ways to prevent the central planning office from becoming a weapon for political power, there is actually no concrete proposal for any institutional changes that could promise to prevent such reactionary consequences. In all these articles and books there is no coherent argument about why we should expect the political changes implicit in national planning somehow *not* to lead to a drastic centralization of political and economic power. Instead there is simply a strong emphasis on the virtues of democratic or local or collective decisionmaking.

Alperovitz and Faux (1977: 3) say that "we must directly confront the need for public control over major economic decisions now in the hands of the private sector" and that "we must develop" (suggesting that we have not yet come up with) "a practical, sensible alternative that uses the power of Government to construct an economy that serves human priorities first." Of course, they insist that we also have to develop "new democratic arrangements to avoid the dangers of centralized bureaucratic power." Yet the only concrete idea they come up with for avoiding this danger is that we "permit citizen suits against public officials for failing to fulfill their responsibilities as trustees for the common interest in our resources" (p. 5). Buell (1982: 24) says that "the Left has an opportunity and an obligation to develop and disseminate a plausible program of *democratic* economic planning. The emphasis on *democracy* is essential; without it, the planning that is surely coming in one form or another will carry a heavy measure of repression."

He seems to think that putting the word "democratic" in italics qualifies as a procedure for ensuring that planning does not, for the first time in history, carry with it any potential for the routine abuse of power. Bluestone and Harrison (1982: 232) simply assert that "under any sort of truly democratic planning (which the New Deal decidedly was not), the actual day-to-day tasks would be performed by those most closely involved with economic affairs: workers themselves, and their own designated representatives." Buell and DeLuca (1977: 4) effectively admit that they have no specific solution to this problem when they say, "Our challenge is to devise a model of democratic socialism which will encourage the full potential for human development—a model that provides the proper institutional supports for a full range of human freedoms. We cannot assume that the good will of socialist revolutionaries will suffice to preserve these freedoms." Indeed they cannot assume this, but it is hard to find anything in all their arguments for planning that goes beyond verbal reassurance that democracy is to be emphasized by the planning agency. Although Crotty and Boddy titled their 1975 article "Who Will Plan the Planned Economy?" they only get around to addressing that question in their last paragraph, and there we are faced again with mere assurances that democratic values will be stressed:

> It seems clear that over the long run the only permanent solution to the economic instability and insecurity which derive from the monopoly, inequality, and imperialism of modern capitalism is to build a democratic, socialist society. A nationwide socialist organization will be necessary to defend ourselves in the short run and to aid us in the task of developing an egalitarian society wherein production is for use rather than profit, and decisions are collectively made by workers, not bosses. (p. 5)

But how are we to defend ourselves from this nationwide socialist organization itself? How are we to ensure that the "workers themselves" or their supposed representatives do not become the new tyrants as they have, for example, in Poland? What are we to expect from a movement inspired by precisely the same rhetoric that drove Lenin to absolute power? Why will this workers' movement be any different? To these questions no answer has yet been proposed.

On occasion it is admitted that the sheer technical aspects of national planning imply that all economic decisions cannot be made by pure democracy, but that experts or representatives will in practice be making the choices for us. Yet once this has been acknowledged, it is incumbent upon the advocate of democratic planning to explain why placing so much power in the hands of experts will *this* time usher in a genuinely progressive society.

Harrington (1982: 423) admits that

> socialists have never argued that the majority possesses technical expertise. We have said—and continue to say—that the majority could make the basic *value choices* better than the elites that speak in its name. But the translation of those value choices into political programs is, under modern conditions, a process that requires computers and experts.

But of course the question is whether such experts can be trusted not to lose something in the translation, especially in light of the difficulties of aggregative planning.

Ginsburg (1982: 8) suggests that the planning agency "would work closely with representatives of business and labor, minorities and women, consumers and environmentalists, regional and community organizations, and other groups which have a vital interest in the successful functioning of our economy." In other words representatives of the very same special interests who now struggle for governmental favor will still do so under national planning. Why these representatives are expected to reflect the democratic will of the people any better than they do now is not explained.

Buell and DeLuca (1977: 4) say, "The economy would have to be planned nationally as well as locally by associations of workers representing various sectors and regions." But how will the representativeness of these associations be guaranteed? Their only answer is that "healthy democratic participation at the local level is the best protection against attempts by any elite to impose its will." But since they admit that this local planning will have to be "integrated" with the national plan, local associations will necessarily be administratively subsidiary to the decisions of the national planning agency. This must mean that, for the protection of our freedom, we will have to rely on the underlings to keep a constant check on their organizational superiors.

Carnoy and Shearer (1980: 5) begin by taking it for granted that the logical vehicle for planning "should be the government—our democratically elected legislature and executive." They then point out that it is "one of the many dilemmas we face" that "the government is heavily influenced (if not controlled) by" the very same corporations that they want government planning to constrain. The dilemma is not resolved 430 pages later, when the book ends.

The closest these writers come to an argument for democratic checks on the power of the planning apparatus may be what is called "counterplanning."[23] According to this idea, government will intentionally finance rivals who disagree with the way the plan is being implemented. One question this raises is, Why have a national plan in order to bring the economy under control if such control is only to be parceled out to competitors anyway?

But the really significant point here is that economic democracy advocates want to retain economic rivalry but want to transform it from a market rivalry, in which competitors try directly to outbid each other for resources, into a political rivalry, in which factions will vie for political power. At least the traditional Marxist notion of planning was consistently against all forms of rivalry as divisive of social bonds. But this new type of planning manages to get the worst of both worlds. Only the market form of rivalry imparts the requisite knowledge to prices which can sustain advanced technology, whereas political rivalry has all the social divisiveness of market rivalry without the advantage of its capacity for knowledge dispersal.

Although these writers condemn the alienation or divisiveness we are now experiencing in our increasingly politicized world, they seem to believe that the sheer existence of a democratic planning organization will transform bitter struggles for power into more peaceful and civilized dialogues about social priorities.[24] On the contrary, I would argue, the sorts of policies these writers favor are certain to *increase* the intensity of the political battles for power that we now endure.

WHY PLANNING?
THE INEVITABILITY ARGUMENT

Why do those who primarily seek decentralized and democratic solutions to our economic woes look to such an apparently centralized institution as a national planning agency? What arguments do economic democracy advocates put forward in favor of this paradoxical solution? Surprisingly, it is hard to find anything that qualifies as an argument on behalf of planning in all of this literature. Instead we are essentially told either that planning is inevitable, or that it is idle speculation to elaborate on how it would work in practice so it is not worth discussing why we favor it. The only matter that is worth debating is who plans and for what purposes.

Leontief (1976: 12) may have inadvertently supplied the answer to the question of why planning advocates so rarely attempt to justify their basic belief in planning when he replied to a question in an interview with the following admission: "I see, now you want me to explain why I think planning will come. I love to answer this question because it is easier for me to explain why I think planning *must* come rather than to persuade people that planning is good."[25]

The tactic of dismissing all substantive analysis of how planning would work as mere utopianism is among the oldest and least respectable doctrines of the Marxist tradition to have survived to the modern era. The basic idea is supposed to be that plans ought not to be constructed "outside of the process of *making* radical social change," as Bluestone and Harrison put it, and that the social scientist's sole responsibility is to supply an appropriately radical critique of our current institutions and policies. Although most of the contemporary Left is less blatant than early Marxists were about using this methodological principle to evade all criticisms of their own proposed institutions and policies, one still finds that as with Marx the preponderance of attention is nearly always paid to the critique of "capitalism" (usually without distinguishing between political capitalism and free-market capitalism). These modern socialists, too, only leave us with vaguely articulated hopes or principles to indicate what positive direction is being advocated.

Of course the clever use of this tactic can conveniently justify ignoring potentially damaging objections that might be raised about the specific policies being recommended. After recommending a multibillion dollar program of federal expenditure, Bluestone and Harrison (1982: 232) conclude by admitting that their discussion "has left *a lot* of very big questions unanswered" such as, "What about inflation?" and "How will such a radical program be financed?," to which they say, "There *are* no answers at this point." But what is even more astounding is their statement that this lack of even the most minimal requirement of a proposed policy—that at least a feasible way be found to *pay* for it—"is as it should be" because the plan ought to "emerge out of the ideas and experience of working people themselves."

There is no better example of the tragic failure of the radical Left to learn from its own history than this. The concluding phrases of Bluestone and Harrison's book might easily have been lifted verbatim from the prerevolutionary writings of Lenin: "*Organizing* is where we have to go from here. The steps after that will reveal themselves in good time" (1982: 264). And so did Lenin believe. He spent his considerable energy writing books on everything from philosophy to imperialism, without a single full page of analysis of how socialism would work. When he came to power he still had no idea of how to implement his dream and only knew for sure that he hated the institutions of capitalism. He began to issue dozens of decrees proclaiming the commencement of the construction of the planned society and the deliberate destruction of capitalism, apparently expecting the workers themselves to work out the details during the process of implementation. Even reading a relatively sympathetic account of Lenin's catastrophic War Communism policies such as that by Trotskyist Tony Cliff (1978: 5–12), one cannot help but be amused by the naïve manner in which the mere issuing of decrees was expected to transform the political economy of a nation. After the Soviet economy sustained a couple of years of the utter devastation that followed from the suppression of profit making and the elimination of market institutions, the once haughty Bolshevik leadership had to retreat in embarrassment and to reintroduce most of the very capitalistic institutions they had tried to destroy.

The danger posed by modern planners is even worse. In Lenin's case the destruction of Russia's relatively backward economy took the form of a substantial reversion to the traditional peasant system that already prevailed in much of the country, whereas in our case today any return of our complex technological system to a peasant economy is out of the question.[26]

The other undesirable legacy of Marxism that survives in the literature on behalf of economic democracy is the old contention (or, more usually, assumption) that there is no need to discuss whether planning is the best policy direction, on the grounds that it is the inevitable policy direction. Lekachman's essay titled "The Inevitability of Planning" (1978) is typical of the literature. One might expect that an article so titled would advance some reasons why planning is unavoidable, but the only reasons given are that "even" many corporate leaders in America such as Felix Rohatyn now favor planning, and that "our European friends already deploy" planning policies (p. 143). He concludes his piece with a mere assertion of his belief that we will get national planning: "I hope and expect that in the next decade under administrations of either party the American polity will grapple rationally with its necessities. It is in that sense that I restate my belief that planning is inevitable" (p. 160). Elsewhere (1982: 198) he explicitly restricts "the realistic alternatives" to corporate planning and democratic planning.

Nor is Lekachman alone. Harrington (1982: 410) breaks the current political spectrum into four main economic philosophies and rightly observes that "all of them, including Ronald Reagan's, assume a degree of national economic planning" differing only on "what plan to implement and how." Presumably the fact that all the major philosophies, which have been responsible for running our economy into the ground, happen to agree in this respect, justifies our taking it for granted that planning is inevitable. He concludes with the statement, "Clearly, as this analysis has demonstrated [assumed?], the crisis of the welfare state is going to be resolved by national economic planning" (p. 424).

Alperovitz and Faux (1977: 2) quote Leontief's statement that planning will come because businessmen will demand it, and they proceed to argue that "the question is not whether America will plan, but how it will plan and in whose interests." Carnoy and Shearer (1980: 78) assert that "most economists have recognized that government management of the economy is a necessity in advanced industrial societies." Heilbroner (1982: 53) confidently predicts that "with all their difficulties and inefficiencies, Government activities will remain and grow," evolving toward "a capitalism in which the line that divides the economy from the polity is redrawn in favor of the polity." He also helpfully informs us that this future development "will last a long time" (p. 55).

Buell and DeLuca (1977: 5) describe a plausible sounding scenario in which the fascist form of planning will evolve if the only alternative, democratic planning, does not succeed in displacing the power of the corporations:

> Such planning may initially take the form of wage and price controls, but controls generally create shortages and economic imbalances. The Government will then be impelled to allocate resources, and to become increasingly involved in various forms of corporate bailouts and economic reorganization schemes. Such measures, in turn, will require Government intervention in the production process itself. Ultimately, political power will be more directly and obviously employed to control workers.

While the logic of this step-by-step development toward fascism is undeniable and indeed is being realized all over the world, it is not obvious why it should be inevitable nor is it self-evident that democratic planning is the only alternative. But naturally, so long as our choice is presented as being between fascism and democratic socialism, the latter will tend to appear as the more desirable option.

The thesis that planning is bound to come to this country is usually joined to the dismissal of the laissez-faire option as a mere myth or rhetorical camouflage for corporate power. Heilbroner (1982: 53)

tells us that "it is futile to think of social evolution as permitting a
return to the 'simpler' ways of the past." "History," he proclaims,
"is a cumulative process that permits no such retreats."

Now first of all it is not clear how Heilbroner has gained access to
information about what history will or will not permit. This procedure of rejecting ideas, not because of flaws identified in the arguments supporting them, but merely because they are deemed historically irrelevant, has seriously marred the political economy of the
Left at least since Marx. However, the evident failure of Marxists or
any other social scientists to predict the future development of capitalism should have taught us by now that nobody can claim any special access to the laws of history. Contrary to the simplistic historical
scripts drawn up by Marxists according to which definite phases of
social organization occur in a predetermined order, actual human
history has proven unwilling to cooperate with any such formulas.
It is time to admit that while social science may be able to tell us
that some imaginable social systems are unworkable, it can never
reveal which of the many workable kinds of systems men and women
will settle upon in the future. If human beings, for whatever reason,
wanted to return to an older mode of social cooperation, and if no
socioeconomic reasons are given as to why this cannot work, then
there is no reason to doubt that history will "permit" such a development. Heilbroner's position seems to suggest that, if human folly
ever takes social evolution down the wrong path, we are for some
unexplained reason doomed never to backtrack and correct our
errors.

Moreover, the belief that we should return to the simpler ways of
the past is attributed by Heilbroner to all opponents of planning
when in fact, while Reagan and other conservatives may indeed be
afflicted with a kind of myopic nostalgia, there is nothing in the
critique of planning that suggests that we should try to turn the
clock back.

When Alperovitz and Faux (1977: 2-3) contend that "the growing complexity of the economy, coupled with the deteriorating economic climate, is forcing businessmen—reluctantly but surely—to
become more open and explicit in their demands for a strong Government authority to implement *their plans*," they combine in one
statement both the fallacy that complexity requires government control, and that support of planning by businessmen somehow justifies
it. Bluestone and Harrison (1982: 200-1) similarly point out that

"as technology has become more complex, we have in the process all become more interdependent" and then proceed to conclude directly from this undoubted fact that "a modern society requires *more* government intervention than an eighteenth-century one."

Lekachman (1978: 159) supplies us with an impressive list of the various complexities of the modern world but says nothing about why this suggests the need for government to take on the monumental task of orchestrating all this complexity.

> The world is an increasingly precarious speck in the universe. It is afflicted by resource shortages (natural or contrived), seemingly intractable population pressures, demands from the Third World for global redistributions of wealth, threats to the environment, background threats of nuclear incidents, and, of course, the persistent political competition of the Soviet Union. At home there are nagging afflictions of unemployment, inflation, urban decay, maldistributed health care, inadequate housing, drug abuse, faltering education, and work dissatisfaction. It is increasingly apparent to political observers of many faiths that these and still other postindustrial dilemmas are interconnected. Solution of one aggravates others. The case for planning derives in the end from the need to coordinate plans for a wholesome environment *and* improving living standards, tax equity *and* adequate capital formation, and so on.

But of course planning is neither the only way people have found for coordinating complicated plans among one another, nor the way that is more capable of coping with complexities. Many of the modern problems Lekachman cites are consequences of disastrous government attempts to coordinate plans in industries such as health, housing, and education.

Carnoy and Shearer (1980: 4) instruct the reader that "America is no longer a nation of farmers and artisans," as if this fact alone justified a reliance on national planning. Indeed the conditions under which they believe a free market could work are amazingly circumscribed: "If everyone worked on small farms and in small shops, if women had the same economic rights as men, if there had been no slaves or racism, then a free market might be the best way to allocate wages and income. But this is not the case" (p. 23).

These passages clearly reflect the confusion between free competition and perfect competition discussed earlier. There is certainly nothing in the case for a free market that demands that all competitors be of any particular size. As for the existence of great injustices in America's past, this is a fact, but one that has little to do with the question of which socioeconomic system best serves people's needs. Descendants of slaves or victims of racism or sexism would like to live unmolested in a prosperous economy, just as much as anyone else. It is not surprising when the champions of economic democracy wonder whether it is "even possible to think about a free market in today's corporate economy" (Carnoy and Shearer 1980: 14). They certainly give us evidence that *they* have been unable to think about it.

These writers, in short, do not counter antiplanning ideas with any substantive proplanning arguments at all. They are content just to dismiss them as eighteenth-century fantasies, or worse, ideological cover for corporate power against the working class.[27] To the extent that any implicit argument for planning exists, it corresponds to the contention of Leontief that the complexity of the economy justifies national planning, while in fact it has been argued that this very complexity is what undermines the possibility of planning.

BAND-AIDS

One might expect the policies of the radical democratic Left to be derived from some sort of principled revolutionary vision of an alternative kind of society. One might hope for bold solutions that cut to the root of our problems as contrasted with the superficial policies of mainstream American politics. And there is an ample amount of radical rhetoric in condemnation of the present economic order that seems to suggest that some profoundly new departures in policy and not mere Band-Aids on their symptoms are called for. Images are painted of a world in which people will reshape their institutions and produce cooperatively instead of competitively. For example, Carnoy and Shearer (1980: 5) say they do not believe "that the best way to work is necessarily to compete individually one against another for bread and status" but that instead we can "produce cooperatively." We ourselves can "decide the best way to produce and how much to produce in a democratically planned economy." They sound as if they are pursuing a radical departure from current policy when they urge, "Rather than discussing the methods for 'fine tuning' the economy we want to shift the debate to strategies for changing the structure of the economy so that it better serves the interests and needs of all Americans" (p. 15). Buell and DeLuca (1977: 3) proclaim that "the highest freedom is not simply the ability to take one's place on the social ladder, but the opportunity to assume control over and constantly reshape the basic institutions of society." Bluestone and Harrison (1982: 118) dramatically call for "a transformation in the organizational form of ownership and management of capital itself," and believe that what makes their proposals radical and different from Rohatyn, conservatives, liberals, and others is the fact that their policy "rejects private profit as the sole criterion for designing and managing a progressive industrial policy" (p. 244).[28]

Shades of the Left's original radical vision of comprehensive planning can be discerned here. But upon investigating the actual policies these writers propose, one finds time and again that they amount only to an endorsement of the well-worn and not particularly inspiring policies that have been used throughout this century by governments all over the world. These writers are, it turns out, not really radicals standing against the conventional thinking of our discredited establishment, as they like to think of themselves. Their opposition is only to the Republican nuances of the contemporary establishment and they are not so terribly uncomfortable with the Democratic party. They wish to cut military spending but otherwise return to the policy directions of the New Deal and the Great Society, of the heyday of establishment liberalism. Without denying that the welfare state is in some serious trouble, they continue to claim that it has been beneficial and to defend its programs from all critics. Their policies can be compared with those of, say, Hubert Humphrey and should bear the slogan "Much More of the Same."

Lekachman (1978: 145) credits these Keynesian and welfare state policies not so much with improving the lives of the poor, which has not yet happened, but merely with having "softened class conflict and promoted social harmony." Does this mean welfare is to be deemed successful as an arm of the police and the National Guard? In any case Lekachman (1982: 207) condemns President Reagan for having allegedly sabotaged the great gains made by these programs "in the sunshine of the Great Society." In truth, however, while many intellectuals and bureaucrats bathed in that sunshine, it largely left the poor in the dark.

Carnoy and Shearer (1980: 329-30) repeatedly explain how each of these welfare state programs has been "plagued with many problems" and then go on to assert that things would have been so much worse had there been no such programs. But when the chief result of the Medicaid/Medicare program, to pick one example, is to raise the costs of medicine, it is not clear that the solution lies in more ambitious national health care programs of the same nature.

Bluestone and Harrison (1982: 206) cite some statistics to try to prove that the proportion of people "classified as poor" declined during the sixties, naturally crediting this to the welfare state, and lament the fact that the liberal policy was "impaired" (by the corporations, of course) before it could "complete its task of . . . ridding the nation of poverty" (pp. 209–10). Harrington (1982: 406) comes right out and says that "throwing money at problems" actually works, and tries to show that Social Security, Medicare and Medicaid have successfully kept one-fourth of the American people who would have been in the poorhouse out of it. Unable to show any actual improvement over time as these programs have rapidly grown, their advocates are forced to argue that things would have deteriorated faster "had it not been for public transfer payments." Of course, to weigh the net impact of these policies, one would also have to take into account the burden of taxes and inflation imposed by them, as well as their effects on incentives. On that basis, it is not clear that poor people are any better off thanks to these programs.[29]

One of the main arguments economists have been leveling at the current system is that the incentives that welfare payments (in combination with progressive income taxes and regressive social security taxes) have set in place have discouraged productivity. The marginal benefit to be gained from looking for a job is likely to be reduced as unemployment compensation (or income taxes) increases. As a result, to some extent it could be said that we can get as much unemployment as we are willing to pay for. Although I do not believe that this incentives problem represents the most serious objection to the welfare system, it is an important point that one would expect defenders of the welfare state at least to try to answer. But the proponents of economic democracy do not address this incentives problem at all; rather they seem satisfied with impugning the motives of anyone who would suggest that some people might be taking advantage of welfare opportunities. Bluestone and Harrison (1982: 232–33) appear to believe that the statement that "productivity is a *social* relation" is enough to establish that to promote productivity "requires *more*, not less, social security" and that increasing the number of recipients of welfare will somehow improve productivity. Thus after an increase in transfer payments is followed by the very fall in productivity that economists had warned of, the only response that advocates of these welfare measures can muster is an assertion that the productivity decline is unrelated to their policies and that in any case what we really need to improve productivity is more welfare measures.

True, it is common for these writers to agree with Leontief that the old Keynesian fiscal and monetary policies are not enough and are particularly useless in these times of inflationary recessions. Harrington (1982: 407) agrees with Herbert Stein that the "Keynesian 'textbook,' which provided the policy framework for a generation, is now obsolete." He also points out that the modern developments in money substitutes make it impossible to gear policy to a control of a money supply that is increasingly hard to define (1982: 409–10, 413). Others who explicitly argue that Keynesian fine tuning is obsolete include Crotty and Boddy (1975: 2), Buell (1982: 21, 23), Buell and DeLuca (1977: 5), Carnoy and Shearer (1980: 15, 40), Hayden (1982: 51), and Lekachman (1978: 149). Heilbroner (1982: 52) points out that "in complex ways, the mixed economy and the welfare state, mighty engines of growth in the 1950s, became mighty engines of inflation 20 years later."[30]

But what is missing in these confessions that fine-tuning policies are impotent in the face of stagflation is any recognition of the causal relation between the Keynesian policies of the 1950s and 1960s on the one hand, which prescribed monetary expansion and budget deficits as a cure for unemployment and the opposite as a cure for inflation, and on the other the present policy dilemma. Somehow Keynesian policies have just become obsolete and must be replaced with even more ambitious attempts to control economic life. Bluestone and Harrison (1982: 141) struggle to make sense of the sudden onset of this new problem and to find somebody else to blame other than the very government they hope to invest with the awesome task of planning the nation's economy:

> Stagflation seemed to be related to the basic institutional facts of life in the new global capitalist system. It was certainly fueled in part by the pricing behavior of giant oligopolies. It was exacerbated by the increased interdependence brought about by the multinational investment policies of these same oligopolies, which contributed to the growing synchronization of business cycles across nations.

The fiscal irresponsibility of governments armed with Keynesian doctrines is listed as a factor that merely "reinforced" these stagflationist tendencies. But how surprised should we be that a policy of deficits and monetary expansion to reduce unemployment would result in inflation without curing the underlying causes of unemployment? Monetary expansion results in a decline in the value of money relative to other goods and draws workers and factors of production into avenues of investment which are unsustainable without additional and accelerating injections of money.[31] Deficit spending results either in monetization by the Federal Reserve System, meaning monetary expansion again, or further crowding out of private investment and rising interest rates.

It seems natural, then, to ask who has had control over money and credit and what they have done to it during the postwar years if we seek an understanding of the causes of our current inflation. And if we pose such questions, we find that it is the federal government alone (with its superficially independent Federal Reserve System) that has had power over these institutions and that this power has been exercised energetically in an expansionary direction throughout the period in question.

Critics of such policies, such as F. A. Hayek, warned from the outset that monetary and fiscal stimulation could not cure the underlying causes of unemployment but could only deliver us into a world in which we are plagued by unprecedented price and interest rate increases *in addition to* unemployment. The response of advocates of economic democracy to all this seems calculated to spread the guilt in order to avoid the painful truth that it has been the incompetence of macroeconomic planners in the Federal Reserve and the government that is responsible. To the extent that these writers ever even raise the question of why Keynesian policies fail, the only answers seem to be either that the fine tuners mysteriously lost their touch or that they were doomed to fail in any case because of the inherent instability of capitalism, which naturally can only be mitigated by far more inclusive and comprehensive efforts at controlling the economy (e.g., Bluestone and Harrison 1982: 207).

While trying to distance themselves from the fiscally irresponsible and increasingly discredited policies of the recent past, these writers seem to have learned nothing from the ordeal. The specific policies they propose are precisely the same ones that have gotten us into this predicament: raising taxes, raising government expenditures, embarking on expensive public works projects, imposing wage and price controls, nationalizing certain key industries, relying on so-called public corporations, borrowing on the future by floating more government-backed bonds, expanding the supply of credit, and channeling new investment through various schemes for credit allocation, tax breaks, and outright subsidies to favored businesses.

Not only is this list of policies depressingly unimaginative, in that every one of them has been tried often and never with any clear success, it is also self-contradictory, in that several of them are bound to counteract one another. Price controls combined with significant credit expansion would result in widespread, systematic shortages that would make our current economy look prosperous by comparison. Increased government borrowing and taxing would worsen the crowding out of private investable funds and reduce jobs as fast as public works projects could create them.

Indeed, unlike the older radicals, who at least tried to address policy issues by means of the consistent application of basic principles, these modern self-styled radicals pride themselves on their pragmatic eclecticism.[32] Carnoy and Shearer (1980: 36) favorably quote C.A.R. Crosland's (1957: 496) statement of what they call the "pluralistic ideal":

> a society in which ownership is thoroughly mixed-up—a society with a diverse, pluralist, and heterogeneous pattern of ownership, with the State, the nationalized industries, the Co-operatives, the Unions, Government financial institutions, pensions funds, foundations, and millions of private families all participating.

Reading Carnoy and Shearer's book in particular, one almost gets the impression that a shotgun tactic is deliberately being used here. The book abounds with diverse examples of government projects that have been tried with mixed results both in this country and abroad, none of which is wholeheartedly defended as a winning strategy. Yet by recounting their several stories, in each case as told by someone highly sympathetic to the particular sort of program in question, the authors seem to depend on the cumulative weight of dozens of tentative endorsements somehow adding up to a single coherent policy. The careful critic who would like to concentrate on systematically rejecting any of these policies would find that there are too many and that too little faith is put behind any one for it to be considered central to the ideas.

The only practical way to respond to this shotgun approach to policy is essentially to shoot back brief answers at each major policy direction these writers favor, hoping that the cumulative weight of criticism will add up to a critique of the policy of economic democracy. However, since each of these policies is only an extension of the familiar programs of welfare state liberalism, this critique will not only comprise a counterargument to this type of planning but will also involve a criticism of the actual failures of the status quo.

For a group that fancies itself a popular democratic movement these writers seem strangely insensitive to the grassroots tax revolt that emerged in the late 1970s. The immensely popular Proposition 13 in California and Proposition 2½ in Massachusetts are callously dismissed by Bluestone and Harrison (1982: 18) as "victories of the corporate sector," when in fact they were vigorously opposed by most major banks and corporations. At a time when other political forces are striving at least to *promise* cutbacks on our immense tax burden, these writers are content to replay the old establishment-liberal refrain, "Soak the rich." Lekachman (1982: 196) says funds "should be extracted from much heavier taxes upon the income and property of affluent Americans," while Carnoy and Shearer (1980: 316) call for a tax reform "that seriously attempts to increase taxes for the rich." But of course the proportion of truly affluent people in this country is minute, much too small to pay for even a fraction of the current expenditures of the federal government, even if their property were completely confiscated.[33] And since these writers call for massive increases in federal expenditures, any rhetoric about taxing the rich has to be seen as either extremely naïve, leaving unanswered where the money to pay for their programs will really come from, or as mere camouflage for broad-based tax increases that will hurt not just the wealthy but the bulk of middle-class America, which is already painfully overburdened.[34]

Naturally most of these writers also favor stiffer taxes on the corporations they so despise, but, as Harrington admits, this is one of the most regressive methods of revenue collection, since "companies simply add all, or most, of that cost to the price they charge, thus imposing the levy on the consumers." Actually Harrington is rather confused about why this happens. Somehow he attributes the corporations' ability to escape really paying taxes to their presumed ability to fix prices at will. In fact, whether firms are competitive or monopolistic, taxing them hurts many parties associated with them—from stockholders to workers, to managers, to consumers—in ways that are unpredictable in any detail and consistent with neither egalitarianism nor economic efficiency. As Rothbard ([1962] 1970: 808-9) put it, the actual process by which the economy reacts to a corporate income tax would be better described not as passing on the cost to the consumer but as a "diffusion of suffering over the economy."

Yet even for Harrington the temptation to pretend that the immense taxes required by ambitious spending programs can really be shifted onto that hated corporate elite is irresistible. Just before telling us that taxing the corporations is irrational, he had argued that paying for his extensive list of new programs is "relatively easy" and can be accomplished "simply by requiring the rich and corporations to pay a part . . . of their fair share of the tax burden" (1982: 420-21).

While these writers do seem intent on reducing taxes for the very poor, there is little prospect for anybody in the lower middle class on up to see the weight of his burden eased in the slightest, and a strong likelihood that it will rapidly grow heavier. This becomes especially clear when one considers the expenditure side of the policies of economic democracy. The only kind of expenditures these writers are at all critical of is military spending, while every sort of domestic project into which tax monies have been poured is to be expanded considerably. These writers are big spenders in the old New Deal-Great Society-liberal sense of the word, complete with their list of social priorities, all of which need quick fixes of federal funds in large doses: health, housing, environment, education, and transportation (especially rapid transit, of course, since the individualist car culture of Americans is to be despised as wasteful and antisocial).[35] Sometimes other categories such as "energy" or "research and development" are tacked onto the list of vital needs for which nothing but massive federal spending programs can suffice.

In short, it is as if we were living in the 1930s and the idea of setting up a giant federal bureau to deal with each of these priorities were still a fresh-sounding notion instead of a historical disappointment. The fact is that we have had federal departments of education, housing, and so on, which have injected massive doses of money into these areas, and yet the problems in these priority areas have worsened.

But the biggest spending hole these proponents of planning want to open up, and usually the highest on their priority lists, is the guaranteeing of jobs by means of public works projects. Indeed, sometimes not just jobs but "meaningful" and "interesting" jobs are to be generously offered by the federal government to anyone who wants them.[36] It has not yet occurred to these people that this sort of policy commitment is bound to utterly bankrupt the already strained resources of the federal government. The more meaningful jobs the government offers, the more taxes or monetary expansion or borrowing on the future it will have to indulge in to pay the bill, and most economists agree that all three of these ways of raising money have the long-run effect of destroying private-sector jobs. Jobs programs are not able to add jobs costlessly to those already offered by the private sector, but can only transfer employment from the private to the public sector. But the desirability of simply putting more people on federal instead of private-sector payrolls does not sound as appealing as jobs bills that promise to put people to work.[37]

When taxes are raised, incomes that would have been spent on consumer goods or saved and thereby made available to investors are instead absorbed by the political system. This both reduces consumption demand (causing a chain reaction in capital goods industries that supply inputs to the consumer goods industries) and increases the cost of borrowing over what it would have been by reducing the supply of investable funds. While the immediate beneficiaries of jobs via government spending are usually easily identifiable, the specific people who lose their jobs because of the indirect effects of tax collection on saving and consumption are virtually impossible to identify.

This raises the question of how these planning advocates propose to cope with inflation. If unemployment is to be solved in the same old way—by massive doses of government spending—and if the jobs are not to be immediately taken away by a sharp increase in taxation, then only two courses of action are open to foot the bill: increase the supply of money or borrow on the future. If the latter is resorted to, then government borrowing, which is already crowding out private investment at a frightening pace, will do so even faster and will certainly mean higher interest rates, higher costs of production, and fewer jobs. If monetary expansion is resorted to instead— as is strongly implied but rarely explicitly admitted to be an integral part of these policies—then the continued burdens of inflation seem to be more guaranteed than job security.[38]

The only answer these writers propose to face this particular challenge is wage and price controls. Although these writers differ as to whether controls ought to be only selective or comprehensive, and whether they should be temporary or permanent, all see some necessary role for politically setting prices as one of the main weapons the planning agency will use to combat inflation. Ginsburg (1982: 13) seems to be suggesting comprehensive controls when he says, "A policy should be adopted, applying equally to all sources of income, which would control increases in profits, dividends, rents, interest, and professional fees," but then he seems to retreat to partial controls when he adds the end of the sentence "as well as selected wages and prices." Harrington (1982: 419) comes out forthrightly in favor of "controls that genuinely seek to contain *all* prices, incomes, rents, and, where required, wages, in any form," even though he concedes that "over time the efficacy of the best system of controls will decline" and hence favors it only as a temporary expedient. Lekachman (1982: 199) on the contrary favors only selective controls but wants them imposed permanently. Carnoy and Shearer (1980: 314) favor "selective price controls for the major corporations" but doubt that their advice will be taken. They claim that the reason the leftist governments of Chile and Portugal in the 1970s suffered such catastrophic inflation was that while they were willing to raise low wages they did not compensate by reducing high wages (pp. 317–21). Crotty and Boddy (1975: 5) put their support behind both comprehensive and lasting controls when they say that since "temporary controls simply reallocate inflation over time" and "suppress market forces" the answer must be to impose "more permanent and extensive controls than we had from 1971 to 1974." Heilbroner (1982: 54) clearly leans toward comprehensiveness and permanence when he endorses W. David Slawson's call for "an anti-inflationary administrative structure as pervasive in our economic life as that of the Internal Revenue Service." Neither his frank admission that such a development is "a disconcerting image" nor that this policy of adding "ceilings and restraints" lacks the ability to "remove the inflationary propensity of the system" is enough to deter him from advocating it. Alperovitz and Faux (1977: 4) favor temporary, selective controls over the prices of basic necessities but go on to argue that price controls are not enough and hence direct public supply of these basic necessities will eventually be necessary.

But the economists' arguments against price controls have been too powerful not to have had their impact, even on these writers who sometimes show so little appreciation for the law of supply and demand. Even as they recommend controls, the very tentativeness of their argument reveals that few expect controls to be very effective for very long without being supplemented by the direct government supply of certain basic goods and services.

Indeed, the logic of this policy progression from selective controls to widening controls to nationalization of key industries is impeccable and was pointed out some sixty years ago by Ludwig von Mises. Since the market system depends on production's being guided by profitability, and since clamping price ceilings on a good renders its production less profitable than it would otherwise be, the market's response to the price control is to cut back on the production of the controlled item. If more extensive controls are imposed to try to hold down the production costs of the first item, the consequence is shortages of all the inputs needed, and the situation deteriorates. Ultimately either the whole economy grinds to a halt as prices completely lose their information-signaling role, or else nationalization is resorted to. Lines of production, having been rendered unprofitable by the first round of interventions, have to be resumed by direct governmental control of the production process—in other words by a larger dose of intervention.

Many of these writers have seen the logic of this interventionist dynamic, and sometimes view it as supporting their belief that planning is inevitable. So long as government insists on pursuing its goals by intervening into the market, this step-by-step deterioration or one much like it is bound to occur, but there is nothing inevitable about society's commitment to intervention as such. It is always possible that we will come to see this deterioration for what it is and reverse the process. This may in fact be our only hope.

But if the pursuit of the logic of interventionism is not abandoned, more direct governmental allocation of resources will be the fruit of wage and price controls. This tends to take the form of either outright nationalization or the construction of semigovernmental public corporations that are to receive special treatment and to be regulated by governmental bureaus. The advocates of economic democracy seem to want more of this halfway policy, since the somewhat embarrassing history of outright nationalization suggests that it "has not proved to be the panacea its proponents had hoped" (to put it mildly) (Carnoy and Shearer 1980: 35).[39] Nevertheless while most of these writers do not explicitly use the unpopular word "nationalization," governmental ownership of certain key industries has its place in their arguments among the main tools of the planning agency.[40]

The fatal premise in their defense of selected nationalization is revealed when Carnoy and Shearer (1980: 83) declare that "we do not intend to bail out the losers of American capitalism" but that their nationalization strategy "relies on government ownership of selected *healthy* firms." Of course the real question here is, How could you know? How can any one agent in a competitive system definitively distinguish between a healthy and a sick firm? Investment is necessarily a speculation about future business prospects, hence nationalizing a firm that has been profitable is no guarantee for avoiding what journalist Andrew Kopkind has called "lemon socialism." Carnoy and Shearer's recommendation of directing investment "toward industries with high rates of innovation" (p. 42) completely misses the point that at the time of an innovation nobody can tell whether the new idea will turn out to be a lemon or not. Indeed they castigate the British for having "nationalized the 'commanding heights' of the economy as they existed in the *nineteenth* century" which, they assert, were "relatively 'sick' utility-type industries ... rather than firms of a more dynamic leading nature" (p. 49). Most of the actual industries that Carnoy and Shearer list in this context, however, such as airlines, gas and electricity, radio, and television were hardly thought of as sick nineteenth-century industries in the late 1940s and early 1950s when they were nationalized. They were in fact deemed to be precisely the leading, most innovative industries of the time, much as the computer industry is today. The fact that many of these investments have turned into lemons cannot be blamed on any sort of backward mentality of British planners. All we can say is that planners are no better at forecasting the future of an economy than anyone else. And of course there remains the definite possibility that the reason these particular industries took ill has something to do with the fact that they were singled out for nationalization.

In any case, while nationalization may be considered necessary in some cases, it is not felt to be the best way to democratize our economy. As Carnoy and Shearer (1980: 83) put it, "Exerting democratic control over investment, rather than nationalizing major firms outright, is the strategic route we believe holds real promise for significant reform in the United States." This control over investment may take many forms, ranging from the channeling of investment funds, cheap loans, or subsidies to private-sector firms, to the setting up of regulated mixed enterprises or public corporations.

Implicit in most of these arguments for direct government supply of goods and services, whether through outright nationalization or other means, is the undefended presumption that publicly owned or regulated corporations will be more accountable to the people, apparently just because they would have to "open their books" on demand, and will thus be more apt to hold down costs than private-sector firms.[41] Indeed, Carnoy and Shearer (1980: 69–91) repeatedly invoke the notion of "yardstick competition" to suggest that one of the key functions of a publicly owned firm is to measure the extent to which its private competitors are honestly reporting their costs.

However, according to the perspective outlined in Chapter 3, this yardstick competition gets matters exactly backward. Private-sector performance cannot be measured by public corporations with their open books, but rather public corporations have to be monitored by the information generated by private-sector competition. Opening up cost accounting to public inspection does not serve as any kind of discipline to public corporations, forcing them to keep their costs down. Accounting costs can always be fabricated. The only discipline that can keep costs honest is the threat of loss a company feels when competitors undercut its operation. A private firm can lie about its costs all it wants, but when it runs out of money it faces bankruptcy. Yet this, the only true cost discipline, is precisely what is absent from governmental corporations. For example, Carnoy and Shearer (1980: 80) point out, "If requested . . . to undertake any activities that were excessively uneconomic yet necessary for social reasons, the public firms would be compensated by direct grants."[42]

What these planning advocates fail to recognize is that, by lending selective government support to certain yardstick competitors, they would not only be failing to generate any useful information about how competitive the other firms in that industry were, but worse, they would be sabotaging the very knowledge-generating process of the market upon which government's own activities must rely. Granting special favors to a public corporation gives it advantages over less privileged competitors and thus permits less efficient methods of production to prevail where unfettered competition would have weeded them out. The public corporation will have no way of knowing which aspects of its operation are uneconomic and would have been abandoned by unsubsidized competitors. Competition is a procedure for discovering and communicating information that can be ascertained *in no other way.* Hence providing selected competitors with special advantages merely introduces "noise" into this telecommunications mechanism.

Yet these writers do not seem even to realize that their proposals imply conferring special competitive advantages to public corporations.[43] Carnoy and Shearer (1980: 82) for instance advocate imposing a sales tax on radios and television sets and turning the money over to local public stations "so that the public network could compete with the private networks on equal terms." They claim that "from a business perspective, the TVA [Tennessee Valley Authority] has been run efficiently," citing low operating costs, and neglecting to see any significance in the fact that of its total congressional appropriation of $2.5 billion, some $1.55 billion remained unpaid as of June 1971 (Walsh 1978: 383). Indeed, when asserting that the federal oil and gas corporation they favor would be economically viable, they point out that "Initial financing is no problem if Congress will appropriate the necessary funds as was done with the TVA" (p. 75). But a project that does not recoup its initial financing costs including the appropriate rate of interest, or that can survive only if supported by a special sales tax, can hardly be said to compete on equal terms or to be economically viable. Though these writers are understandably reluctant to admit it, the fact is that public corporations have only been able to survive in competition with private corporations by exploiting the substantial advantages associated with official ties to government.

Carnoy and Shearer (1980: 77) illustrate their misunderstanding of the competitive system when they state that public enterprise "has not significantly threatened private enterprise" on the grounds that such public corporations have often "subsidized and promoted the growth of private business." But of course helping capitalists is not to be equated with helping capitalism. If the virtues of the market order stem from the knowledge generated by free competition, then there is no surer way to threaten this system than by subsidizing selected competitors.

When Harrington (1982: 418) calls it "the key strategy" to "make any subsidies to corporations dependent upon their conforming to a democratically determined plan," he shows the importance these writers typically attach to the basic idea of an institution patterned after the Reconstruction Finance Corporation as one of the central instruments of the planning process.[44] In fact of all the kinds of policy endorsed by advocates of economic democracy, the one that they seem to support most wholeheartedly is the one they share with the advocates of reindustrialization: government allocation of investment funds to selected private enterprises (though they disagree about which industries ought to be favored). Since the next chapter will take up this policy in more detail, I will here only reiterate that the basic problem of this proposal remains the same as the problems of deciding which industry to nationalize or which price to control at what level: How is the new RFC to know what it is doing and whether it is operating effectively? The only way these writers differentiate their RFC from that of Felix Rohatyn is that they (like Robert Reich) want theirs to be subject to the extensive democratic constraints from which Rohatyn wants his to be well insulated. Buell (1982: 24) talks about a National Development Bank that would be "held democratically accountable, not 'insulated' from political pressure." Harrington (1982: 419) urges that the Federal Reserve Board take charge of credit allocation so that "funds are channeled to genuinely productive, socially valuable uses" and that "the Fed should be subjected to democratic controls" to ensure that it does not simply serve the banks. Lekachman (1982: 195; see this chapter's first epigraph) makes it clear that his disagreement with Rohatyn is not over the nature of the new RFC but simply over the goals such an institution is to pursue. Ginsburg's (1982: 10) National Industrial Policy Board and Infrastructure Financing Bank are explicitly patterned after the RFC.

This difference between an "insulated" and a "democratic" RFC may seem profound to those who take for granted that planning will come and thus focus their attention exclusively on the issue of who controls the planning process rather than on whether this process can be conducted rationally. But from the point of view of the present critique, as well as from Wassily Leontief's perspective, the issue of who runs this RFC has to be treated as quite secondary to the question of whether whoever runs it can possibly gather the knowledge to do so rationally.

The most compelling criticism any of the other advocates of planning would be able to make of economic democracy is that there does appear to be a contradiction in the whole idea of planning from the bottom up. If there is to be national planning at all, then all policies have to be precoordinated with a single responsible agency, a central planning office of some kind. To the extent that proponents of economic democracy can escape from this critique, their policies shade into those of reindustrialization, since they end up relying on their investment-guiding institution, their version of the RFC, to play the crucial role of central coordinator for the otherwise decentralized policies. To the extent that they insist on genuinely decentralized decisionmaking they are proposing the arbitrary and uncoordinated injection of contradictory policies by all levels and departments of government. In other words they have a prescription for chaos, not rational planning.

NOTES TO CHAPTER 5

1. Most important, some economic democracy advocates (such as the anarchocommunists) are not in favor of even the most minimal national economic planning and thus, while they may in many cases be criticized on other grounds, they are completely immune from the critique of this book.

2. The older three of these are available from *The Progressive* as reprints. John Buell, an associate editor of the magazine, wrote the more recent article "After Reaganomics, What? Democratic Socialism If We Dare" (the cover story of the July 1982 issue) and co-authored "Let's Start Talking about Socialism" (1977) with Tom DeLuca, a political scientist from Marquette University. "Building a Democratic Economy" (1977) is by Gar Alperovitz and Jeff Faux, co-directors of the Exploratory Project for Economic Alternatives, which was established "to define practical approaches to restructuring the American economy." James R. Crotty and Raford Boddy, economists from the University of Massachusetts and the American University, respectively, are the co-authors of "Who Will Plan the Planned Economy?" (1975).

3. "A Path for America: Proposals from the Democratic Left" was the lead article in the Fall 1982 issue. Its author, Michael Harrington, is one of the best known advocates of planning in this country.

4. Heilbroner's article "Does Capitalism Have a Future?" (1982) appeared in the *New York Times Magazine*.

5. Lekachman's "Inevitability of Planning" was presented at the Columbia University Seminar on Technology and Social Change in 1976 and was published in Goldstein (1978).

6. Hayden's book *The American Future: New Visions Beyond the Reagan Administration* (1982) and Lekachman's *Greed Is Not Enough: Reagan-*

omics (1982) are popular and somewhat polemical criticisms of President Reagan's policies and rhetoric from an economic democracy perspective. Bluestone and Harrison, co-authors of *The Deindustrialization of America*, represent significant examples of advocates of economic democracy who operate under the banner of reindustrialization and thus will be discussed further in the next section. Two more recent books that are very much along the same lines are *Beyond the Waste Land: A Democratic Alternative to Economic Decline* by Bowles, Gordon, and Weisskopf (1983) and *A New Social Contract: The Economy and Government After Reagan* by Carnoy, Shearer, and Rumberger (1983).

7. Lekachman calls this book an "acute analysis" while Heilbroner calls it an "eye-opening tour through a series of options that informed citizens should know more about."

8. As Buell and DeLuca (1977: 5) put it, we need "an alternative to the authoritarian socialism of Eastern Europe and the emerging corporate control of the state in the West."

9. The use of political power to secure profits has been aptly called the "parasitic involution of capitalism" by Andreski (1966: 76–86).

10. See the last section of Chapter 3. Hayden (1982: 53) remarks that there are "certain new realities that cannot fit the theoretical supply and demand model" but then proceeds to show that he does not understand what the model is.

> The concept of "supply" is not as obvious as an infinite pot of gold. Supply of resources, for example, is declining, or being contaminated and therefore made more costly, or cartelized and therefore withheld until prices rise. The traditional notion of supply also ignores as immeasurable the role of *human* energy which, by *labor*-intensive processes, could alter the very meaning of supply itself from a quantitative to a qualitative concept.
>
> Demand is equally ambiguous when carefully defined. Is a market survey a real measure of "genuine" demand when billions are spent each year on advertising to stimulate over-consumption? Does a demand for more goods and services have a higher moral value than a demand for less?

Of the six remarkable sentences quoted here, all but the first one, which makes no sense to me at all, reveal different shortcomings in Hayden's own understanding of supply and demand. Contrary to Hayden's suggestions, such phenomena as the exhaustion or contamination of a resource, or the withholding of production by a cartelized industry, cannot be understood *except* by reference to the theory of supply and demand. Indeed, these are exactly the sorts of examples economists use when they teach the idea to introductory students. The traditional notion of supply does not ignore the qualitative aspects of labor, which were recognized by all the classical economists. While many modern economists have narrowed their attention to measurable quantities and ignored certain qualitative differences, this only represents a clumsy use of the law of supply and demand, not a limitation of its applicability. No economist I know thinks that a demand for more goods is necessarily superior in any way, morally or otherwise, to a demand for fewer. Few think that market surveys are a very good measure of genuine demand. The fact that Hayden finds the effects of advertising on demand socially undesirable because advertisements stimulate other people to consume more than he thinks they should, again, does not in the least challenge the validity or applicability of the law of supply and demand.

11.   Harrington (1982: 411) and Buell (1982: 21) assert that the economy is "out of control" just a few pages away from their complaints that the corporations control things. Ginsburg (1982: 8) tells us that "our vast social, industrial, governmental, and economic problems—domestic and international—cannot be left to the pressures and priorities of countless private interests" but must be subjected to conscious control by a planning agency. Hayden (1982: 40) frets about our "uncontrolled technology" and repeatedly warns us that "things are out of control" (p. 48, p. 49). Lekachman (1982: 198) observes that the private sector is "irresponsible" because "it eludes control by elected officials." In his 1965 book *The Accidental Century*, Harrington's critique of the technological revolution of the last hundred years is based on the charge that it has been "accidental," by which he means out of control. He views this lack of control as the central problem of our time: "The hope for the survival and fulfillment of the Western concept of man demands that the accidental revolution be made conscious and democratic (1965: 42).

12.   Heilbroner (1982: 22) blames the "instability" of the nineteenth-century economy on "cutthroat competitive tactics" and the "destructive competitive wars" which were mitigated by twentieth-century cartels aimed at minimizing "the vagaries of the market." These cartels, he says, were able to reduce but not to eliminate competition, and still found themselves buffeted by "the unruly forces of the market" (p. 38).

13.   Harrington (1982: 412) is bothered by the fact that our economy is "awash with money being used to 'rearrange' assets rather than to produce goods and services." Ginsburg (1982: 9) suggests that government investment will be needed because private investment "may be overseas, or purely financial or speculative, or may in fact be corporate mergers and takeovers. . . . Such moves add nothing to the nation's productive capacity." Buell (1982: 23) praises Marxist economist Harry Magdoff for his observation that "more and more of the work force in the monopolized segment of the economy is assigned to advertising and other essentially unproductive activities" including "finance, tax avoidance, merger activity, speculation, and the like." Bluestone and Harrison (1982: 6) say that "the essential problem with the U.S. economy can be traced to the way capital . . . has been diverted from productive investment in our basic national industries into unproductive speculation, mergers and acquisitions, and foreign investment." This is the same point that reindustrializa-

tion advocate Robert Reich argues in his chapter "Paper Entrepreneurial-ism" (1983: 140).

14. Harrington (1982: 408) goes so far as to refer to an "epidemic" of mergers. Buell (1982: 22) blames inflation on the concentration that results from mergers. Bluestone and Harrison (1982: 122–26) write ominously of three distinct "waves" of corporate mergers involving such presumably horrifying consequences as "diversification with a vengeance" and a situation where "whole businesses were nothing more than commodities to be bought and sold" (p. 124).

15. Harrington (182: 409) says that corporations have become "addicted to debt" while Crotty and Boddy (1975: 4) complain that the American economy is overleveraged in debts. These writers unfortunately do not place the blame for this excessive indebtedness on the cartelized central banking system, which regularly injects large doses of cheap credit into the economy as a means of stimulating business. Instead, businesses are blamed for accepting the credit that is offered to them.

16. Lekachman (1982: 196) asserts that "the American economy in the last decade has not been afflicted by a capital shortage. Its growth has been sabotaged by misdirection of available funds." Harrington (1982: 411, 413–14) calls it a "critical truth" that "it is not the *supply* of capital that is problematic, but the *use* made of it."

17. Hardin and Denzau (1981: 1) report that "during the past four years, the annual supply of funds advanced in credit markets has remained generally unchanged . . . while the share of credit utilized by the federal government has bloated from about 30 percent in 1978 and 1979 to approximately 43 percent in 1980 and 1981." See also Stilwell (1983).

18. Alperovitz and Faux (1977: 5) ridicule "wasteful, mindless consumerism" citing Polaroid cameras as an example of something we waste money on. Buell and DeLuca (1982: 3) find American interest in "vicarious sports thrills" and "insipid 'entertainment' shows" quite beneath them, and make fun of those who view freedom "in terms of the choice between an aerosol deodorant and a roll-on." That people get pleasure out of individual car ownership rather than use public transit systems seems particularly bothersome to Buell and DeLuca (1977: 3), Buell (1982: 22), and Hayden (1982: 13). Hayden also gets infuriated by seeing ads for "cancer-causing, mind-dulling cigarettes and liquor," Big Macs, and "a camera modelled by Cheryl Tiegs." (This in a book whose cover was adorned by a picture of its author's famous wife, Jane Fonda.) He laments our "decline of ethical fiber" (p. 13) and tells us we have been "swept up in the self-indulgences of consumption" (p. 32). Instead he urges that all people pare down their material expectations to "what they really need" (p. 41). Carnoy and Shearer (1980: 76–77) wax eloquent about the virtues of the BBC in England, where the public gets to watch "quality" tax-supported

television while Americans are "forced" to spend nothing to watch com-mercial-supported TV that is geared to the masses, but they fail to observe that the BBC appeals only to the tiny, educated elite of Great Britain.

It should be borne in mind that the "unnecessary consumer gadgets" that these Western intellectuals denigrate happen to be the very conve-niences and fascinating forms of entertainmnet that the vast majority of people living all over the world have enthusiastically desired whenever they have had the good luck to be exposed to them. The progressive intel-lectuals in Eastern Europe understand that we in the West are fortunate to be able to enjoy the luxury of a (relatively) consumer-oriented society. One does not have to claim that the artistic merit of commercial televi-sion rivals that of Bach in order to appreciate the virtue of a society that caters to the tastes of both the majority and tiny elites.

These writers seem to find it demeaning to imagine that most Americans really want to do things like pursue vicarious sports thrills and eat fast food, and so they focus their outrage on advertising. But is it not far more demeaning to view Americans as such dupes as to consume whatever the corporate elite's advertisements tell them to consume?

19. Hayden (1982: 13) actually argues that modern Americans with our con-sumption ethic "have less to offer to oppressed people in an Iran than Khomeini does." What he finds so lacking in our culture turns out to be "any endeavor requiring personal sacrifice for a larger purpose." The two examples he cites of such grand endeavors in our past are the public works programs of the New Deal and the military production effort for World War II.

> In both cases, the work was intrinsically very hard. But most Americans threw themselves into it willingly and with satisfaction. There was a connection between their individual labor and social good. We were not producing unnecessary con-sumer gadgets. We were creating the projects, services, equipment and technology which would lead to economic recovery and victory in the war. Only during such a process can people begin to feel whole, an integration of their personal, economic, and citizenship roles. (p. 43)

Similar attitudes are found among the advocates of reindustrialization, as when Etzioni (1983: 188) talks about the need for a "Core Project." These sentiments unwittingly underscore Walter Lippmann's point: "There is only one purpose to which a whole society can be directed by a deliberate plan. That purpose is war, and there is no other" (1936: 90). War, he pointed out, "is incomparably suited to the creation of a collec-tive sentiment in which all lesser purposes are submerged" (p. 93). One might hope, in any case, that people could find ways to feel whole without having to sacrifice themselves to anybody's grandiose social causes. To me, the great virtue of Americans is their diversity. These United States are liv-ing proof that a nation need not be very united in order to be great.

20. Government intervention has been extensive in energy production, and this *has* led to a serious crippling of the industry. For a detailed study of the effects of intervention in the oil industry, see Bradley (1984).

Alperovitz and Faux (1977: 4) ominously refer to "the coming period of scarcities," and Hayden warns that "the planetary limit is being reached," citing the gloomy but discredited Global 2000 report as evidence. He supplies us with a unique historical perspective by discovering that in the good old days of the frontier "resources . . . were cheap and plentiful" whereas "it is obvious that they become increasingly scarce and expensive as time and exploration go on" (Hayden 1982: 15). In fact, energy sources, adjusting for inflation, are not generally any more expensive than they used to be and, even if they were, there does not appear to be any cause for alarm. After all, that is what prices are *for*, to tell us how to allocate resources more effectively according to their relative scarcities. Scarcer energy sources command higher prices. This brings forth a greater allocation of resources toward energy production, including new alternative sources, and a withdrawal of resources away from energy consumption, including new methods of conservation. Shortages are a consequence of faulty pricing, not of some sort of physical depletion of resources. In fact, Simon (1981) has argued convincingly that natural resources in general are becoming more abundant, not scarcer.

21. Since economic democracy advocates are unaware of the knowledge problem argument, I have had to try to construct this counterargument for them from their general perspective.

22. Mancur Olson (1982) attributes the decline of most societies to their diversion of scarce resources from productive to rent-seeking activities.

23. Harrington (1982: 423) calls this a basic principle which the democratic Left should adopt. His aim is "that wherever planning decisions are to be made, public funds be available to significant groups that wish to engage in counterplanning."

24. Thus Carnoy and Shearer (1980: 72) declare that a nationalized bank "would be free of conflicts of interest caused by interlocking boards of directors." Buell and DeLuca (1977: 5) assert that, under democratic planning, "conflicts of interest and viewpoint would remain, but when the economic security of all is guaranteed, such divisions lose their present brutal nature." Similar assumptions will be found among the structuralists of the next chapter.

25. The published title of this interview makes another inadvertent point: "The Alternative to Not Planning May Be Chaos: A Conversation with Wassily Leontief."

26. Note that I am trying to turn the tables on the planners' argument that the complexity of the modern economy makes their policy necessary. I am arguing that this very complexity increases the danger posed by planning.

The market has so removed most of us from our roots in traditional methods of production that, were it to be crippled by some new visionary who wants to replace it with planning, our very survival as a civilization would be threatened.

27. The charge happens to be from Harrington (1982: 422) in reference to "Milton Friedman and his ilk" but is the typical attitude these writers hold of those who are consistently opposed to planning. Hayden (1982: 9–30) is particularly fond of this technique of dismissing free-market ideas by simply tagging them as old and, in his case, also equating them with a frontier mentality, for which he finds General Custer to be the suitable image.

   In fact, justifications for active government control over the economy are both older and, as I will argue in Chapter 7, far more complementary to militarism, than are free-market ideas. The latter were born in opposition to mercantilist-colonialist justifications for government interference at home and abroad. Of course it is true that free-market ideas have often been used as an ideological disguise by contenders for power who never genuinely believed them. But surely this is true of every set of ideas, including economic democracy.

   When arguing against a set of ideas, one is obligated to try to defeat the best scholarly minds one can find among the advocates of that set of ideas. One should be looking, say, for someone like a distinguished professor of economics who has devoted his life to the clearest possible articulation of the position. To focus a critique of free-market ideas on the popular rhetoric of Ronald Reagan would be something akin to my directing this book at demolishing the ideas of Walter Mondale.

28. In fact, of course, all these mainstream perspectives insist on overriding the dictates of the profit and loss signals in favor of governmentally enforced alternatives.

29. For an alternative view of the causes of the problems in the medical profession, see Goodman (1980). On the question of whether the welfare system benefits the poor, see Browning (1978), Anderson (1978), Murray (1984), Tullock (1983), and Piven and Cloward (1971).

30. Lekachman and Heilbroner do not mention that when, in the 1950s and 1960s, they were both promoting Keynesian policies, their critics were warning them that such policies would invariably turn into "mighty engines of inflation."

31. For a concise discussion of some of these perils of monetary expansion, see Leijonhufvud (1981: 227–69).

32. Carnoy and Shearer (1980: 400–1) illustrate this eclecticism when they reproduce a chart (prepared by Shearer and Bert Gross, in Gross 1979) matching up kinds of policies (price controls, spending, taxes, credit, energy, transport, housing, food, medical care, and insurance) on the verti-

cal axis with levels of government (federal, state, and local) on the horizontal axis. They seem to be trying to say, "We have something for everyone." Their pragmatism arises from the fact that they confine their attention to policies that have been tried rather than try to invent wholly new ones. Thus Alperovitz and Faux (1977: 3) argue that we should "begin to build an alternative to corporate-dominated planning with those ideas that have already been developed and those trends—however modest—that are already in motion." The "building blocks," we are told, are "already at hand," and all that is left is to "cement these pieces together" (p. 6).

33.   Hazlitt (1973: 114–15) has shown (using figures from 1968) that even if all the income of the roughly 0.6 percent of the taxpayers who reported incomes greater than $50,000 were completely confiscated (instead of only 36 percent of it), the addition to revenue would only have totaled about $24 billion, a fraction of a year's federal budget. And this does not even take account of the disastrous effect on incentives such confiscatory taxation would entail.

34.   Ginsburg (1982: 15–16) sets out an eight-point agenda for cutting back on the government's "tax expenditures," the revealing way that these writers refer to the policy of letting people keep some of the government's money. The first on his list of ways "to restore vital revenues and correct glaring tax expenditures" is to place a cap of $700 on tax cuts for the personal income tax. Referring to tax breaks for foreign investment, Bluestone and Harrison (1982: 130) describe the situation as corporate managers being "rewarded with windfall profits from the IRS." They propose that "we should stop granting IRS business-tax incentives of any kind, and for any purpose" (p. 233). Somehow we are supposed to consider the money people keep out of the hands of the IRS to be "glaring," or as Harrington (1982: 421) puts it, "outrageous," while money we turn over to the government restores vital revenues.

35.   Just to be safe, a miscellaneous category is usually added to the list of priorities. Alperovitz and Faux (1977: 3) supply two such lists on one page: "health, housing, environment, education, and other areas of need" and "energy, housing, solar development, medical care, and other sectors." Hayden (1982: 43) tells us, "There are three priorities" [he means "I have ..."], the first of which alone includes "food, shelter, education and health care"; the second involves energy; and the third promises to swallow up computers along with television and satellites. Lekachman's (1982: 196) list of priorities cites "housing, public transportation, and health care," in which, by the way, he claims private enterprise has "conspicuously failed to meet the needs" of Americans. That these areas have received intense interference by government is not considered as a possible reason for the failure. Bluestone and Harrison's (1982: 247–48) "inven-

tory of unmet needs" includes "housing, energy, health care and both freight and passenger transportation." Carnoy and Shearer (1980: 88) have a staggeringly expensive list of "unmet public needs," which involve "better and more universal health care, low-income housing and neighborhood revitalization, rebuilding of cities and economic rebirth of rural areas, pollution control, transportation upgrading, environmental enhancement, energy retrofitting, and many other projects whose costs run into the billions and even trillions of dollars."

36. Ginsburg (1982: 7) wants to offer "a meaningful job for every person willing and able to work" while Bluestone and Harrison (1982: 244) favor policies that will give us "more interesting" work environments. Harrington (1982: 418) envisages "the conscious and planned creation of an entire new industry" in order to create jobs. (In his particular case he's fond of railroads as the technology of the future.) Alperovitz and Faux (1977: 3) agree with Ginsburg that the answer to unemployment was already contained in the original Humphrey-Hawkins bill of 1975, which designated the federal government as the "employer of last resort."

37. However, Lekachman (1982: 196) does set out as an explicit goal the achievement of this transfer to the public sector: "As fractions of total investment, the share of the private sector should diminish while that of the public sector increases."

38. Ginsburg (1982: 14) advocates that we "use short-term control of the money supply as an anti-inflation tool, and bring down high interest rates" (by which he really means we should contribute to inflation by expanding credit), and he says we should "raise [the Federal Reserve System's] targets for money growth in 1982 to accommodate healthy economic expansion."

39. As Carnoy and Shearer (1980: 38) admit, "Many of the high hopes of the European Left for nationalization have not been realized in practice." Yet it often seems that the major reason these writers shy away from nationalization is the fact that it would be unpopular to Americans rather than any inherent objection to the policy. Carnoy and Shearer state that "proposing outright and complete nationalization of any industry or group of major firms would be both politically infeasible and unduly costly, given Americans' genuine concern about big government . . . " (p. 79). Hayden (1982: 208–9) admits, "Nationalization seems an unattractive alternative to corporate power," although he does not want to rule it out as a "legitimate alternative" and actually recommends it for the oil industry.

40. Alperovitz and Faux (1977: 4) favor "more public control and ownership of land." (Governments now own nearly half the land in this country, in some states over 90 percent.) Ginsburg (1982: 10) favors nationalization as a last resort when he says, "If direct investment in an ailing industry

becomes necessary, the nation should receive equity in the enterprise in return for the investment." (Of course, by "the nation" is meant the government.)

Carnoy and Shearer (1980: 84) agree with this approach of viewing failing private-sector businesses as "fruitful opportunities" for attaining increased direct governmental control over these industries; they even suggest that government specifically buy out firms that are "convicted of criminal behavior" as a form of punishment. I will not go into the rather bizarre incentives such a policy would put in place.

Carnoy and Shearer (1980: 330–31) also specifically attribute the failure of our health care system to the fact that Medicare and Medicaid were mere systems for regulation instead of being "run directly by federal or state governments," which they think would somehow have kept costs down.

Bluestone and Harrison (1982: 248) favor "selective nationalization" for the oil business and "especially in the production of expensive capital equipment, where private firms are unable or unwilling to provide a reliable flow of high-quality products at affordable prices."

41. This perspective on public accountability is also evident when it is suggested that even where investment decisions remain in the private sector, these can be improved if we only open up their accounting records to public view. Thus Harrington (1982: 419) demands that "all the corporate books must be opened; all of the major investment decisions must be subjected to scrutiny." Bluestone and Harrison (1982: 248) think that a government oil corporation could, unlike private corporations with their closed books, "be held accountable by Congress for publicly reporting its true operating costs, thereby keeping the private companies honest about the true cost of drilling, refining, and shipping the product."

Such statements are indicative of a serious misunderstanding of the nature of profit and loss accounting. There is no way a third party can scrutinize a corporation's books in order to objectively determine whether it acted competitively or not. While accounting records are extremely valuable to the corporation that keeps them (and potentially valuable to any rival businesses who might like to take advantage of such public scrutiny) they are not particularly valuable for anyone who would like to make corporations more publicly accountable.

Alperovitz and Faux (1977: 5) typify this naïve view when they assert that "publicly owned firms tend to be more accountable to the public (their books are open), and more responsive to major economic policy needs. For example, it makes economic sense for a public enterprise to consider the social costs of its location decisions since its owner, the public, will have to pay them."

42. When Carnoy and Shearer (1980: 73) support Senator Adlai Stevenson III's call for a nationalized energy corporation, they contend that it "would serve as a standard against which to judge the performance of private firms with regard to operating costs, prices to the consumer, and other variables." They suggest that public enterprises would apply "competitive pressure" to private businesses, challenging them "to follow their lead" in producing innovations such as "a longer lasting light bulb, a safer high-mileage car, or a readable insurance policy." Such public companies would "provide vital information to the government on the actual costs and processes involved in the industries, and thus serve as a standard for social responsibility" (p. 80).

43. This is the only way to make sense out of the frequent assertions by many of these writers that, as Alperovitz and Faux (1977: 5) put it, "public corporations can be at least as efficient as private ones," or as Carnoy and Shearer (1980: 77) would have it, "Most public enterprises in democratic mixed economies are run efficiently." The only way such amazing statements can be made is if their authors ignore the costs of initial funding, generally through government-backed loans, and tax-free interest rates and other special tax breaks that are afforded public corporations. When these true costs are taken into account, it becomes clear that public corporations represent some of the most wasteful boondoggles in economic history. The recent book by Bennett and DiLorenzo (1982) is one of the best accounts of some of the subtler ways public corporations have found to waste other peoples' money.

Perhaps Carnoy and Shearer (1980: 83) have admitted the whole case when they say they want to "run these utility-type enterprises in an efficient manner (though not necessarily one that is commercially profitable)." The point that eludes them is that aside from commercial profitability there is no way of knowing whether an operation is efficient or not.

44. Heilbroner (1982: 53) refers to "the deliberate encouragement and guidance of investment" as the "key" to economic planning. Carnoy and Shearer (1980: 63) boast on the RFC's behalf that in a couple of years it had "pumped more money into the American economy than had the House of Morgan from 1919 to 1933." The next two chapters will discuss the nature of the RFC in more detail.

6

REINDUSTRIALIZATION
Shoring Up the Economy's "Structural" Sectors

I recognize that "planning," and even worse, "long-range planning," have become buzzwords. Government planning is equated in some quarters with Soviet five-year plans and thus has about it an aura of communism or, at the least, socialism. And that is very strange, because it is considered perfectly splendid, indeed a necessity, for business and industry to have long-range planning. But applied to government, it becomes somehow unsavory. In recognition of this unfortunate connotation often given to planning, we have substituted the term "foresight capability." It is a euphemism, to be sure, but one which seems necessary if the subject is to be discussed with objectivity. What we are talking about here, of course, is not a planned society, but rather the use of planning to meet society's needs.

Russell Peterson (1981: 2–3)

We cannot become a nation of short-order cooks and saleswomen, Xerox-machine operators and messenger boys. . . . These jobs are a weak basis for the economy. . . . To let other countries make things while we concentrate on services is debilitating both in its substance and in its symbolism.

Felix Rohatyn, as quoted in Alpern (1981: 29)

Finally, we will need political institutions capable of generating large-scale compromise and adaptation. Some of these institutions will be at local and regional levels. But we will also need a national bargaining arena for allocating the burdens and benefits of major adjustment strategies. Such an arena would enable the nation to achieve a broad-based consensus about adjustment. It would enable government, business and labor to fashion explicitly agreements to restructure American industry.

Robert B. Reich (1983: 275–76)

173

THE STRUCTURE METAPHOR

The word "reindustrialization" has become the political slogan of the season precisely because it is vague enough to include anybody's program and sounds innocuous enough to be negotiable as ideological currency. In some sense everybody favors revitalizing and modernizing America's industry.[1] Unlike "economic democracy," this slogan has the advantage of referring to the less controversial *goal* of national policy, achieving a second industrial revolution, while leaving the more contentious *means* unspecified. As a result, confusion reigns about what reindustrialization means in terms of any concrete measures for stimulating the economy. In popular usage the term spans a spectrum from radical leftists (including some of the economic democracy advocates) to establishment liberals and even populist conservatives on the other extreme. One leftist writer attributes its origin to Congressman Jack Kemp, and condemns it as fascism, while others on the extreme Left try to appropriate the slogan for themselves.[2] Its true coinage seems to have been due to sociologist and former Carter adviser Amitai Etzioni, who stakes out a moderate position distinct from either extreme.

Despite the wide spectrum of political thinkers associated with reindustrialization, an important subset of these seems to be emerging that is distinguishable from both conservatism and economic democracy. These writers share certain typical attitudes, see a particular sort of role for national economic planning (although most of them would prefer to use some euphemism), and promote the establishment of an institution patterned after the Reconstruction Finance Corporation of the 1930s (or after modern Japan's similar agency, MITI) as the main policy instrument to implement their agenda for planning. While a significant degree of heterogeneity exists among those who make up this perspective, it has already been singled out by one enthusiastic writer as a "New Economics" that is "at the frontiers of economic thinking" in much the same way Keynes had been in the 1930s, and has even been christened with another name almost equally ambiguous: "structuralism."[3]

Even though the common grounds that can be discerned in this diverse group are much too nebulous to earn it the designation of an economic school of thought, the term "structuralism" does capture a key attitude typical of most advocates of reindustrialization. This common attitude consists of an extended use of a kind of civil engineering metaphor: The economy is like a great structure, a building in which certain stories (industries or regions) are the foundations that have to remain firm in order to support the whole edifice of the relatively superficial upper stories. Planning is advocated in order to shore up the weakening beams and supports upon which the survival of the rest of the structure depends. A new RFC is promoted as a sort of crack team of specialists to be assigned the responsibility for identifying any structural weaknesses in the economy and for patching them up with federally guaranteed loans, grants, and the like.

So long as we remain on such a vague and metaphorical level there is a remarkable degree of unanimity among these writers, but as we delve more deeply we can discover the differences among them: Which sectors (snowbelt versus sunbelt, for example) are deemed structural and hence ought to be shored up? What is the ultimate purpose of the patchwork (to protect stockholders' and bankers' investments or to save workers' jobs from plant closings)? What are the root causes of the deterioration of the "basic" industries (excessive worker demands, the mobility of capital, foreign competition, and so on)? While these differences are politically significant in terms of the intense conflicts and battles we can expect over control of the new RFC, the main economic objections I will raise to reindustrialization will be unaffected by such quarrels.

Thus it will not seriously weaken the thrust of my case if, out of the many structuralists, I choose two as the main examples of the perspective: Felix Rohatyn, Wall Street financier and head of New York's Municipal Assistance Corporation ("Big MAC"), and Robert Reich of Harvard's John F. Kennedy School of Government. For the most part, to the extent that the other advocates of reindustrialization differ from Rohatyn and Reich their viewpoints tend to shade into economic democracy (for example, Bluestone and Harrison or Ronald Müller) and therefore need not be reexamined at length in this section.

The RFC agencies envisaged by these two structuralists would appear to be starkly different in two respects. Rohatyn prefers an "insulated" planning agency and wants it to funnel aid to sunset industries, while Reich prefers an "open" one and wants it to funnel aid to sunrise industries.

The prominent Rohatyn variant of reindustrialization seems to have precisely opposite attitudes from those distinctive of the advocates of economic democracy. Whereas the proponents of economic democracy favor workers' control and curbs on profits, Rohatyn favors forcing austerity measures down the unions' thoats to keep wage costs from rising too high.[4] Where the former insist on democratizing government policymaking or planning both as an end in itself and as the primary means toward most of their other ends, the latter proposes protecting government experts from the fray of political battles by insulating them from democratic pressures.[5] If the former seem primarily motivated by a desire to fight the corporate elite, the latter is a millionaire investment banker who epitomizes this very elite and who openly seeks to promote its interests.[6] While the former insist that there is no shortage of capital but only misuse of investment funds for unproductive uses, the latter admits that capital and savings are in short supply and imagines that this problem can be resolved by pumping investment monies into the economy through an RFC and by shifting taxes from investment to consumption to encourage savings. Where the former blamed the recent recession on mergers and corporate takeovers, Rohatyn is touted as one of the very financial wizards who has made his fame by masterminding such mergers and acquisitions.[7]

On the other hand Robert Reich's notion of a "national bargaining arena" seems to have more resemblance to the democratized planning agency that is imagined by the advocates of economic democracy. The same consensus that Rohatyn thinks can be achieved by insulating the new RFC from open political debate, Reich (1983: 276), with the economic democracy advocates, believes can be reached by establishing an open forum, a single arena where proposals can be "debated in full view [of those] groups on whom their costs would fall." Reich's argument that Rohatyn's closed RFC would represent a dangerous concentration of power is convincing. So is Rohatyn's argument that Reich's open RFC would become a politicized struggle among special interest groups for government largesse. Neither offers any compelling reasons why closing or opening the new RFC to direct political scrutiny would reduce its likelihood of being exploited by special interests.

In addition, Rohatyn's emphasis on salvaging the declining older industries is in direct contrast to Reich's emphasis, similar to many proponents of economic democracy, on promoting newer, high-technology, or as he prefers to call them, "flexible-system" enterprises (Reich 1983: 278). Rohatyn wants to channel investment funds toward steel plants, highways, and subway systems, while Reich wants it for promoting those industries which are, according to Reich's expectations, destined to be the technologies of the future. As Reich (1983: 13) puts it[8]:

> The industries in which the United States can retain a competitive edge will be based not on huge volume and standardization, but on producing relatively smaller batches of more specialized, higher-valued products—goods that are precision-engineered, that are custom-tailored to serve individual markets, or that embody rapidly evolving technologies. Such products will be found in high-value segments of more traditional industries (specialty steel and chemicals, computer-controlled machine tools, advanced automobile components) as well as in new high-technology industries (semiconductors, fiber optics, lasers, biotechnology, and robotics).

But the proponents of reindustrialization fully concur with the most important attitude of economic democracy advocates. The economy is described alarmingly as out of control and therefore, by that fact alone, presumed to be in need of concerted government action in order to be rescued. Rohatyn (1980a: 3) begins one of his articles with these words: "It has been apparent for some time that our economy was out of control." Reich begins his latest book (1983: 3) by declaring that "since the late 1960s America's economy has been slowly unraveling," and later warns ominously that "the U.S. economy is grinding to a slow, painful halt" (p. 134). To meet the challenge of such international competitors as Japan and West Germany "requires far-reaching economic and social changes," but we are "not organized for changes of this magnitude" (p. 14). Hence what is needed is an institution for "orchestrating adjustment," (p. 14) and "more strategic policies to shift citizens to higher-valued production"; that is, we need to gain control over the "unraveling" American economy (p. 267).[9]

The crisis is generally depicted as stemming from a variety of causes, including international circumstances beyond our control and unwise government policies of the past, rather than being blamed, as with economic democracy, almost exclusively on corporate investment decisions, but the solution is essentially the same: central government direction of investment—that is, national economic planning. Both Reich and Rohatyn see the essential problem as the withdrawal by private corporations of capital funds from avenues of investment that the planners think ought to be financed, whether "high tech" for Reich and most proponents of economic democracy, or older industries for Rohatyn. Both want to make up for this by setting up a special RFC-like institution that would undertake the desired capital investments.

In particular, reindustrialization advocates generally lament the withdrawal of capital from what are called "structural" components of the national economy. The one attitude that is common to all advocates of reindustrialization is their propensity to employ this structure metaphor to promote the salvaging of certain industries that are designated as basic. Some flavor of what is usually meant by basic industries may be revealed by Rohatyn's remark (quoted in Alpern 1981: 29) that services are a "weak basis for the economy" and are somehow "debilitating, both in . . . substance and in . . . symbolism." The kinds of industries which Rohatyn views as more appropriate to our country's symbolic self-image and which constitute the necessary foundation of the industrial structure are the manufacturing sectors, especially the heavy industries such as steel and automobiles. Rohatyn (1981a: 16) views it as a national crisis that "McDonald's hamburger chain employs more people than U.S. Steel" and concludes that a massive effort is needed to rescue his favored industries.

Reich (1983: 132) agrees that "the nation cannot rely on services" because these "depend on the vigor of its future manufacturing base." The fact that the "nations of Western Europe and Japan have been selling America more manufactured goods than it has been selling back to them" is taken as evidence of the decline of this country's economy. The crisis is the fact that "America's basic steel, textile, automobile, consumer electronics, rubber, and petrochemical industries are becoming uncompetitive in the world" (p. 126).[10]

Similar preferences for certain basic, substantive (one could almost say macho) industries over nonbasic (namby-pamby?) sectors is to be found among most other structuralists, as well. Bluestone and Harrison (1982: 5) find it "shocking" that

> in terms of dollar value, the number one Japanese product sold to America was passenger motor vehicles, followed by iron and steel plates, truck and tractor chassis, radios, motorbikes, and audio and video tape recorders. In contrast, America's top seven exports to Japan, in order of dollar value, were soybeans, corn, fir logs, hemlock logs, coal, wheat and cotton. The . . . United States has been reduced to an agricultural nation trying desperately to com-

pete with the manufacturer of the world's most sophisticated capital and consumer goods.

Similarly Lane Kirkland (1982: 21), president of the AFL–CIO, proposes that a new RFC "be concerned with the industrial base of the country" rather than "support more McDonald's and K-Marts," while William Winpisinger (1982: 22), president of the International Association of Machinists and Aerospace Workers, believes we should invest in "modern steelmaking plants and equipment" instead of "chemicals and dixie cups."

One need not be a complete cynic to notice that one common factor that seems to underlie all the "basic" industries besides their machismo symbolism is that they all represent highly organized labor forces that are backed by a considerable bloc of voters and political clout. Whether particular reindustrialists come across as antiworker (Rohatyn) or proworker (Kirkland and Bluestone and Harrison), their policies appear calculated to increase the power of union leadership.

Despite frequent insinuations that the proper image of a proud nation should depend on something tough and physical like steel plate and truck chassis rather than something soft and gushy like soybeans and hamburgers, there is nothing of any substance in this literature to suggest what exactly is so shameful about this state of affairs. For over two hundred years economists have taught that the wisest course for any nation to take is to permit free trade so that each country may produce those goods for which it has a comparative advantage and then exchange these for the goods that are efficiently produced by others. Only in this way can we obtain command over the maximum quantity of all the goods we would like to consume. While it might damage some peoples' sense of patriotism to face the fact that America exports several agricultural products to Japan in exchange for manufacturing goods, surely this is a development with which mature adults can learn to cope. It seems to me that our primary concern ought to be whether we *have* jobs and what the quality of life is that these jobs enable us to afford, not whether the goods we happen to be most efficient at producing might promote the symbolic image we have of ourselves.

Rohatyn and Reich do suggest that there are substantive as well as symbolic reasons to resist the decline of the basic industries, but offer only occasional clues as to what these reasons are.[11] They each try to construct an argument to the effect that we should salvage some (basic) industries because they constitute the main source of demand for other (nonbasic) industries.[12] Such connections between sectors can be multiplied at will, and of course Reich and Rohatyn have differing opinions of which industries need to be helped. For example, much of the steel the United States has been able to produce competitively has been the kinds needed for high-technology industries, such as microprocessors. Hence one could construct an argument that granting cheap credit to the latter will help put the former on its feet (Reich) or that aiding the former will help put the latter on its feet (Rohatyn). The point is that such relations between the health of different sectors of a modern economy are so intricate and complex that it is the height of pretense to claim that any single agency could take them all into account in its decisions to reallocate credit to certain sectors.

While Reich agrees with Rohatyn that the uncontrolled decline of these basic industries constitutes the main problem that economic planning is supposed to solve, he completely disagrees, as we have seen, about how to respond to this decline. While Rohatyn wants to retard the structural changes, Reich wants to hasten them. Rohatyn is for shoring up the old structures; Reich (1983: 130) for "restructuring" them. Reich believes the national bargaining arena should "negotiate a package of public adjustment assistance designed explicitly to buttress their most competitive operations, retrain their work force, and shift other resources to more profitable uses" (p. 276).

But, Reich is quick to assure us, "This does not mean that industrialized countries must abandon their older industries, like steel, chemicals, textiles, and automobiles," which are "the gateways through which new products and processes emerge" (1983: 130). Nor, he says, should these industries be merely propped up as they are now through government subsidies (1983: 178–79). Rather, we should "restructure them toward higher valued and technologically more sophisticated businesses" (p. 130).

But what Rohatyn and Reich have not told us is who is to carry the burden, which industries are to be pressed into decline in order to pay for the sunrise or sunset industries that are to be aided. In all of this literature one finds many more suggestions of potential expenditures of money by the new RFC than of possible sources of revenues. It has to be borne in mind that any argument for offering subsidies in the form of cheap credit to some favored industries, whether old or new, is also an argument for penalizing other (possibly unidentifiable) industries.

At any given time an economy has only a limited supply of investable funds to allocate to its various possible production projects. In a free credit market entrepreneurs have to compete with one another to discover profitable projects in order to secure future command over such funds. To the extent that government agencies disperse favors in the form of cheap credits, the competitive discovery process is subverted and politically favored projects succeed at the expense of others that may have been more economically efficient. The microprocessor and steel industries, as well as the economy as a whole, would be far healthier if we permitted them to compete fairly for investable funds rather than provide cheap credit to one of their current customers.

This crucial point is rarely admitted, and its significance as a critique of the whole idea of an RFC is never noticed, by advocates of reindustrialization. Thus for example Eugene Keilin, Big MAC's first executive director and a senior vice president of Rohatyn's firm, Lazard Freres, admits that "to the extent you succeed in raising capital and channeling it, it does mean that capital is somewhat less available and somewhat more expensive for everybody else," but he does not let this dampen his enthusiasm for Rohatyn's RFC proposals (quoted in Rothenberg 1983: 44). Frequent references in this literature to the idea that an RFC agency would supply or raise capital are simply false. All this sort of agency can do is transfer capital, not create it. It can only channel investment away from the avenues market signals would have attracted it into and toward those it prefers.

The point is that the only way we even know which lines of production are better suited to concentrate on and to what extent is by observing the outcome of market rivalry. Whether we are squandering resources by over- or underinvesting in microprocessors or steel can be revealed only by the message contained in the relative profitability of rival firms in these industries. But this is precisely the information we garble when we channel money toward one or another of the contenders. Deprived of its elimination process, the market would no longer be able to serve its function as a method for discovering better and eliminating worse production techniques. Without the necessity of responding to consumers' wants or needs, businesses would never withdraw from unprofitable avenues of production. One need not be a crude Social Darwinist in order to understand that we could no more expect the Market to function as the economy's coordination process while simultaneously bailing out unresponsive firms than we could expect biological evolution to function without any species' becoming extinct.

The only support advocates of reindustrialization give for their claim that the particular industries they call "basic" should be considered necessary for the survival of other industries seems to be an excessively literal interpretation of their own metaphors. The term "industrial base" connotes some sort of firm foundation that is holding up the economy's structure (appropriately made of solid things like steel) without which the whole building will collapse. Thus, we are told that we need to shore up our industrial base before we find it "coming apart at the seams," leading to a collapse of the whole structure.[13]

But articulating an analogy between an economy and a building does not constitute an explanation. There is no reason why the steel industry constitutes any more crucial a linchpin of our economic structure than any other industry, whether its product be as tough as nails or as soft as software. There is no reason a country might not find itself most prosperous by specializing in selling intangible services to other nations, in which case its industrial base would be invisible. In any case, to sustain an argument that an expensive rescue operation is needed to salvage certain selected industries, it is necessary to go beyond architectural analogies and specify why the overall economy can expect to benefit from such an operation.

It turns out that the older structural industries are not all that Rohatyn wants to shore up through federal assistance. He urges that large doses of money be offered to America's "older cities, as well as our older industries." Here again a structure metaphor is made to carry most of the weight of the argument, only this time it is in terms of the so-called infrastructure, which includes the nation's cities, harbors, and transportation systems. We are told that we cannot afford to allow our cities to deteriorate, but we are given no more reason why the rest of the country would benefit from assuming the burdens of the bad management of various mayors than we had been given for taking on the losses that have resulted from the decisions of the managers of steel plants.[14] If New York City's government cannot pay its bills, why should Idaho taxpayers be compelled to come to the rescue? As in the case of bailing out basic industries, would this not amount to a program for rewarding bank-ruptcy? Would this not be a policy virtually guaranteed to call forth a rash of defaults in order to win federal loans? If, as Rohatyn admits, the precarious financial situation of so many major metropolitan governments is a direct result of their irresponsibility, how can these salvage operations be expected to make the recipients more responsible?

Rohatyn's response to such charges of rewarding failure is that his RFC would impose onerous austerity conditions on anyone, whether in city government or in basic industries, who is to receive federal assistance.[15] Nobody will see these bail-out schemes as a prize to try to win, because the conditions on the loans will be so stringent as to discourage any further fiscal irresponsibility. We will shortly return to the plausibility of this response, but for now I would only remark that it seems to require a rather strong assumption that the financial experts within the RFC are considerably cleverer than those whom they are bailing out. We have to assume that these experts are able to devise schemes that the managers of the recipient institutions did not think of, whereby cities or businesses can be saved without also being benefited in such a way as to attract others into the now lucrative business of going broke.

But perhaps the real reason Rohatyn wants the country to bail out its older industries and cities is much more straightforward: It may simply be a matter of special pleading. As he openly admits, "I like big cities. . . . Civilization grows there. Religion develops in open air, I suspect. But civilization—that is in the cities." (Quoted in Alpern 1981: 26.) But such an argument takes us out of the realm of social science and into the streets of political struggle. How could Rohatyn respond to, say, a religious rural dweller who cares little about the so-called civilization of big cities and wants an RFC to bail out small farmers and bankrupt churches at the expense of steel companies and city folk? So long as we can find no plausible case for the special status of the older industries and cities—a case that could show that the health of other sectors and regions would somehow benefit from this opportunity to finance the massively expensive rescue operation involved in Rohatyn's reindustrializing—there is no reason why those who do not share Rohatyn's tastes should be expected to endorse his policy prescriptions.

There is no better illustration of the political warfare national economic planning will invariably ignite than the divergence between two of its leading proponents about which sectors ought to be shored up. Although we actually have no definite assurance that there is any expenditure which either Reich or Rohatyn would not approve, it is evident that Reich cares little for Rohatyn's older cities, and that Rohatyn is relatively unimpressed by Reich's new-fangled technologies.

While most of those who clamor for reindustrialization largely concur with Rohatyn in designating basic industries as structural supports of the economy, which therefore require shoring up, and many would agree about the older cities, Rohatyn's third major category of potential recipients of RFC funding, the banks, is much less popular. While, for example, the major unions have a clear interest in propping up many of the heavy industries Rohatyn likes, and are strongest in some of the cities he wants to help, they are not always so enamoured of the idea of coming to the aid of Chase Manhattan.

But the logic of Rohatyn's position is no different in this case than in the other two. Banks are referred to as "weakening financial structures" and thus transformed by the strength of the by-now-familiar metaphor into necessary supports for the rest of the economy. Needless to say, Rohatyn (1982a: 7) concludes that we must take "steps that would shore up the domestic banking system" because "the private banks, alone, cannot carry the burden." To solve this crisis, Rohatyn (1982a: 7) proposes that "both the taxpayers and the bank's stockholders will have to assume a part" of the burdens resulting from overextended credits to Third World countries "if the banking system is to be protected." Almost as if he wanted to mock the Left, Rohatyn proposes a sort of bankers' welfare system that would involve supplying "a safety net for our American banks" (p. 6) and "doubling the IMF's capacity to lend money" (p. 7) to help prop up "our" banks' shaky investments overseas (p. 6). And, comparable to his argument for saving the cities, Rohatyn's case for rewarding the banks for their financial irresponsibility amounts to little more than the fact that he likes them: "Our banking system is one of the most precious assets of our economy and of the free society itself" (p. 8).[16]

The real issue in all of these crises of weakening structures that demand shoring up is the same. Whatever the underlying causes of the deterioration of basic industries, older cities, and overextended banks, their long-term salvation cannot lie in propping them up with federal monies. Bailing them out can only perpetuate and reward inefficient uses of scarce resources at the expense of more efficient ones. It can only obstruct the competitive discovery process on which the genuine health of our economy ultimately rests.

The idea of an economy's capital as a structure—in the sense of an interconnected, interdependent network of relationships between sectors—is an invaluable metaphor for understanding how productive processes must be coordinated with one another. But the first principle of any analysis of the capital structure has to be the clear recognition of the fact that, unlike a physical structure such as a building, it is continually changing. Its parts are forever readjusting to one another on the basis of profit. Profit and loss signals are the only information that can guide producers of higher order capital goods toward the production of the kinds of intermediate goods that will contribute to the production of lower order consumption goods. This intricate network of relations among the thousands of orders and sectors of capital goods is continually being restructured by the forces set in motion by differential profit rates. Thus, a call for governmental restructuring or shoring up of this self-ordering system amounts to a destruction of the very mechanism that tends to keep the sectors of the capital structure integrated.

Indeed, the radical reindustrialists Bluestone and Harrison (1982: 208) reveal the essence of the structuralist position by obligingly taking it to its ridiculous extreme. They identify as one of the main causes of our economic malaise "the increase in the velocity of capital mobility." The problem, then, is alleged to be the mobility of investment per se, not just its withdrawal from basic industries or beloved cities and banks. Since capitalists are compelled by the profit motive to look constantly for ways to cut costs, they invariably can be found pulling out of less cost-effective investments. They are therefore deindustrializing older facilities. The proposed solution to this "problem" is to pass plant-closing legislation to make it difficult for capital to move. This, of course, will mean that less and less of our nation's productive plant will operate cost effectively as time goes on and as economic circumstances continue to change. Taken to its logical conclusion, reindustrialization is a pathologically reactionary call for economic rigidity, for preventing the competitive process from stimulating rational adjustments to changing circumstances. To borrow one of Leontief's analogies, it is a prescription for pouring glue down the economy's steering column.

The fact that Robert Reich (1983: 278) seems to want to accelerate many of the very changes that Rohatyn and Bluestone and Harrison want to slow down does not make his policies any better. To favor "flexible-system production" is to desire an outcome, not to specify any means for its attainment. To propose that the planning agency guide and accelerate market forces is to presume that the investment-guiding agency can anticipate future developments better than the market can; it is to assume that the agency's individual intelligence exceeds the social intelligence of the competitive process. How will the investment-guiding agency know exactly which up-and-coming firms to direct funding toward? Whether resisting or promoting the market's structural changes, the advocates of reindustrialization must assume that the new RFC agency know enough to intervene intelligently in the market process.

The structuralists often seem unaware of the fact that progress requires abandoning less effective modes of production precisely in order to release resources for more effective ones. Rejuvenating the American economy cannot be accomplished without relying on the knowledge supplied by competition as to which specific lines of production to discard as well as which to pursue. By taking their own metaphor too seriously, the structuralists presume that shoring up the economy is a task essentially similar to that undertaken by a civil engineer who repairs the structural supports of a building. That is, they treat a dynamic spontaneous order which is sustained by the social intelligence generated by competitive processes as if it were a single static project under the supervision of an individual intelligence.

THE EXPERT COORDINATORS

Although there are substantive differences in attitude between leftist adherents of economic democracy and corporatist or neoliberal reindustrializers like Rohatyn and Reich, they are similar in their reluctance to supply any genuine arguments as to why national economic planning is the policy most likely to solve the problems they describe. In lieu of arguments for planning, there are the same sorts of terse dismissals of the free-market alternative as "just a theory," as appropriate only for the simpler circumstances of previous centuries, or as representing the nonpolicy of doing nothing in the face of real problems. The moderate and corporativist structuralists first dismiss the only coherent alternatives to planning and then argue that their particular variant of planning is desirable because the only other alternative, economic democracy, would be so much worse. In much the same way, proponents of economic democracy refuse to consider any alternative to their program but Rohatyn's to be "permitted by history" and then base their case on the undesirability of his corporativist planning. Each of these advocates of planning makes a good case against the only alternative they consider. Rohatyn is correct that the policies of economic democracy would be uncoordinated, irresponsible, and chaotic, and would probably ensure the utter ruin of America's industry. At the same time, proponents of democratic planning are equally correct in pointing to the dangers and undesirability of permitting the concentration of power Rohatyn wants in order to salvage his friends among the corporate elite. Each version of planning gives us good reasons to be opposed to the other versions but has little to offer beyond undefended beliefs and assertions about why we need *any* kind of planning.

Rohatyn's (1980b: 24) response to his leftist critics is symptomatic of this tunnel-vision: "To cries of elitism or the fear of creating a new 'establishment' I say that where we are going otherwise is infinitely worse." Yet all he has to say against any nonplanning alternative is that "both the known facts and the potential problems argue against a policy of hoping to muddle through with a little bit of luck" and that "the risk of inaction is simply too great" (Rohatyn 1982a: 3). But actually to bring about a free-market system would be a far cry from inaction. On the contrary, it would require a drastic reversal of the policy directions of the present century; it would entail the substantial modification of several major components of our economy from our credit and monetary institutions to the scope and dimensions of our property rights system. *It is, in short, the planners who are asking us to muddle through with more of the same policies we have been trying for years.*

Even if all these drastic reforms were made and a free market were instituted, the resulting system could hardly be called "inactive." It is indicative of a peculiar view of society when the (voluntary) actions of millions of market participants are dismissed as inaction merely because active (coercive) involvement by the government is minimized.

Reich's (1983: 232–35) dismissal of the free-market alternative is just as misguided. First he identifies all market advocates with the position that the economy, once disturbed, automatically finds its way back to a new equilibrium. Then he points out that this equilibrium "is a vanishing mirage." But instead of offering a critique of this abstract equilibrium theorizing, he proceeds to adopt some of its worst underlying assumptions. He quite agrees with such theorists that the economy will adjust to equilibrium on its own, and only wants to select a less painful and more rapid path to a new equilibrium. "There are many routes that the adjustment can take—some far easier, more socially equitable, and more efficient than others," he writes.

However there are also many routes that the adjustment cannot take, paths so severely inefficient that, if we were to embark on them, economic survival would itself be threatened. Like many of the very equilibrium theorists Reich ridicules, he assumes that he can foresee the costs and benefits of alternative future paths of economic evolution, that he or anyone can consciously choose a feasible route for the future economy to traverse.

The case for the free market does not rest on any sort of belief that market forces bring the economy to some ideal equilibrium state of full adjustment. It argues that market forces drive a process of plan coordination in which full coordination can *never* be attained, but which uses more knowledge than any single agent or organization can command. But Reich simply takes it for granted that this process could be altered at will, that informed industrial policy could "promote market forces rather than supplant them." The crucial questions remain unanswered: How do you know? How could you even find out? [17]

Rohatyn (1982b: 72) has even less to offer in critique of the free-market alternative. Like the proponents of economic democracy, he chooses to equate this philosophy with Reaganomics and Thatcherism, which he can easily reject as "uncaring and backward." Like most critics of the market, he has never examined any of its more sophisticated proponents. [18] Where Rohatyn does discuss a more sophisticated critic of planning, Milton Friedman, it is only by associating his ideas with the failing policies of British Prime Minister Margaret Thatcher that he is able to answer them. But Friedman is not on record as being in favor of sharp increases in excise taxes on consumer items, or of increasing the overall level of government spending (to 47 percent of the GNP) and of borrowing (so that the budget deficit increased from 8.5 billion to 11.5 billion pounds sterling in fiscal year 1980-81), or of adding between 4 and 5 billion pounds to government expenditure in order to bail out certain basic industries (like British Steel, British Leyland, Rolls Royce, British Shipbuilders, and British Airways). Yet these actual policies of the Thatcher government are remarkably similar to what Rohatyn does recommend.[19]

Thus an account of the failure of conservative policies is joined to assertions that merely relying on a "hands-off government and a blind faith in the market process" (Rohatyn 1982b: 82) will not bring us recovery—while presuming that a blind faith in hands-on government policies, despite their repeated failures, will. Rohatyn (1982b: 74) asserts, "I believe that large social, economic and political problems can be handled only when there is a conviction that government has not only a right but a duty to intervene when imbalances become too great."

Reich (1983: 14) also takes it for granted that our response to the structural changes of the economy must be "orchestrated" by a government agency:

> For America's next stage of economic evolution, the government's role in industry must become not so much more extensive as more open, more explicit and more strategic. This is not because public officials are somehow wiser or more far-seeing than private managers, but because renewed national prosperity depends on certain social investments that executives (judged by the profits of their separate firms) cannot be expected to undertake and on a broader economic perspective than private managers can attend to.

Clearly Reich believes that the individual intelligence of the new RFC agency will be such as to enable it to plan explicitly those parts of the economy that are now left to spontaneous and tacit market processes. He urges that we "make explicit the hard choices that otherwise will be made implicitly" (Reich 1983: 273) and then "fashion explicit agreements to restructure American industry" (p. 276). But besides these doubtless sincere confessions of belief, the structuralists offer no reason why such large problems can only be handled by explicit government intervention. Nor do they have any answer to those who charge that such problems (to the extent that they *are* problems) have actually been caused by intervention.

It is unnecessary to repeat here the argument that the complexity of the modern world is not only an insufficient condition for the advisability of national economic planning but is, on the contrary, a reason for relying on the social intelligence generated by market forces. Unlike the explicit programs of an RFC, the market can take advantage of implicit knowledge that is imparted to the system by the competitive process. Rohatyn and Reich show much concern for visible "imbalances" such as the decline of the cities of the Northeast, which they do not even demonstrate are harmful to the overall economy. But who will correct the less visible imbalances resulting from government intervention itself if the only source of knowledge concerning how best to coordinate the various parts of the capital structure—the competitive process—is being sabotaged?

The only quasi-argument for planning that Reich and Rohatyn employ (and which advocates of economic democracy would be less likely to use) is their reliance on the experts or strong leadership to figure out how to rescue the economy. It is the responsibility of a strong leader to *coordinate* the actions of the rest of us. It is significant that while Reich and Rohatyn repeatedly use the verb "coordinate," it is always in its transitive form. Coordination in their view cannot occur spontaneously among interacting individuals but must be imposed by a coordinator upon the coordinated.

· Reich (1983: 275) points out that "much will depend on the quality of America's future political leadership" and that "we will need leaders who are not afraid to recognize frankly the political choices that are entailed in major economic change and who are willing to choreograph openly the bargaining about them." Thus despite all Reich's references to open arenas for bargaining and debate, it is a peculiar bargain indeed that is choreographed by a courageous leader. But given the nature of the participants to these bargaining sessions (political representatives of special interests), and the sorts of issues being debated (that is, who gets special benefits and who gets penalized), it is inevitable that if any consensus is ever to be reached it must be by stacking the forces on one side among the contenders.[20]

But the key issue here is not how courageous the leadership is but how it knows what it is doing. On this question Reich offers no argument. He takes it for granted that the only reason our economic decisions are so often made implicitly is that there is some kind of reluctance on our part to face up to tough choices. His repeated calls for replacing the implicit decisionmaking of the market with explicit political decisionmaking ignore the possibility of any sort of limitation on the capacity of the individual human mind to articulate all the information that is used by the competitive discovery process. It is simply assumed that anything the market does implicitly can be done as well by explicit government policy. Yet the whole argument of this book has been that the market system's ability to generate as much wealth as it can is primarily due to the fact that it can make use of tacit knowledge in a way that Reich's explicit politics cannot.

It is also on the issue of expert leadership that Rohatyn places most of the burden of his argument, for it is his own much trumpeted success as chairman of the Municipal Assistance Corporation in salvaging New York City that convinced him to attempt to "go national" and set up a bigger MAC for the whole country.[21] We are continually reminded by Rohatyn about how, through his own expert guidance, New York was saved, and thus since the nation's problems are similar, the answer must lie in putting a financial expert like him in charge of the nation. Every one of his several popular articles makes at least passing reference to his extensive financial experience both in business and in rescuing New York and thus leaves the definite impression that his whole case for planning amounts to little more than a personal advertisement: Put me in charge of a new RFC and your troubles are over.[22]

Hence it does not seem unfair to ask just what did happen in New York, in order to see whether Rohatyn's efforts there inspire any confidence in his financial expertise and in the kinds of policies he wants to extrapolate for the nation. Unfortunately, what we find is not so much that Rohatyn's success in New York argues for putting him in control of some sort of National Assistance Corporation, but rather that his failure there instead necessitated a national agency to bail him out.

The bankruptcy of the New York City government was preceded by a ten-year increase in borrowing for current expenses from $26 million in 1965 to $724 million in 1975, while during the same period the overall short-term debt rose from $250 million to over $4.5 billion. One of the biggest factors in this debt debacle was the mushrooming of so-called Off Budget Enterprises, or OBEs, as quasi-private agencies whose borrowing could escape the constitutional limits placed on official government borrowing. The "courageous" (Rohatyn's word) solution that Governor Hugh Carey devised to solve this problem was the creation of even more OBEs, in particular a state-level Municipal Assistance Corporation led by Rohatyn which was authorized to issue an additional $10 billion in new bonds. And in fact these bonds were sold only when the federal government agreed to offer over a billion dollars in loan guarantees and other forms of support. Indeed, Rohatyn admits that "there is a real question whether the market can absorb the billions in New York-related securities," but says that this makes the argument for a new RFC more compelling. But he cannot eat his cake and have it too. Rohatyn cannot both plead that the dire financial circumstances of New York make an RFC necessary and rest his case for the prospects of a successful RFC on the shining example of his rescue of New York from its threat of bankruptcy.[23]

In other words, Rohatyn was able to save the city by spreading its burdens to state and national taxpayers. All that his going national really amounts to is more such bail-outs for other localities that try to live beyond their means. It was not some mysterious financial wizardry that worked its magic on New York City, nor the much vaunted austerity Rohatyn repeatedly insists he imposed on the unions, banks, and political institutions there.[24] It was, on the contrary, the rather pedestrian idea of letting someone else pay its bills that got New York temporarily out of trouble. The problem is, there are no higher levels of government to pick up the tab for our national problems, though as Rohatyn admits, if given the chance, he would love to "go international" and ply his trade at the International Monetary Fund to try to get somebody else to pay the federal government's bills.

But if Rohatyn's own success in New York City generates little confidence, what of the RFC itself? While anything invented by Herbert Hoover can hardly be called a new idea, an RFC would at least be a departure from current policy. No single agency of government now has access to the kind of capital Rohatyn would like this institution to control.[25] The agency Hoover set up in 1932 over a period of thirteen years dispersed over $35 billion[26] and, Rohatyn says, thereby "saved thousands of banks, railroads and businesses, financed public works and ultimately defense plants in World War II." Indeed, Rohatyn declares that on top of bestowing these blessings on the economy, the original RFC even "returned a profit of $500 million to the taxpayers."[27]

This profit figure, however, was arrived at by an imaginative arithmetic manipulation (performed by none other than the head of the RFC in his self-aggrandizing book about it), which manages to leave out of account some $12 billion of RFC notes that Congress generously cancelled. If any private credit agency were to take this kind of beating on its loans, it would become the laughing stock of the financial world. In fact, of course, the RFC was designed to make what other credit institutions would consider bad-risk investments—that is, to aid businesses that might fail without its subsidized aid. Thus, the idea that it could turn a profit by adhering to a loan policy of propping up losing businesses that could not get loans from the private credit market is simply ludicrous. The new RFC would necessitate, as the old one did, considerably increased taxes and a hefty dose of government borrowing to foot the bill.

If the consequences of paying these hidden costs are taken into account, it is hard to credit the old RFC with having saved any businesses on net. How many firms were taxed out of operation or squeezed out of credit markets because of the generous loans of this agency? The plain fact is that investment funds cannot be created by government fiat; they can only be rearranged. The RFC, like any single organization, is necessarily limited by the capacity of an individual intelligence and has no crystal ball to tell it where the best future investment possibilities lie. Its activities can only tend to divert capital from the politically inept but economically efficient (to whom the social intelligence of market processes would have channeled it) to the politically adept and economically inefficient.

Thus the knowledge problem indicates that the task Rohatyn would like a new RFC to take on, rejuvenating America's industry as a whole, is beyond the powers of any such agency, and indeed that it would almost certainly reduce the nation's real wealth. But the totalitarian problem suggests that in practice the new RFC may prove quite capable of achieving a rather different task, namely, the reallocation rather than the net increase of wealth. Whereas the old RFC was a dismal failure when judged against that first standard, it was a stunning success as a dispenser of special privileges to those with high political connections at the expense of those without. Although Houston millionaire Jesse H. Jones (1951: 11) boasts that during his tenure at the RFC "there was not a single instance of fraud in the entire organization," his book is one long Santa's list of favors, many of them just happening to be to friends and relatives of the heads of the RFC.

For example the first chairman, Eugene Meyer, Jr., a long-time promoter of the J. P. Morgan financial empire, made sure some of the first RFC loans ($44 million) were to railroads to help them to repay their loans to Morgan banks. The first president, General Charles Dawes, resigned and three weeks later coincidentally found that the Chicago bank he headed was getting a loan ($90 million) nearly equal in size to the bank's total deposits. Dawes's successor as president, Atlee Pomerene, authorized a loan ($12.3 million) to the Guardian Trust Company, of which he was a director, while Meyer's successor as chairman, Jesse Jones, spent his years dispensing favors mainly to western, non-Morgan interests like Henry Kaiser ($200 million) of aluminum (and steel) fame, helping him while his rival Alcoa desperately tried to fend off a trumped-up antitrust suit. In other words, the RFC has proven a very potent weapon in the extra-economic competition among big businesses to secure privileges from the state.[28] The old RFC's only success was in its role as what humorist Will Rogers called "the caviar of big business" (Jones 1951: 5).

Although Reich's favorite model for emulation is Japan's Ministry of International Trade and Industry (MITI) rather than our own country's RFC, he recognizes the close family resemblance between these institutions and sees the latter as an important experience. It was in such planning projects, he says, that government, business, and labor "learned to communicate and bargain smoothly, orchestrating decisions through their hierarchical control over vast reservoirs of complementary resources" (Reich 1983: 52–53).[29] Reich's national bargaining arena would differ from Rohatyn's RFC only in the particular industries to be supported and the openness with which the agency would arrive at its decisions. But Reich offers no more justification than Rohatyn for the belief that this investment-guiding agency would know how to repair the weakening industrial structures of our economy.

Reich attributes the Japanese miracle of rapid economic growth since the Second World War to MITI's farsighted industrial policy. Unlike the tale of the rescue of New York, there is no question that this success is genuine. Japan's real GNP has grown from 21 trillion yen in fiscal year 1951 to 191 trillion yen in 1980.[30] The only question here concerns the extent to which we are justified in attributing this success to the positive actions of MITI.[31]

Reich paints MITI as an elite of experts who have consistently fostered Japan's most successful industries. There have been so many winners like Sony and Honda, we are told, because MITI had the foresight to *pick* them. Having spent a lifetime studying the Japanese economy, however, G. C. Allen (1981) points out that MITI's record in selecting sunrise industries on net has been anything but awe-inspiring. MITI bureaucrats were so unimpressed with the technological possibilities of the transistor in the 1950s that they tried for two years to prevent Sony from buying manufacturing rights from Western Electric (Henderson 1983: 113). They tried to dissuade Japan's automobile manufacturers from getting into the export market, then tried to force its ten auto firms to merge into two, Nissan and Toyota (Gilder 1982: 12-13). Fortunately for the Japanese economy, all of this advice was ultimately ignored. (See Sunwall 1983; Sakoh 1983; Trezise 1982.) If MITI has made fewer of these sorts of errors than most other bureaucracies, it is only because it exerts less power.

Thus, if Japanese industrial policy is to be credited at all for the economic miracle it would have to be on the grounds of how *little*, relative to other industrialized countries, it interfered with entrepreneurs' decisions. Although Reich credits the remarkable success of Japan's semiconductor industry to its government's industrial policy, in fact the U.S. government has been spending ten times as much on its semiconductor research and development as Japan has been spending. The Japanese *economy* employs more people in R&D than Britain, France, and West Germany put together. (See Beckner 1983: 51 and Casement 1982: 5, 14.) But government channeling of investment funds, the central policy goal of the reindustrializers, involves a relatively small proportion of Japan's capital formation.[32]

When the old bureaucratic class, the *zaibatsu*, was removed from power after the war, the productive forces of entrepreneurial competition were unleashed. Japanese government expenditure is still only about 25 percent of the GNP, compared to 35 percent in the United States, and 44.5 percent in Britain (Macrae 1980: 7). From 1951 to 1970 Japan's taxes fell steadily from over 22 percent of national income to under 19 percent, while taxes in most industrialized nations were rising.

But probably the single most significant factor in Japan's economic success has been its high rate of savings. In 1980, for example, savings were over 19 percent of personal income. And here again it is the *lack* of government involvement which appears to be largely responsible. Depending on the kind of savings program, the first $13,600 or $22,600 of an individual savings is tax exempt (Henderson 1983: 114).[33] The result of this is that the reserves of capital available to Japanese entrepreneurs are estimated to be at least twice what is available to American businesses (Gilder 1982: 15).

In short, while Reich is right that we can learn an important lesson from Japan, he has learned the wrong lesson. As Richard Casement (1982: 21) points out, by and large "the market is king in Japan and companies respond rapidly to its changing fashions." What is admirable about MITI is not what it has done or can do, but what it hasn't and can't.

There is no substantive argument for planning among the structuralists other than this appeal to the expertise of people presumably like Reich or Rohatyn themselves, whose arguments and history in fact give us little comfort that the new RFC would be able to "orchestrate" clever solutions to the financial difficulties we face on the national level. Instead, we should expect solutions offering generous rewards to those who run their businesses or governments into debt—policies that in themselves would require the federal government to increase taxes, inflation, or its own debt. Reich's policy of rewarding prospective winners does not stem from any better conceptual foundation than does Rohatyn's of rewarding losers and is as sure to encourage a gross waste of scarce resources and to make a bad economic situation worse.

MORE BAND-AIDS

The structuralists, like their economic democracy counterparts, present their program as if it represented a sharp departure from the kinds of policies that have been practiced by the U.S. government both currently and over the past few decades. Rohatyn (1980a: 6), for example, declares that what the economy needs is not the "continued application of Band-Aids" but rather a dose of "strong medicine." Reich (1983: 202) agrees with Rohatyn that the traditional tools of Keynesian macroeconomic policy are "too broad and too blunt" and that we are therefore "beyond economic 'fine tuning.'" (See also Müller 1980: 28–29.)

But, again like the advocates of economic democracy, the structuralists offer us nothing but old policies that have extensive histories of failure. While there are discernible differences in policy between most reindustrialists and the advocates of economic democracy, neither lives up to its rhetorical promise of a radical alternative to the status quo: increasing taxes, worsening unemployment, runaway money supply and inflation, deteriorating public services, skyrocketing government expenditure and indebtedness, and in general, more government domination of the economy.

For example, on taxes the proponents of reindustrialization are no more sensitive to the genuinely democratic tax revolt than are the self-styled democratic planners; they just favor increasing different taxes. Whereas economic democracy proposals typically urge the closing of tax loopholes, especially those involving income from capital investment, reindustrializers tend to want to open up and create new loopholes and even to use such tax incentives as the main instruments of planning.[34] But the tax revenues lost to these loopholes are to be more than made up for by imposing heavy taxes on consumption. Both the corporate taxes preferred by leftist planners and the consumption taxes to which the neoliberal and corporativist planners are partial are in fact likely to be most heavily borne by some of the poorest and already overtaxed segments of society. Having learned of the damage government has caused the economy by stifling investment with capital gains and profits taxes, most structuralists want to impose excise taxes to stifle consumption instead.[35]

Despite their "age of limits" rhetoric, the structuralists are just as prone to the sort of ambitious, visionary government-spending agendas as were traditional liberals, as is demonstrated in the titles of Rohatyn's, Etzioni's, and Reich's latest books: *The Twenty-Year Century: Essays on Economics and Public Policy, An Immodest Agenda: Rebuilding America Before the Twenty-First Century*, and *The Next American Frontier.* While paying lip service to the need to bring government spending under control, the structuralists promise massive spending projects that are guaranteed to increase the total size of government expenditure dramatically.[36] Reich (1983: 275) says, "We need a political revitalization," and envies West Germany, France, and Japan, where "traditions of legitimate government involvement in orchestrating economic change were firmly established" and where there are "more government-sponsored training and retraining, more generous unemployment assistance, and health benefits that are distributed more widely" (pp. 14–15). Rohatyn (1982b: 72) talks casually about spending a trillion dollars on rejuvenating the country's physical plant. The advocates of reindustrialization join the democratic planners in routinely jumping to the defense of all the welfare programs currently in place, defending them against even the tiny cutbacks proposed by the Reagan administration. Again, about the only part of the massive Reagan budget that these writers criticize at all is the military spending, and there they are less critical than the advocates of economic democracy.[37]

Rohatyn likes to joke that Reaganomics is "Keynes in drag," a program dressed up as fiscally responsible but underneath a prescription for deficits caused by tax cuts instead of by spending.[38] But in Rohatyn's own policies it is hard to see how Keynesianism and increased government borrowing could be avoided. Unwilling to challenge either defense or nondefense spending in any fundamental way, and prepared to add the immense cost of a new RFC to the already bloated budget, the structuralists cannot be expected to do much to reduce the federal deficit.[39]

In addition, Reich (1983: 273–74) seems to believe that merely adding the adjective "explicit" to the intellectual arsenal of establishment liberalism is enough to turn old unworkable policies into promising new ones: "An explicit regulatory policy would let Americans deal sensibly with the hard choices about the social costs of a given path of economic development—the concrete sacrifices of health, safety, and the environment that it would entail and upon whom the burdens would fall." Similarly he expects an "explicit training and retraining policy" (p. 274) to work where implicit training programs have failed. In these and other cases, the same assumption is made that matters such as where the burdens of any given regulation will fall are only unknown because Americans are too secretive or in any case unwilling to face up to the "hard choices" they confront. That such issues might *have* to be decided implicitly because the remote effects of policies are not ascertainable in advance is a possibility Reich does not seem to have entertained.

In short, the advocates of reindustrialization seem to be just as sure to worsen the burdens of inflation as are the economic democrats. All Reich (1983: 274) has to add to the failed incomes policies of the past is that he wants to make them "explicit" so that the government can make "aboveboard choices about how the burden of fighting inflation should be allocated."[40] And Rohatyn repeatedly calls for a renewed bout of credit expansion by the Federal Reserve in order to reduce unemployment (at least temporarily) and to rejuvenate the housing and construction industries with lower interest rates.[41] And, like the proponents of economic democracy, Rohatyn (1982b: 90) admits his ambitious spending programs run the risk of inflation, and so halfheartedly suggests that perhaps the (by-now discredited) policy of wage and price controls could be resorted to as his only inflation-fighting policy.[42]

Figure 6-1. The Planning Spectrum.

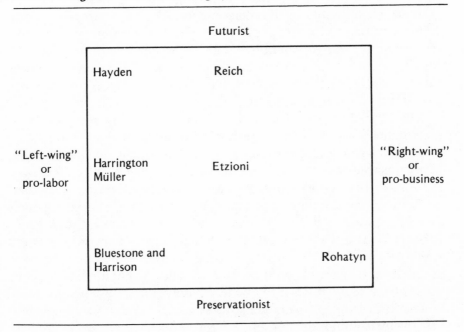

The noble-sounding aspiration of both economic democracy and reindustrialization is to achieve some sort of social control over the process of investment through a government planning agency rather than simply to let the shape of capital investment be determined by the turbulent, undesigned, and anonymous forces of supply and demand in competitive capital markets. The likely result of these pleas for a national planning agency is that the turbulence will remain— as indeed the current battles between these planning factions already show—but that the rivalry will be fought with political weapons in addition to financial ones. The upshot of these political rivalries will not be more control over investment by society at all. Indeed, the wastes involved in these political battles for government privilege will ensure that society as a whole suffers.

As we survey the planning spectrum, we cannot help but notice the wide range of purposes to which the desired planning agency is imagined to be committed. The figure on this page shows that the range of opinions is not limited to the usual Left-Right political spectrum (roughly, the horizontal axis in the diagram), but also encompasses the contrast (vertical axis) between the preservationist extreme (represented by Rohatyn and Bluestone and Harrison), which emphasizes saving older declining sectors, and the futurist extreme (represented by Hayden and Reich), which stresses picking winners among the newer industries. Intermediate points of view on the vertical axis, representing neither the preservationist nor the futurist extreme, themselves constitute a wide divergence of political opinion along the horizontal axis, from Harrington's democratic socialism to Etzioni's moderate liberalism.

What the diversity of this collection of planning advocates suggests is the kind of intense conflict we can expect over control of a new RFC agency. Notwithstanding the insistence by all planning advocates that one of the main purposes of setting up such an agency is to explicitly resolve conflicts among special interests, what they are really doing is holding out a new and very tempting prize for such divergent interests to struggle over. Thus, I would argue, the real way for society as a whole to be served by the investment process is for us to relinquish all the current efforts to control these decisions by governmental agencies, both on and off budget, not to enhance and concentrate such efforts into one immensely powerful bureau.

The knowledge problem constitutes a challenge to planning advocates which could be put in the form of the rude question: "If you're so smart about investment, why don't you just go out and make yourself a profit by investing?" This may sound not only rude but irrelevant, but it strikes at the heart of the basic difficulty with planning. Both Reich and Rohatyn, we have seen, rest their case, at bottom, on their own expertise. They are touted by their supporters as "financial wizards" who *know* how to guide investment. But of course, since they disagree, they can't *both* know the best way to guide investment.

The only proven testing ground in which their competing views of investment advice could be effectively weighed is that of free and open competition. The competitive market implicitly compels the "smart" investor to put his money where his mouth is. Instead, Reich and Rohatyn want these battles to be fought explicitly within the federal government. Rather than try to persuade investors to aid sunrise or sunset industries by participating in the competitive process, they each want to lead government attempts to exert control over that process. It is the main conclusion of the argument I have called the knowledge problem, however, that *there are no rational grounds upon which Reich could ever convince Rohatyn or vice versa on such matters as are involved in economic change.* As a result, such battles are sure to be fought with weapons other than those of carefully reasoned argument.

We can now see the relation between the knowledge problem and the totalitarian problem. The first suggests that neither Reich nor Rohatyn nor any proponents of planning can possibly know which industries ought to be picked in order to enhance industrial growth. The second then constitutes a warning that since the case for any particular use of the planning power lies beyond the capacity of human reason to establish, that power will instead be wielded in response to political clout rather than careful debate.

The call for planning, then, amounts to nothing more than a plea for more of the same kinds of blind government intervention into the market that has brought us our current difficulties. Wherever any of these kinds of policies have been implemented, and most of them have been implemented all too often, the result has invariably been severe discoordination of market processes rather than conscious control over them. In short, noncomprehensive planning, while not impossible altogether, as is comprehensive planning, is yet so utterly counterproductive that literally doing nothing and preserving—but at least not aggravating—all our current problems would be preferable.

But doing nothing is, contrary to the repeated assertions of planning advocates, not our only alternative to planning. The next chapter will briefly turn to the more positive task of suggesting the policy direction that can break us out of our ailing status quo and point the way toward a workable, radical alternative.

NOTES TO CHAPTER 6

1. During the 1980 presidential campaign Paul Blustein (1980) remarked that "Ronald Reagan and John Anderson are all for [reindustrialization], in one form or another. Jimmy Carter is too, though he often calls it 'revitalization' partly to make sure not to sound too much like Mr. Reagan or Mr. Anderson." Similarly for the 1984 election we found Walter Mondale, Gary Hart, and Fritz Hollings all enthusiastically endorsing Robert Reich's latest book on reindustrialization.

2. Respectively, Sidney Lens (1980: 44) and Bluestone and Harrison (1982). The latter would also call some reindustrialization advocates fascist, but they promote their own policies as a democratic variant of reindustrialization. These writers (understandably) consider Rohatyn a politically

dangerous corporativist or fascist and yet refer to their own program as "reindustrialization with a human face," a throwback to the phrase popular a decade ago among Eurocommunists and Eastern European dissidents who hoped to create a "socialism with a human face." One may legitimately wonder, however, whether putting a "human face" on what are essentially socialist, or in this case fascist, policies can somehow transform them from reactionary into progressive ones or whether it only succeeds in disguising their true nature. See Levy (1979).

3. Karen W. Arenson (1982: sec. 3, pp. 1, 24) includes under this term everyone from Paul Samuelson, an old-time establishment Keynesian, to neoliberal Robert Reich, to Bluestone and Harrison on the radical Left, to Felix Rohatyn on the corporativist Right.

4. Instead of trying to find ways of making the rich and the corporations assume most of the burdens of expensive planning measures, Rohatyn wants to ensure "evenly distributed burdens" (1980b: 24) to pay for programs that often come primarily to the aid of the rich and the corporations. Reich also calls for planning in order to arrive at "a fair sharing of the burdens and benefits of industrial change" (1983: 256). They undoubtedly differ, however, on exactly who should bear the burden for whose benefit.

5. Rohatyn complains that there are too many democratic checks on the discretion of our leaders and favors constitutional change "so that a president with a real vision of the future will be able to put his program through," which he admits would be "obviously a risk for democracy" but apparently one he is willing to take (1980b: 24). He wants his new RFC to be "publicly accountable, but sheltered from political pressures" (1982b: 80). Whether such an institution can plausibly be expected to resist the intense political pressures that will be occasioned by its very existence is another matter (to be taken up later), but Rohatyn and other proponents of reindustrialization intend to have it be kept immune from all influence peddling. As Adlai Stevenson III put it, the new RFC ought to be "insulated as carefully as possible from politics, including organized labor and organized business, in order to make neutral economic decisions with respect to government support" (quoted in Daly 1980: 24).

6. Rohatyn frankly admits that he is not interested in "changing the structures of authority that exist in this country" (quoted in Serrin 1981: B10). Many of the other main supporters of reindustrialization besides Rohatyn are also leaders of the very corporate and banking elite that is so despised by the Left. Grinder and Fairgate (1975: 2) point out that "supporters of the RFC concept have included Henry Ford, former chairman of the Ford Motor Company; William McChesney Martin, former chairman of the Federal Reserve Board; Alfred Hayes, president of the Federal

Reserve Bank of New York; and Gustave Levy, senior partner of Goldman Sachs." Among some of the other prominent corporate leaders behind reindustrialization can be found recent and current chairmen of Dupont, Norton Simon Inc., and B. F. Goodrich: Irving Shapiro, David J. Mahoney, and John D. Ong.

7.   Rohatyn for example guided the sale of Avis and the Hartford Fire Insurance Company to ITT and pulled off mergers between Kinney and Warner Brothers and between Loew's Theaters and Lorillard Corporation (cited in Serrin 1981: B1). Reich for his part argues for reorganizing industries which are "too small and fragmented to compete internationally" by "dividing the industry into fewer firms of larger scale" (Magaziner and Reich 1982: 338).

8.   Reich's numerous discussions of the kinds of industries he sees dominating the future have the ring of an advertisement for a Wall Street investment house. But we must keep in mind that his intention is not to *persuade* people to invest in these industries.

9.   See also Magaziner and Reich (1982: 258), who contend that America's economic problems are attributable to "the absence of any single agency or office with overall responsibility for monitoring changes in world markets or in the competitiveness of American industry, or for easing the adjustment of the domestic economy to these changes."

10. The claim that the manufacturing sector as a whole is declining is itself disputable. See DiLorenzo (1984).

11. Rohatyn occasionally suggests that the real reason for the priority of structural industries is national defense. Now, to the extent that one takes a radical perspective on the military, this argument carries little weight. But even if we favored a stronger military and admitted the likelihood that Japan might blackmail us for its steel, it is not only things like steel and truck parts that foreign governments could withhold to hurt our military production. For a world that is increasingly interdependent, it is difficult to think of any products, other than nonessential consumer items, the withholding of which could not somehow, directly or indirectly, harm the interests of national security. To defend itself from such potential blackmail, the United States would have to become virtually autarkic. But of course even to approach that condition would reduce our productivity so drastically as genuinely to endanger our national defense.

12. Rohatyn (1982b: 80) points out that "the auto industry is one of the largest customers of microprocessors as well as of industrial robots and many other high-technology products" in order to argue that to promote such glamorous industries we must first save so-called basic industries. Reich (1983: 132) similarly argues that, since so much of the service sector is "directly linked to the manufacturing base of the country," it ".surely will diminish as merchandise trade declines."

13. Bluestone and Harrison (1982: 16) use the latter phrase. The phrase "shoring up the system" recurs throughout this literature. David L. Barnett (1980: 60) closes his article on the reindustrialization debate with the prediction that out of it "will come action that will shore up America's economic might." Etzioni (1983: 190, 313) talks about "steps needed to shore up the economy" and asserts that "all agree that the foundations of the American economy have weakened and need shoring up." Rohatyn (1982a: 3) refers to "a coordinated process that would shore up the system and avoid a crisis."

14. Rohatyn (1980b: 23; 1982b: 80). Again Rohatyn (1980b: 23) asserts that other people's economic survival is wrapped up in the fate of this particular structural component:

> Our older cities, our older industries, our hardcore unemployed are all tied to the same umbilical cord. An independent financing entity is needed to cope with the fundamental restructuring of older industries, with the renewal of the physical plant of older cities, and to make use of the work potential of the inner-city unemployed.

But beyond an assertion that "no democracy is workable half rich, half poor" (1981a: 14), he offers no explanation of why subsidizing the declining "snow belt" regions at the expense of the prospering "sun belt" would benefit the country as a whole. Since businesses have been moving south for definite economic reasons, reversing this process would diminish economic efficiency, resulting in a democracy that is less than half rich and more than half poor, instead.

15. Thus Rohatyn (1982b: 82) explains:

> In the industrial field the RFC's investments would be limited to those basic industries such as automobiles and steel that could be made competitive. The RFC would provide funds only if there were concessions on the part of labor, management, suppliers, and bankers sufficient to make the company competitive with the best foreign producers.
>
> Similarly, in the public-infrastructure field the RFC's capital would be available only if local support—such as tax changes, union productivity and wage concessions, fare and user fees—assured the viability of the projects. These would include mass-transit systems, sewers, roads, bridges and so on.

Similarly Charls E. Walker, a leading conservative champion of reindustrialization, answers this charge by saying the new RFC board would have to be run by a "hardnosed, take-charge financial type" (Shaw 1981: 13).

16. I am not minimizing the dangers involved in the U.S. banking system's shaky international commitments. The default of a couple of Third World countries could bring down several major banks and cause immense financial difficulties in this country if significant reforms to the banking system are not undertaken first. The issue is not how bad these banking problems are, but whether propping up the very institutions that brought about the problems and rewarding the very decisionmakers who got us into this dan-

ger is the best way to resolve them. The banking system is the oldest cartel in the United States and the most in need of fundamental reform in the direction of more competition, not, as Rohatyn would like, more government involvement. See Weber (1983).

17. See also Müller (1980: 279), who repeats the assertion that planning is inevitable: "The crucial issue has moved beyond the question of whether we have planning or whether we do not. Planning already exists. The question is what kind of planning are we going to have and who is going to control it."

18. I have in mind such Austrian school works as *Competition and Entrepreneurship* and *An Essay on Capital* by Israel Kirzner, *Capital and Its Structure* and *Capital, Expectations and the Market Process* by Ludwig Lachmann, *Antitrust and Monopoly* by D. T. Armentano, *Economics as a Coordination Problem* by Gerald P. O'Driscoll, *Law, Legislation and Liberty*, volumes 1 and 2, and *Individualism and Economic Order* by F. A. Hayek, and *Human Action* by Ludwig von Mises. Of all these writers, only Hayek has ever expressed any sympathies with the policies of the Reagan and Thatcher administrations. In some recent interviews Hayek has unfortunately invited this kind of association with conservative politicians, but he has explicitly argued ([1960] 1972: 395-41) why he does not, in fact, view himself as a conservative. Actually the kind of social change he envisages is diametrically opposed to conservatism.

Of course, there are many other sophisticated defenders of free-market policies outside of the Austrian school, such as Friedman, Stigler, Brozen, Demsetz, Buchanan, Bauer, Wagner, Rowley, and Sowell, none of whom is as easy to dismiss as Reagan or Thatcher.

19. See Burton (1981). Though these are British figures, "billion" here follows the American usage: 1,000 million.

20. It is worth noting that the original, idealistic aspirations for fascism in Italy were to set up the very same kind of bargaining arena for settling conflicts that Rohatyn and Reich now promote, and that there too a kind of choreographed bargaining process was promised. See, for example Luigi Villari (1932: 98-99): "The National Council was created to coordinate all the productive forces of the nation. . . . The Council is further intrusted with the duty of coordinating the interests of the various branches of trade; this is a particularly important provision, and implies the settling of such conflicts as may arise, as for instance between agriculture and industry, or between two or more rival industries."

21. The salvation of New York City is described as having "required the courageous political leadership of the governor" (Rohatyn 1980b: 20), while the nation's problems will also "require inspired political leadership" (p. 22). This "leadership" should extend internationally as well. One

might legitimately wonder what people in other parts of the world would think of the dramatic words with which Rohatyn closes one of his articles:

> The United States, I suggest, should speak for the West. It must speak for opportunity, for growth, for social justice, and it must speak with confidence and power. That will only happen when a majority of Americans will decide that the drift has got to stop, and a president with a sense of the future gives direction to the power that will be unleashed. This will not happen today, but it will come sooner than we think. (p. 26)

Surely Americans would be made rather uncomfortable if, say, some German statesman, were to talk like this about the Federal Republic of Germany speaking for us with its vision of the future and unleashing its power.

22. See for example Rohatyn (1980b: 20), where the austerity measures he imposed on New York are declared to be "what saved the city," or Rohatyn (1981a: 16), where "cooperation among business, labor, and government coupled with a wage freeze, cost control, and sales tax revenues driven up by inflation," most of which were engineered by Big MAC, are credited with having "saved New York City." Rohatyn considers himself courageous for not having disguised the magnitude of the city's problems, despite the fact that many feared that this disclosure would bring on bankruptcy, and boldly calls for a similar act of bravery in the case of the nation's difficulties: "Those of us who were asked to help the city chose to disclose the facts while at the same time coming forth with a plan to resolve the crisis. It was a correct, if probably inevitable, decision. The same must now be done on a much vaster, more complicated scale." (Rohatyn 1982a: 3)

23. See Rohatyn (1981b). This account is taken from a more extensive examination of OBEs by Bennett and DiLorenzo (1982), especially their ch. 5.

24. McClelland and Magdovitz (1981) report that a private auditing firm found a deficit of over $700 million in 1978, two years after Big MAC's supposedly tough austerity measures were firmly in place. In spite of Rohatyn's frequent appeals to the need for honest accounting procedures, the city reported a *surplus* of $32 million in that year.

25. Instead there are over 150 federal loan guarantee programs administered by different agencies which guide a total of some $100 billion in loans annually. In addition, various parts of the federal government control some $30 billion in direct loans (see Bennett and DiLorenzo 1983). Rohatyn's RFC proposals are not large in comparison to these totals, but they would concentrate a much greater amount of discretionary power in the hands of a single agency than now exists.

26. This is the total amount Jesse H. Jones (1951: 3) says the RFC "loaned and spent, invested and gave away" during his tenure as its head.

27. Rohatyn (1982b: 80) must have gotten this bogus profit figure by reading Jones's book (1951: 4) in which the statement that all of the $10.5 billion

used "in the struggle against the depression" was "returned to the Federal Treasury with approximately $500,000,000 profits, after paying the Corporation's operating expenses and a fair rate of interest on the money which it borrowed to finance this phase of its operations." On the same page, however, Jones refers to cancelled debts that turn this half-billion dollar profit into an $11.5 billion loss.

Randall Rothenberg (1983: 44) makes a different but equally misleading statement in his article on reindustrialization when he remarks that the old RFC paid for itself because "when Congress closed its doors, the RFC returned $6 billion to the Treasury."

28. On the early history of the RFC see Rothbard (1963: 261–65) and Zaid (1973). See also Grinder and Fairgate (1975).

29. Reich (1983: 98) explicitly credits Hoover with having anticipated "the kind of government role in industrial development that Japan's MITI would undertake forty years later."

30. These figures were computed in terms of market prices in calendar year 1975, as reported in the Comptroller General's report (1982: 2) to the Joint Economic Committee of the U.S. Congress.

31. Chalmers Johnson (1982) supplies an excellent historical survey of MITI and its antecedent institutions, but he merely assumes that the Japanese miracle of the past three decades is due primarily to MITI's policies.

32. David Henderson (1983: 114) cites a study by Philip Trezise at the Brookings Institution which shows that the Japan Development Bank provided only 1 percent of private, nonhousing capital formation.

33. If giving industry tax breaks is a spur to the economy, I suggest that this is because it is a species of the economically more encouraging policy of tax reduction.

34. Etzioni (1983: 317–41) relies primarily on tax incentives as the mechanism for his "semi-targeted" planning. Rohatyn (1981a: 14) is particularly fond of federal "programs for incentives for local tax reductions as a way to give stimulus to areas suffering the greatest economic hardship." Although I agree with the general policy direction of reducing taxes, the basic knowledge problem arguments apply just as much to governmental attempts to steer the economy through *differential* taxation as they do to the use of other policy tools.

35. A *U.S. News & World Report* article on "Rebuilding America" cites Jerry Jasinowski, one of the architects of the Carter administration's industrial revitalization plan, who argues that "the American appetite for consumption is one reason for lagging investment" and favors consumption taxes to kill some of this appetite (Barnett 1980: 57). The special issue of *Business Week* "The Reindustrialization of America" concludes that "to jolt Americans out of their low-saving habits so that the nation has the wherewithal to finance its required investment growth, the first essential is to change the tax system substantially" (*Business Week* 1980: 47). The only

thing they can't decide on is whether to try a value-added tax which bites into every stage of production but which bites the consumption stage hardest, or to settle for a traditional sales tax on consumption goods.

Amitai Etzioni (1983: 317) says that "what ails the country is over-consumption . . . and underinvestment" and that we should "release resources to the private sector, but channel them to the infrastructure and capital goods sectors, away from both public and private consumption."

Robert Reich (1983: 242) urges that the government "replace the personal income tax with a progressive tax on consumption" according to which the "tax rate would be greater the more money was spent." Reich assures us that his scheme "would not be difficult to administer," because it would be implemented by the banking system, which would assess the tax as money was withdrawn from savings accounts.

Felix Rohatyn (1982b: 74) finds the Reagan administration's 5-cent-a-gallon gasoline tax increase to be "grossly insufficient" and instead wants to phase in a 10-cent-a-gallon increase each year for the next five years and would like to use this money to pay for mass transit systems. But this will not worsen our price inflation, because, when his "stiff" gasoline tax is imposed, "energy prices should simultaneously be removed from the Consumer Price Index" (1981a: 16). This politically imposed increase in consumers' energy costs is then to be "coupled with an import fee on crude oil" partly in order to "prepare us for the next OPEC shock" (1982b: 74). (To me this makes about as much sense as shooting oneself in order to prepare for the next war.) In any case the fact that the next shock proved to be a dramatic lowering of oil prices shows how adept these people are at forecasting.

36. Rohatyn (1982b: 80), for example, admits that "slowdowns in the growth of Social Security and healthcare costs are absolutely essential" if they are not to end up completely bankrupting the federal government. He criticizes Reagan's modest attempts to cut back on welfare programs not because he finds the operation of these programs actually to *be* fair, but on the grounds that "a democracy, to survive, must at the very least appear to be fair" and that "this is no longer the case in America" (1982b: 90). Presumably were Rohatyn in charge he would keep up appearances of this kind.

37. Under the Carter administration Rohatyn (1980b: 23) was saying that part of his gas tax "should finance tax cuts that will lead to increased investment and an increase in military spending." Now that Reagan has promised us this program, Rohatyn is saying things like "our defense program cannot be immune from . . . retrenchment" (1982b: 74). In any case he can hardly be called a radical critic of military spending.

38. Rohatyn frequently mistakes Reaganomics the rhetoric for Reaganomics the actual policies of the current administration when he describes the

latter as "massive tax cuts and huge increases in defense spending combined with tight money" or as "a huge budget cut coupled with a huge tax cut and restrictive monetary policy" (1981a: 14). In fact federal spending is setting a ten-year record under Reagan, increasing in real terms by 8.7 percent from October 1981 to May 1982, while revenues from taxation rose in real terms in 1982 by 6.2 percent, the fastest increase since 1977. The tight money supply (M2) grew at an annual rate of 9.7 percent during the third quarter of 1982. The deficit under Reagan will be large indeed, but its cause is not tax cuts but the more familiar problem of runaway spending. What we have here is not "Keynes in drag" at all. We still have Keynes.

39.   Reich (1983: 120) tells us not to worry about rising deficits or taxes because, as percentages of the national product they are not too high. The *Business Week* (1980: 27) issue on reindustrialization suggests that the federal budget be divided into two parts, a current accounts budget, which "should show a substantial surplus" and a reindustrialization budget, which "would have to run a large deficit for some time." Thus, other governmental projects will have to tighten their belts, while the part that is needed "to help rebuild the eroded capital base" should not be "distorted by efforts to create the illusion that income will match outgo immediately." Rohatyn (1981b) insists that running his new RFC with "lending capacity of $25 billion to $30 billion, mostly provided by Government-guaranteed bonds" would have only "limited impact on the Federal budget," but if its operation is anything like that of its namesake we can expect this to directly cost something on the order of $10 billion for every $30 billion it lends out, not counting its crowding-out effects on the capital markets.

40.   Apparently it has not occurred to Reich that the way inflation works makes its redistributionary effects far too complicated to be sorted out. Those who get the newly created money relatively sooner benefit at the expense of those who face higher costs before they receive inflated incomes. The only way to allocate these burdens fairly would be to trace the detailed flow of money expenditures throughout the whole economy. But if that were possible, we could dispense with the market altogether and adopt comprehensive planning.

41.   Rohatyn (1982a: 7) advocates the creation of "sizable new credits from the banking system" in addition to debt extensions and moratoriums in order to shore up our weakening financial structures. He says that "we can have no real growth until our interest rate structure is lowered" (1980b: 23) and thus considers it "our most urgent national objective" to achieve "the reduction of unemployment through high economic growth rates and low interest rates." This, he realizes, requires "a commitment on the part of the Federal Reserve to accelerate its downward pressure on interest rates" (1982b: 74), or in other words vigorous monetary

expansion to artificially lower the price of credit. It has been precisely this policy of credit expansion that Hayek's work in monetary theory (e.g., [1931] 1935, [1933] 1966, [1939] 1975) has shown leads to both inflation and unemployment. Although the immediate effect of lowering interest rates is stimulative, the extra investments this policy encourages are not coordinated with genuine consumer demand, but rather are dependent on further injections of money. When the credit expansion is reduced in order to fight the inflation this policy created in the first place, the investments that had been artificially stimulated are suddenly revealed to be unprofitable, and a recession results. See also White (1984).

42. Rohatyn (1981a:16) calls for a "temporary freeze of wages and prices to deal with inflationary behavior that does not respond to other measures" and then offers no other measures that would even fight the symptoms of inflation (as do controls) much less the causes (as would monetary stabilization). Like the economic democracy advocates, he declines to say what he will do after these temporary measures are lifted and prices are again allowed to reflect the relative scarcity of goods. He has admitted that "wage and price controls in an advanced industrial society cannot work for long" (1982b: 82), although on an earlier occasion (1980b: 23–4) he favored temporary controls as a way station to a tough and apparently permanent incomes policy to be implemented by using tax incentives: "To begin to control inflation, an incomes policy that relates wage and price increases to productivity is essential. This should be administered through benefits and penalties of the tax system rather than through a new bureaucracy. A freeze of both wages and prices should be imposed until such an incomes policy can take its place." Monitoring the prices, wages, and real productivity of all factors of production throughout the U.S. economy and trying to influence these through tax incentive schemes might not require a new bureaucracy, but it would certainly require a considerable extension of the size and powers of some of the old ones.

7 WHAT IS LEFT?
Toward an Alternative Radicalism

World War I shaped the superstructures of industrial management. In the war America found a singleness of public purpose perfectly compatible with large-scale industrial efficiency. Ideas and institutions which were born then lived on, in various guises, through World War II and on into the cold war. . . .

The institutional legacy was powerful. Key economic functions of the federal government—which came to be taken for granted by the end of the management era [1970]—had their beginnings in World War I. The War Finance Corporation which underwrote bank loans to war industries, for example, was the precursor to decades of active government involvement in providing low interest loans to specific industries and firms. It was the direct precedent for Hoover's Reconstruction Finance Corporation, designed to bail out banks and railroads, and for the various schemes of government-backed loans and loan guarantees which marked the New Deal.

Robert Reich (1983: 93–94)

That we should foreswear all principles or "isms" in order to achieve greater mastery over fate is even now proclaimed as the new wisdom of our age. . . . If I am not mistaken, this fashionable contempt for "ideology" or for all general principles or "isms" is a characteristic attitude of disillusioned socialists who, because they have been forced by the inherent contradictions of their own ideology to discard it, have concluded that all ideologies must be erroneous and that in order to be rational one must do without one.

F. A. Hayek (1973: 58)

211

I have argued that a general respect for truth is all that is needed for society to be free. The way freedom and truth have proved identical in the battle against Stalinism bears out my views. I hope to see a modern theory of freedom, conceived on these lines, emerging from this battle.

Michael Polanyi ([1946] 1963: 19)

PLANNING AS REACTION: WAR, MONOPOLY POWER, AND THE LEFT

Until now I have largely granted advocates of planning the presumption that the origin and essential nature of their ideas are radical, that theirs are sincere attempts to expand the power of the people against that of privileged elites. I have analyzed planning proposals as misguided attempts to attain noble ideals. I have assumed, as most of their proponents do, that the intellectual roots of planning policies can be traced back in an unbroken sequence to the ideas of Karl Marx, Frederick Engels, and other nineteenth-century radicals, and can be viewed as modified, more practical versions of the embryonic planning ideas of such revolutionaries. Even though very few contemporary advocates of planning would defend many of the extreme views of Marx and other traditional socialists, it is from these origins that they borrow many of their attitudes about the market and much of their vocabulary and analysis. It is from this legacy that their radical credentials are established. After all, these nineteenth-century socialists were, for the most part, opposed to monopolistic privilege, dictatorial regimes, militarism, conscription, all varieties of political exploitation, and aggressive nationalism.

From this perspective, then, the totalitarian excesses of Stalinism are seen as a tragic deterioration of the true planning ideas of the Left. Planning, these radicals insist, need not mean simply an intense concentration of political power. Indeed, on the basis of its heritage in nineteenth-century revolutionary thought, planning has often been taken to mean something fundamentally different: a rational vehicle for realizing democratic aspirations. If planning in practice has often (always?) been transformed into an instrument for reaction instead, this presents a problem and a challenge for progressive intellectuals and activists—indeed, perhaps *the* challenge. It is not taken as sufficient reason to abandon the basic notion of national economic planning itself. Since the Left awakened to the true nature of Stalinism, it has been struggling to revise and correct planning, to create what its originators were supposed to have wanted. The intention is not to step backward into some sort of military and industrial feudalism such as exists in the Soviet Union, but to step forward to a "socialism with a human face." It has been generally assumed that what is needed is a system of firm democratic safeguards that will keep planning in the hands of the people and prevent the aberration of Stalinism from rearing its ugly head. Stalinism, then, is portrayed as the accidental betrayal of Marxism and of the ideals of true planning—that is, as a "tragic failure."

This account of the failure of planning leaves less extreme notions of planning unscathed. First of all, it is said, the main problems planning ran into in practice are due to the fact that its early advocates, such as Marx and Engels, paid no attention to the question of how it would work. The consequence of this unfortunate neglect naturally led their followers, such as Lenin, Stalin, Mao, Castro, and so on, to make serious errors. Economically, insufficient attention was paid to the need to permit market institutions to flourish alongside planning; politically, insufficient attention was given to the dangers to basic human liberties presented by an overcentralized planning apparatus. Moreover these ideas were rooted in classical economics and its now abandoned labor theory of value instead of the modern marginalist value theory of neoclassical economics.

Later on the Left is thought to have resolved these problems when liberal adherents of planning such as Abba Lerner and Oskar Lange—recognizing the flaws in the Marxist model but admiring its ideals—formulated a revised program for "market socialism," thereby solving both economic and political problems by allowing for a reconciliation of planning with market institutions. This more moderate kind of planning ideology is thought to be pro-market *and* pro-planning and is often considered to be what underlies the policies of, say, Sweden, England, or France rather than those of the Soviet Union, China, or Cuba. Thus, this account goes, planning ideas were born, but unspecified, in the mind of Marx, and only elaborated in the market socialist theories of the 1930s and 1940s. The tragic performance of Lenin and others is due to the fact that they were trying to implement the embryonic (comprehensive) rather than the mature (noncomprehensive) theory.[1]

This whole perspective suggests that while Marx proved to be wrong on certain details concerning the way planning would work, because of his neglect of such practical questions, his antagonistic attitude toward the competitive behavior of market systems should be preserved. A new kind of "market," without private property in the means of production and the wastes of competition, was to be constructed. Thus the Left retained a basically antimarket orientation and simply toned it down from "Abolish it" to merely "Control it."

But the modification from comprehensive planning, which seeks to completely *replace* market competition as the coordinating process of the economy, to noncomprehensive planning, which seeks to reconcile planning with market institutions, is hardly an alteration of some minor details. It is the toppling of the basic pillar of Marxist analysis. Marx may be justly accused of paying insufficient attention to the way planning would work, but he paid volumes of attention to the way the market system worked. He understood that capitalism, precisely because of its market institutions, was, as he put it, anarchic. It worked, as well or as poorly as it did, by means of unplannable forces of competition. To preserve money, prices, and so on is to abandon Marx's whole system.[2] It is by no means evident that the Marxist critique of the market order which modern planners still implicitly employ, can stand up once it is admitted that markets are necessary and that planning is to consist merely of interference in this unplannable system. Can this profound retreat be treated as a mere modification of planning? Does it not, rather, call into question the whole attitude of the twentieth-century Left toward both markets and planning?

What follows will tell a rather different story. I believe that it is fundamentally misleading to view planning in practice only as a *failure* to achieve the progressive ideals embodied in the various planning theories described so far. I think it can just as well be said that planning in practice has been a stunning *success* in achieving some entirely different goals. The true origins of the *idea* of planning must be traced further back, and find their genesis in some rather authoritarian pre-Marxist doctrines, while the legacy of *practical* planning procedures traces to an unambiguously reactionary beginning.

I do not doubt that many, perhaps most, advocates of planning are sincerely in pursuit of progressive ideals, but I will be arguing that those who are sincere are in fact being used by the *true* ideologists of planning who have no radical heritage at all, nor even a clearly articulated ideology. I will contend that there were two successive mutations in the development of the Left, when it was fundamentally transformed from a progressive, if sometimes seriously mistaken, revolutionary ideology into a combination of innocent victims, naïve dupes, and paid agents of the very forces of reaction it had been born to oppose. Stalinism, then, is not an aberration or a betrayal of true planning or a failure of its designers to attain Marxist ideals but, rather, a successful realization of reactionary ideals. In other words the problem is not that planners in practice have been unable to attain their radical goals; the problem is that the Left has been co-opted into cloaking an essentially nonradical policy in radical garb.

The story really begins long before Marx, in the numerous popular revolts against the society of empire, feudalism, mercantilism, and privilege on behalf of principles of natural law or justice, from which none, not even kings and popes, are exempt.[3] Some of the earliest to formulate these vague principles into more specific shape were the Levellers of the English Civil War (1642–1647), the radical liberals during the French Enlightenment of the late eighteenth century, and the American revolutionaries.[4] Here was the original Left, the radicalism that opposed government power not by merely putting forth a set of reforms for the state to implement but by insisting on a set of rules—or natural laws, as they called them—by which all human beings, including those in positions of power, are to be equally limited in order that they be equally free. Reason, the power of systematic thinking, was to be our sole guide in the spelling out of these rules. In this way, it was hoped, the day would come when war, militarism, monopoly, and, in general, the exploitation of some men by others would cease to be regular, systemic parts of the human condition. They would become relics of our barbaric past.

The libertarian Left was opposed to the intervention by any government into the lives of anyone, domestic or foreign. Thus, it combined an adamant opposition to international interventionism with an equally adamant aversion to domestic economic intervention into the market process. Unrestrained trade and migration, domestically and internationally, are, they understood, perfectly compatible with economic and cultural development. Noninterventionism at home and abroad was the consistent principle of the radical liberals. Any ambition to plan society's development was rejected as nothing more than a return to the society of status, power, and privilege.

This libertarian radicalism sought to carefully establish the rules of permissible conduct in such a way as to allow the competitive forces of the free market to do their progressive work. The evolution of the economy would be driven by the unplanned flux of market competition regulated only by the principles of natural law. Social progress was to be the indirect consequence of the competitive engagement of human minds with one another, not the direct result of the conscious planning of any single organization of minds. It was to be a society where no person was to coercively rule over another but where each one was to be persuasively influenced by others.

The sharp divergence of the Left from these libertarian beginnings may be traced through various influences, but perhaps the clearest symbol of this transformation lies in the writings from 1814 to 1825 of Henri Saint-Simon, among the most important of the early visionaries of the planned economy. Originally influenced by such radical liberals as Charles Comte, Charles Dunoyer, and Augustin Thierry, all of whom held to the kind of ideals sketched in the previous paragraphs, Saint-Simon was gradually to reject the ideal of discovering rules for the equal protection of liberty, substituting in the last eleven years of his life the alternative ideal of setting up an elite for the rational control of society. Where the earlier radicals saw reason as a means for the discovery of the natural laws that were to protect all people equally, Saint-Simon saw reason as a means for the deliberate reconstruction of society by a special organization of scientists, industrialists, and bankers. Where the earlier radicals saw danger in monopolies and sought to cultivate an open and competitive market, the followers of Saint-Simon saw danger in competition itself, and sought to institute a complete monopolization of economic activity under a unified plan. Where the earlier Left was groping toward a conception of the economic order as a spontaneous resultant of the system of legal constraints, the later came to adopt a concept of economic order as the designed product of the deliberations of a committee of social engineers. The liberation of humanity came to be seen as the special task of an intelligentsia.

The conception of planning that is contained in Marx's system of "scientific socialism" (a phrase first used by the Saint-Simonians) was profoundly shaped by the followers of Saint-Simon.[5] Virtually all of Marx's immediate influences in German revolutionary thought, from Ludwig Feuerbach to Moses Hess to D. F. Strauss had been infected with Saint-Simonian ideas. It was the chief expositers of the Saint-Simonian system, Enfantin and Bazard, not Karl Marx, who first clearly articulated the goal of a comprehensively planned society: a hierarchical organization of the whole world's industries into "a vast workshop, laboring under a common impulse to achieve a common goal" (Halevy 1965: 60).

To be sure, Marx and the Young Hegelians often proposed democratic processes for the carrying out of the common plan, while the Saint-Simonians were quite authoritarian. But the very notion of organizing industry according to a common plan traces directly to Saint-Simon and had as its original models military and feudal organizations. Saint-Simon patterned his various chambers or ministries of planning after a number of permanent advisory bodies that had been created by Napoleon and Louis XVIII (Halevy 1965: 48–49). The Saint-Simonians longed for "a kind of return to medieval theocracy," but one "imbued with the spirit of science and technical progress" (Kolakowski 1981a: 190). They conceived of their "Industrial Society" as a hierarchical administration of the whole of society's resources under the direction of the "captains of industry," among whom bankers are prominently included.

When the great historian Elie Halevy (1965: 52–53) points out that Saint-Simon was not a democrat, he understates the matter. Saint-Simon had little but contempt for "the masses" and explicitly recommended that those who refused to cooperate with the visions of the ruling intelligentsia be "treated like cattle" (quoted by Hayek 1944: 24). This authoritarian attitude was not unique to Saint-Simon but permeated the whole school of revolutionary thought that arose after his death. As Halevy observed, the Saint-Simonians, although advocates of international peace, "did not call for the abolition of armies; they proposed changing their purpose. Following Fourier's idea, an *industrial army* should be established" (Halevy 1965: 87).

In short, when the theoretical ideal of the planned society was born, it was already linked with practical organizational procedures that had been borrowed from military institutions. Of all pre-Marxist theories, the Saint-Simonian doctrine had, as one eminent historian of Marxism put it, "the strongest effect in diffusing socialist ideas among the educated classes" (Kolakowski 1981a: 192), serving as a direct inspiration not only for leftist revolutionaries such as Louis Blanc, Ferdinand Lassalle, and the Young Hegelians but also for reactionaries such as Napoleon III (Hayek 1955: 166). Contrary to the usual story, the notion of planning was not born in the mind of the young radical revolutionary, Karl Marx, but rather in the mind of an elitist admirer of medieval order, military discipline, and rule by an intelligentsia made up of engineers, industrialists, and bankers. Although this initial connection with reactionary elements does not prove that planning is inherently nonradical, it is not without significance that the central policy prescription of radical Marxism was borrowed from a writer with such definite authoritarian leanings.

Karl Marx began his intellectual career as these ideas were sweeping the European continent. His notion of comprehensive planning was an outgrowth of the sort of engineering mentality typical of the Saint-Simonians. What Marx added to this notion of planning was the insight that comprehensive planning represents a fundamentally different method for coordinating economic activities, a method that logically precludes any role for market institutions. The Saint-Simonians had condemned the irrationality of competition. Marx showed what the abolition of competition taken consistently implies. All acts of buying and selling, profit and loss accounting, the very use of money, can and must be dispensed with in the comprehensively planned economy. Marx's critique fueled a growing animosity on the Left toward market institutions. By the end of the nineteenth century, "radicalism" had come to mean socialism and classical liberalism was in retreat.

It is important to realize that at this time, while the Left was already seriously misguided in its endorsement of comprehensive planning (a policy I have argued is impossible to implement), it was still by and large a radical movement. Despite Saint-Simon's authoritarian elitism, the Marxist Left retained the democratic attitudes of the older radicalism. Its goals were still anti-imperialist, antimilitarist, and antiprivilege. The period from 1889 to 1914 has been aptly called "the golden age of Marxism," days of confidence, impressive scholarly output, and brave promises of the possibilities of the planned economy.[6] Because so many radicals thought that a planning bureau could rationally and democratically control the cultural and economic development of society for the benefit of all, the ambition of the Left came to be not just the complete equality of rights, as important as that was still thought to be, but the more grandiose ideal of equality of wealth. Thus the aboliton of all inequality of wealth, through the planned redistribution of income, was added to the traditional goals of the Left. Attention was re-directed from coercive exploitation to a more subtle Marxist notion of capitalist exploitation, whereby the wage earner is seen as a wage-slave. But this development did not yet diminish the widespread belief in the original goals, the upholding of individual rights, which remained the main source of the Left's popular appeal. That appeal has always been and continues to be the greatest where the none-too-subtle exploitation of the common man by a privileged class has been the most severe.

It was during—and because of—World War I that the subversion of the Left was completed and the movement lost what was left of its radicalism. The war led directly to a split of the formerly antimilitar-ist Socialist International into nationalistic factions, which began to see themselves as defenders of their native governments instead of as protectors of all peoples against their governments. Nationalist mili-tary intervention around the world was transformed from the greatest enemy of progressive society to its most cherished tool. At the same time the war indirectly resulted in the collapse of the Russian govern-ment and in Lenin's attempt to implement the Marxist idea of plan-ning, conceived as the abolition of all market relations. Both of these effects, the Left's embrace of militarism and the coming to power of a ruthlessly committed Marxist, have in fact served to undermine any claim the Left could make from that time on to speak for the oppressed peoples of the world.

And just as proponents of radical causes became increasingly hos-tile to market institutions, classical liberal proponents of the free market increasingly lost touch with radicalism. They began to see themselves as defenders of existing, partially free markets against the threat of radical socialism. They increasingly couched their arguments in practical, economic, utilitarian terms rather than in terms of morality and justice. The newer radicals, meanwhile, were speaking eloquently of higher principles of a social justice which seemed to surpass the mere individual rights of the older radicals. By World War I the old radicalism had been replaced by one that was profoundly antagonistic to market institutions.

But if the First World War caused the destruction of the radical nature of the Left and seriously undermined its original Marxist theory of comprehensive planning, it also provided the fertile ground from which sprouted a different and extremely nonradical concep-tion of economic planning. Whereas the old radical notion of planning was never successfully implemented and thus always remained an abstract theory, the new nonradical conception was born in practice and never had any theoretical basis.

The market-socialist theories of liberal neoclassical economists such as Lange and Lerner, frequently put forward as the intellectual foundations of noncomprehensive planning, actually have played no role whatsoever in the practical implementation of economic planning. These ideas were not even introduced until a form of noncomprehensive planning, inspired by a clearly nonradical prototype, had been firmly established for several years.[7] Indeed, it may be seriously doubted whether the market-socialist theories can possibly be implemented in the real world. Based on the increasingly discredited perfect-competition model, a particularly useless part of neoclassical economics, these ideas have never found anything remotely resembling implementation in the real world.[8] The descendants of these models still occupy the imaginations of theoretical economists but cannot be taken seriously as guides for actual planning policies.[9]

It is not correct to say that planning was modified from its Marxist origins to take on its modern, noncomprehensive forms. It would be more accurate to say that comprehensive planning and the radical movement it inspired were utterly defeated and replaced root and branch by an entirely different idea with an entirely different heritage, by a movement driven not by popular resistance to oppression but by ruling groups themselves. The radicals' chief purpose was not just modified but completely reversed: from ending all wars and exploitation to conducting a world war of unprecedented destruction; from avoiding the monopoly power of big corporations that they feared unrestricted competition would permit, to handing these corporations the very weapons they needed (and could not have gotten under a free market) to secure monopoly power for themselves. The Left, in short, was duped into cloaking the corporations' monopoly-building agenda in its progressive-sounding anticorporate rhetoric.

The real fathers of planning, *as it has actually been practiced in this century*, are neither Marx and Engels nor Lange and Lerner, but Bernard Baruch, David Lloyd George, and General Erich Ludendorff. It was in their efforts to mobilize, respectively, the American, British, and German economies for the purpose of fighting World War I that the specific procedures for implementing a noncomprehensively planned economy were first ironed out. Their policies were not derived from the principles of any ideologists of the Left but were pieced together gradually from the day-to-day experience of trying to direct the war effort. Their aspirations were not to achieve any utopian vision but to secure for the major corporations effective isolation from the rigors and uncertainties of competition. Planning in practice was born as a mutual protection society for a corporate elite.

While the Saint-Simonians *anticipated* several aspects of what this kind of authoritarian planning would be like, it is unlikely that they *inspired* the fathers of modern planning, who saw matters in much more pragmatic terms. Even so, to call the directors of the American War Industries Board, the British Ministry of Munitions, and the Prussian war ministry the "fathers" of planning is probably to credit them with more originality than they deserve. Their activities were not wholly unprecedented; they were extensions of the same kinds of policies for government control over the economy which Bismarck had developed in the late nineteenth century, which Adam Smith had earlier attacked in the days of mercantilism, and which have legacies stretching back into prehistoric times. But the peculiar mix of institutional relationships of these World War I planning agencies was entirely new at the time and seems to have become the direct or indirect model for every implementation of national economic planning of this century. The common pattern of specific planning procedures was never actually designed by the highly visible heads of these agencies but rather evolved from a sequence of experimental measures and only after much initial confusion.

The procedures that emerged involved the use of government power to rigidify the existing structure of industries, to carve up the market among the established firms, and to protect their investments by shielding them from the potential competition of as-yet unestablished or politically impotent firms. In Chapter 2 it was argued that the unprecedented productivity of the Market organizing principle relative to Tradition was due to the rapid profit and loss selection process by which new habits could be tried, old ones revised, and either, where profitable, preserved. The essence of planning as it is practiced is to sabotage this very feature of markets, to slow down or prevent the revision of established routines. These rigidification policies are implemented by using the traditional mercantilist tools for government interference into the competitive process: licensing restrictions, wage and price controls, credit allocation, and the dispensing of subsidies to special interest groups—that is, the policies surveyed in the preceding two chapters.

It was argued forcefully by the American liberal Walter Lippmann that the implementation of these rigidification policies is essentially a *militarization* of the economy, the most complete forms of which have been National Socialism and Stalinist communism. Defenders of planning, or as he calls it "collectivism,"

> refuse to believe that the dictatorship, the terror, the conscription of life and labor, which have prevailed in Russia for eighteen years [1918-1936], are integral in a collectivist order, or that their striking resemblance to martial law in a state of siege is more than superficial and transitory. I venture to suggest that this is an illusion. I contend that a close analysis of its theory and direct observation of its practice will disclose that all collectivism, whether it be communist or fascist, is military in method, in purpose, in spirit, and can be nothing else. (Lippmann 1936: 67)[10]

We must remind ourselves, Lippmann says, "not only why collectivism is necessary in war but why war is so favorable to collectivism." It provides the Grand Social Mission that can inspire widespread "loyalty and enthusiasm."

> Under the system of centralized control without constitutional checks and balances, the war spirit identifies dissent with treason, the pursuit of private happiness with slackerism and sabotage, and, on the other side, obedience with discipline, conformity with patriotism. Thus at one stroke war extinguishes the difficulties of planning, cutting out from under the individual any moral ground as well as any lawful ground on which he might resist the execution of the official plan. (Lippmann 1936: 67)

Economic historian E. H. Carr has called the German war economy of World War I "the first more or less fully planned national economy in modern times" (quoted by Robert Conquest 1972: 98). The ministry of war's raw materials department was established in 1914 to secure war materials for military use, and by 1916 under General Ludendorff's direction the idea of "national service," of systematically involving the whole society in the war effort, became the order of the day. In January 1918 Ludendorff drafted tens of thousands of striking workers to form "labor battalions" for the war. Germany was to become a vast munitions factory. Planning was understood to mean the systematic militarization of economic life.

A single agency vested with immense powers set itself the task of coordinating the activities of all the major industries of the economy, of rapidly mobilizing the nation's labor and capital for war production (see Johnson 1983: 90).[11]

In Britain, David Lloyd George's Ministry of Munitions was established in 1915 when, as with Germany, problems emerged in supplying materials for the war that each side thought would be over quickly. War planning interventions expanded step by step until by the end of the war half the national income was in government hands. One sympathetic observer called the Ministry of Munitions "the major supply innovation of the war" and credited it with having transformed a "primarily free enterprise system of weaponry production" into a "primarily statist system" (Trebilcock 1975: 155).

In this country in 1915 President Wilson set up an Industrial Preparedness Committee, the IPC (formerly a part of the Naval Consulting Board), to plan for wartime production, and a Council of National Defense was established in 1916 that joined the federal government's secretaries of the interior, agriculture, labor, and commerce with the secretaries of war and the navy. After the United States entered the war, this council set up the War Industries Board, which lasted from July 1917 until November 1918. As with Germany and Britain, the planning agency from the start was seen as a rationalization of industry by the corporate leaders themselves. As Howard E. Coffin (1916), vice-president of the Hudson Motor Company and chairman of Wilson's IPC, put it:

> In any problem as big as the question of industrial organization of this country for the service of the government, in any problem as big as the analysis of the industrial resources of the country, we cannot, of course, depend upon any small corps of men or board which may be created for the purpose. Such work must be done by the men who themselves have developed the industries of the country.

And indeed this is exactly what happened. In the initial Advisory Commission a railroad executive was put in charge of transportation, a Sears executive was put in charge of supplies, a conservative labor union leader was put in charge of labor. Coffin himself became head of manufacturing and munitions, while a wealthy Wall Street financier named Bernard Baruch assumed control over raw materials. When the War Industries Board was formed, Baruch became its czar. When his powers were expanded, the WIB intervened in virtually all aspects of the economy in order to "secure maximum production with the least possible disruption of normal business routine and with the least political disturbance" (Weinstein 1968: 222; see also Cuff 1973). In effect this meant ensuring that Baruch's friends in industry profited from military production. The board, as its official historian put it, "was really the town meeting of American industry, curbing, disciplining and devoting itself" (Clarkson 1923: 73).[12] While allegedly authorized to fix maximum prices to protect society from war profiteering, the board actually used these as minimum prices to protect specific business interests (Weinstein 1968: 224–25). The board's price-fixing committee became the forum for the enforced cartelization of American industry.

Moreover, this cartelization process must have had a systematic effect on the size of firms that survived. The enforcement of fixed profit margins in order to eliminate "profiteering" or "windfall profits" constitutes a definite bias against small businesses, which, having a smaller volume of sales, need to be able to recoup a higher margin per sale. This point was admitted even by Herbert Hoover, who, discussing his experiences with the Food Administration during World War I, noted that "the larger establishments can do business on narrower margins than the small establishments. To have fixed margins too narrow during the war would drive the smaller concerns out of business, leaving us at the mercy of large monopolies after the war" (Hoover [1920] 1941: 17). Nevertheless, this policy of setting fixed profit margins was followed by both Hoover's Food Administration and Baruch's War Industries Board.

As Robert D. Cuff (1973: 266) showed in his revealing history of the War Industries Board, this planning agency combined a public-relations image of unity, central coordination, and patriotic cooperation, with an actual practice that was "marked by loose, informal understandings, ad hoc arrangements, calculated risks of infringement, and pervasive bargaining."

> Baruch and the WIB have since come to represent the greatest concentration of delegated authority in American history, while at the time Baruch and his men floundered in an organizational maze over which they never had sufficient control. Baruch has since taken on the aura of economic dictator, although at the time, economic interest groups and the military service bureaus reached into the WIB organization to shape specific programs, oftentimes against his will. The symbol of Bernard Baruch, the WIB's high priest of cere-

mony, has given an image of unity and form to what in retrospect was an extraordinarily chaotic, disjointed process. (Cuff 1973: 270-71)

Yet the image of Baruch as economic dictator is not as mythical as Cuff here implies. Planning in practice is characterized precisely by this public image of comprehensive control combined with an intense concentration of arbitrary government power but inevitably lacking the detailed knowledge to exercise that power intelligently. It is in the very nature of planning that an imagery of unity (stemming from the aspirations of comprehensive planning) be joined to a reality of chaos (generated by arbitrary interferences into the market process that constitute noncomprehensive planning). Cuff's point (1973: 265) that there is a "gap between the rhetoric and reality of the WIB experiment" can be generalized to all the twentieth-century experiences with planning. But the fact that such planning agencies lack "sufficient control" to do what their rhetoric says they are doing does not in the least mean that men like Baruch are not economic dictators. In fact, Cuff shows that the WIB and other wartime agencies represented a "sweeping usurpation of traditional prerogatives and responsibilities" (p. 270; see also Grant 1983). Cuff succinctly summarizes the importance of these wartime transformations in the opening paragraph of his book:

The Great War produced an unparalleled expansion of the state in the United States, as it did in every country under arms. An administrative army marched into Washington before a military force sailed overseas. Networks of agencies spanned the nation and cut deeply downward through the country's social structure. State agencies organized and administered social and economic functions normally left to private, uncoordinated decision-making. The Committee on Public Information, the Food and Fuel Administrations, the Allied Purchasing Commission, the United States Railroad Administration, the War Finance Corporation, and other wartime experiments produced the greatest concentration of public bureaucratic power to that point in American history. (p. 1)

Thus, the origins of planning in practice constituted nothing more nor less than governmentally sanctioned moves by leaders of the major industries to insulate themselves from risk and from the vicissitudes of market competition. It was not a failure to achieve democratic purposes; it was the ultimate fulfillment of the monopolistic purposes of certain members of the corporate elite. They had been trying for decades to find a way to use government power to protect their profits from the threat of rivals and were able finally to succeed in the war economy.[13] While these corporate leaders often shrouded their actions in democratic rhetoric—frequently aided in this effort by progressive intellectuals and reformers—the implementation of planning policies was from the outset a simple matter of practical, politically influential business leaders protecting themselves from the forces of the market. As Cuff (1973: 272) pointed out, "The command posts of the WIB were staffed by a special group of men" who were neither economic entrepreneurs nor philosophers or ideologues of planning but were "business politicians." "A thoroughgoing pragmatism far more than ideological commitment to the ideal of business-government cooperation characterized private business leaders who negotiated with the WIB in Washington" (pp. 272–73).

All three of these experiences with war planning, all relatively successful from the point of view of those implementing them, had to be severely cut back after the war. The war experience became, however, the practical model for later schemes for planning all over the world. Nazi Germany spawned a successful rejuvenation of Ludendorff's planning agencies, just as England's World War II experiences with planning echoed the policies and organizational form of Lloyd George's Ministry of Munitions.[14]

In the United States the experiences of the War Industries Board of 1917–18 "illustrated to businessmen the advantages of large-scale industrial combination rather than competition and the unexpected benefits of close government-business cooperation" (Wilson 1980: 27). The same model, and many of the same personnel were to be called upon in the 1930s when the Reconstruction Finance Corporation was created. Herbert Hoover, who created the RFC, had been food czar during the American experiment in war planning. Bernard Baruch was his first choice as the RFC's head and although Baruch turned down this offer, his former aide, Eugene Meyer, ended up with the job. Meyer had been managing director of the War Finance Corporation, which was the main surviving institutional remnant of the WIB and which was actively extending credit to agricultural interests from 1919 to 1920 and then again from 1921 to 1929 (Baruch 1941: 137). Meyer was originally an investment banker in New York; his RFC has now become the model for New York investment banker Felix Rohatyn's proposals for reindustrialization.

One begins to see a certain regularity here. One begins, perhaps, to see that the real forefathers of contemporary proposals for national economic planning were not intellectuals of the Left but the big businessmen, bankers, and industrialists who sought to use planning agencies as weapons against competition, and found the war and the Great Depression convenient chances to wield those weapons.

But the war economy probably found its most successful realization not in its native lands but as an export to Russia, culminating in the Stalinist-type centrally planned economy. Now it might be objected that this cannot be true because neither Lenin nor Stalin was a member of the corporate elite. But the essentials of the war economy were explicitly pursued by Lenin and attained their purest realization under Stalin's rule.

We should recall that Marx had said virtually nothing about how planning would work except that markets were to be utterly abolished. Thus, when Lenin found himself in power, he had to look elsewhere for practical models. The Soviet concept of planning had its origins in the improvised central industrial administration of War Communism, encouraged by Lenin's admiration for the "war socialism" of German economic planning during the First World War.[15] As one historian put it, Ludendorff was "the man who really inspired Soviet economic planning" (Johnson 1983: 90). Lenin ([1918] 1965: 547) was quite explicit about viewing wartime Germany "with its splendidly organized bourgeoisie," as his model for *economic* planning at the same time as it embodied his clear *political* and military antagonist:

> Here [with Germany] we have "the last word" in modern large-scale capitalist engineering and planned organization, *subordinated to Junker-bourgeois imperialism*. Cross out the words in italics, and in place of militarist, Junker, bourgeois, imperialist *state* put *also a state*, but of a different social type, . . . that is, a proletarian state, and you will have the *sum total* of the conditions for socialism.

> . . . History . . . has taken such a peculiar course that it *has given birth* in 1918 to two unconnected halves of socialism existing side by side like two future chickens in the single shell of international imperialism. In 1918 Germany and Russia have become the most striking embodiment of the material realization of the economic, the productive and the socio-economic conditions for socialism, on the one hand, and the political conditions, on the other. . . . While the revolution in Germany is still slow in "coming forth,"

our task is to study the state capitalism of the Germans, to spare *no effort* in copying it and not shrink from adopting *dictatorial* methods to hasten the copying of it. (Lenin [1918] 1965: 339-40; emphasis in the original)[17]

However, despite his attempt to emulate Ludendorff's war planning and regardless of the fact that his policies during the War Communism period represented in many ways a similar intensive militarization of the economy, Lenin's planning was different. It was significantly more destructive of wealth, and this was the case precisely because of his adherence to Marxism. Lenin was quite consciously and consistently trying to destroy the institutions of the market and to replace them with the administrative planning methods he so admired in the Prussian ministry of war, whereas Ludendorff and the others were only trying to severely limit competition, not to completely eliminate it. The fathers of planning were trying to secure the profits of certain businessmen; Lenin was hoping to eliminate profit making altogether. He was for comprehensive planning; they for noncomprehensive. And the result of this important difference was, on the one hand, that Lenin's more ambitious form of comprehensive planning was a catastrophic failure necessitating wholesale retreat and a restoration of some market institutions under Bukharin's direction during the "New Economic Policy." On the other hand the noncomprehensive planners were able to avert such complete disaster because they merely obstructed and distorted the market process instead of eliminating it.

Planning, one might say, is a social parasite. It cannot survive without a reasonably healthy host, that is, one in which the market process is permitted to operate. Attempts at planning by radical ideologues like Lenin—who want to take it to its logical, Marxist, conclusion and abolish the price system—are doomed to failure for the same reason that a leech that kills its victim is. Pragmatic, inconsistent planning can actually work as a device for monopolization and coercive wealth redistribution—even if it cannot improve an economy's overall performance—simply *because* it is inconsistent and refrains from destroying its host.

Paul Johnson (1983: 94) concludes his summary of the debacle that was Lenin's comprehensive planning as follows:

Thus ended, in total failure, the first major experiment in what it was now fashionable to call social engineering. Lenin termed it "a defeat and retreat, for a new attack." But soon he was dead, and the "new attack" on the peasants was to be left to the bureaucratic monster he left behind him. Lenin believed in planning because it was "scientific." But he did not know how to do it.

But if Lenin's planning was too faithful to its Marxist principles to survive, Stalin's version was a successfully inconsistent implementation of war planning, a rigidification and militarization of the economy on the Ludendorff model, which managed to preserve its host. Stalin grossly interfered with prices, money, competition, and profit and loss accounting, but he did not utterly destroy them. The monopoly power of the Communist party and its government bureaucrats was successfully secured; the economic system was brought to serve the interests of a New Class (see Djilas 1957 and Konrad and Szelenyi 1979). The fact that the beneficiaries of this monopoly power did not consider themselves capitalists is an incidental detail. Stalinism is not, as Leninism is, unsuccessful Marxism; it is successful Ludendorffism: a permanent war economy in peacetime.

Stalin had spent the War Communism period as a political commissar at the front in the war, and as Stephen F. Cohen puts it, these years Stalin spent serving the Bolshevik regime during its ill-fated attempt to mimic Germany's war economy "seem to have been a crucial experience in his life; and warlike approaches to social problems were congenial to what has been described as his 'warfare personality.'." His intensification theory held that the class struggle was to be intensified as the country approached true socialism and justified an increasingly militarized and dictatorial control over the economy. Cohen (1974: 314–15) explains the true intellectual roots of Stalinism:

Military rather than traditionally Marxist in inspiration, Stalin's intensification theory was perhaps his only original contribution to Bolshevik thought; it became a *sine qua non* of his twenty-five-year rule. In 1928, applied to Kulaks [landowning peasants], "shakhtyites" [named after some anti-Bolshevik miners who revolted in the Donbass industrial complex in March 1928] and anonymous "counter-revolutionaries," it rationalized his vision of powerful enemies within and his "extraordinary,"civil war politics. By the thirties, he had translated it into a conspiratorial theory of "enemies of the people," and the ideology of mass terror. Its murderous implications were clear to Bukharin when he first heard the theory in July, 1928: "This is idiotic illiteracy. . . . The result is a police state."

Stalin was able to perfect the war economy, from which nations that had democratic traditions had to retreat in peacetime, by declaring a permanent civil war within his own country's borders. The culmination of the planning policies that were initially aimed at the mobilization of the economy's resources for the war effort was the perpetuation of the military mentality during peacetime. Soviet planning has itself been the model throughout much of this century for numerous experiments in centralized planning, especially in the developing countries. It has universally led to what can only be called the militarization of economic life. It is time we came to realize what Walter Lippmann was trying to tell us nearly fifty years ago: Planning does not accidentally deteriorate into the militarization of the economy; it *is* the militarization of the economy.

> We may go further and say that, though the planned economy is proposed as a form of social organization which will provide peace and plenty, thus far in all its concrete manifestations it has been associated with scarcity and war. From 1914 to 1918 all the belligerents were driven step by step into a planned and politically directed economy. The bolsheviks . . . were driven into it by the civil and international war they were forced to fight. They have continued with it under the Five Year Plans, which, in their strategy and in the order of their priorities, are fundamentally military. The fascists have adopted collectivism, more or less frankly proclaiming their intent to solve their social problems by developing their military power. In all the nations which are still democratic and capitalistic, plans are drawn for their rapid transformation into totalitarian states. . . .
>
> That, I believe, is where all planned economies have originated and must in the very nature of things originate. For it can be demonstrated, I am confident, that there is only one purpose to which a whole society can be directed by a deliberate plan. That purpose is war, and there is no other. (Lippmann 1936: 89–90)

When the story of the Left is seen in this light, the idea of economic planning begins to appear not only accidentally but inherently reactionary. The *theory of planning* was, from its inception, modeled after feudal and militaristic organizations. Elements of the Left tried to transform it into a radical program, to fit it into a progressive revolutionary vision. But it doesn't fit. Attempts to implement this theory invariably reveal its true nature. The *practice of planning* is nothing but the militarization of the economy.

It is unnecessary to repeat the account of the immense degradation and annihilation of human life to which the Left's romance with central planning has led us. Today, after Solzhenitsyn, it is enough to say the word *gulag*. But there is another tragic consequence of this whole episode of which most of us are still insufficiently aware: it has helped to drive a wedge between our deepest desires for action that is both "practical," that is to say, rational or scientific, and "moral," that is to say, consistently principled. The most consistent advocate of planning, the one who is most moral according to the principles of his own ideology, is also the least practical. In other words there is a premium on immorality, on unprincipled action. By aiming at an unworkable utopia, a comprehensively planned, egalitarian society, the Left has soured us on the commitment to *any* ideal society, and left us with the kinds of connotations of the words "ideologue," "utopia," and even "radical" which make it so difficult to stand for—or even to discuss—principles or fundamental change.

We must not, however, let the decay of planning as an ideal for the Left destroy our hopes for radical change. What is wrong with that form of radicalism which aspires to the planned economy as its utopia is not the simple fact that it was a radical movement, that it sought to inspire popular support by its appeal to an imagined alternative kind of social organization. What is wrong with it is that its specific utopia happens to be completely unworkable if carried to its logical conclusion, and essentially reactionary if not.

From this point of view it becomes evident why the contemporary Left is completely paralyzed by modern conservatism as epitomized by Ronald Reagan. By its largely rhetorical devotion to the free market and its actual policies of constructing a permanent war economy, conservatism helps to perpetuate the myth that it is the policies of free markets rather than those of planning that have been obstructing peace, and that it is an existing market economy rather than an established system of noncomprehensive planning which is responsible for our current economic distress. In fact, Reagan's rapid militarization of the American economy, in spite of the rosy pictures of free-market economies that fill his speeches, is the very *essence* of national economic planning.

Over the history of this country the increase of government's role in the economy, of noncomprehensive planning, has been steady. We have seen state-enforced cartelization of industry after industry, from the public utilities in communication and energy to the regulated cartels of the insurance, medical, and transportation industries.

We have seen the size of government and its involvement in our lives grow virtually unchecked. We have seen our monetary and banking systems erode, our economies stagnate. Yet the only alternatives to this decay we have seen in our current political climate are the Right's militarization of the economy and the Left's industrial policy or national economic planning.

I submit that these alternatives are fundamentally equivalent both to one another and to the worst of the decaying regimes of the present world. To varying degrees every economic system of the modern world is, in the final analysis, of one kind. Whether called capitalist or socialist or fascist or communist, it is a system of noncomprehensive planning. Whether its aim is military or not, its method of organization most certainly is. And whether this militarization of the economy is left naked (Hitler) or is dressed up as progressive reform (Baruch), Marxist communism (Stalin), or free-market ideals (Reagan), its true nature remains the same: it is national economic planning.

AN ALTERNATIVE TO THE PLANNED ECONOMY

The first part of this chapter has given an overview of the failure of planning to achieve the democratic, progressive ideals of most of its supporters on the intellectual Left. The one consistent theory, Marx's comprehensive planning, was abandoned long ago as completely unworkable, while the various forms of noncomprehensive planning to which the Left retreated have proven to be convenient tools for the forces of reaction. It seems to me that the reason for this tragedy is that *the Left has retreated to the wrong line of defense.* Comprehensive planning may have once been a plausible position for a radical movement to try to defend, albeit one that has now been, and should have been, thoroughly repudiated. But the kinds of attitudes toward market institutions that the advocacy of comprehensive planning instilled in its followers made it psychologically if not logically impossible for them to endorse the radical ideal to be sketched here. It is not easy, psychologically, to turn immediately from vehemently condemning the market (for its inability to attain what turns out to be an impossible standard) to warmly embracing it. But since I believe this is precisely what logic and what economic science tell us we should do, I think the radical movement must find itself making exactly that dramatic reversal.

The world's history is riddled with the triumph of popular national uprisings, of radical movements for liberation, but it is equally filled with rapid reversals of these triumphs, with revolutionary heroes transformed overnight into the new oppressors.[18] Over a hundred years ago Marx wrote that "all political upheavals perfected this machine instead of smashing it. The parties that strove in turn for mastery regarded possession of this immense state edifice as the main booty for the victor" ([1871] 1974: 238). And again that "all reactions and revolutions had only served to transfer that organized power—that organized force of the slavery of labor—from one hand to another, from one fraction of the ruling classes to the other" (p. 249). Instead, the goal of true radicalism was to be "to break down this horrid machinery of class domination itself" (p. 249). "Freedom," for Marx, "consists in converting the state from an organ superimposed on society into one thoroughly subordinate to it; and even today state forms are more or less free depending on the degree to which they restrict the 'freedom of the state'" ([1875] 1974b: 354).

Unfortunately, it can still be said today that all revolutions have only served to transfer rule from one hand to another, and the Left is still looking for a way to transcend this level of political struggle. As the French radicals Daniel and Gabriel Cohn-Bendit (1968: 250-51) put it, "Democracy is not suborned by bad leadership but by the very existence of leadership. . . . We are convinced that the revolutionary cannot and must not be a leader." The essential goal of radicalism has always been not to change the current personnel in power but more fundamentally to transform institutions in such a way as to make the very exercise of power by one human being over another extinct.

There are important lessons, then, to be learned from both the successes and the failures of the twentieth century's revolutionary movements. The triumphs of these popular revolutions seem to me to be evidence of the *power* of ideology, while the reversals are evidence of the *weakness* of most of the particular ideologies that have driven these revolutions. They have generally striven to drive the current oppressors out of power, only to replace them with new rulers. If an ideology is found, however, that can transcend this mere replacement of rulers, aiming instead at a society without need for rule of some of its members by others, but in which, in some sense, the people can democratically rule themselves, then the triumph might be secured.

The Left, as Polish philosopher Leszek Kolakowski has shown, is defined and fueled by its vision of a better world, its utopia. The very word "utopia" conjures up the image of a fanciful, impossible world which impractical social dreamers construct, but which practical men and women cannot afford to take seriously. A common reaction of many of those on the Left who have come to realize the utter failure of the ideology of planning has been to abandon all ideology. Having realized that an adherence to the utopia of planning leads to either totalitarianism or economic collapse—that is, something substantially worse than the status quo in Western countries—they have all too often lost hope in radicalism per se.[19]

Many, perhaps most, utopias that have inspired people in the past have been inherently unachievable, and their pursuit has often led to immeasurable social harm. But there is really no alternative for anyone who recognizes the gross injustices of our modern world—and, for that matter, of virtually the whole of human history—but to lie down and resign oneself in defeat or to try to get up and devise a new utopia, a new vision of a fundamentally different world with which to reinspire an international movement. For if we settle for anything less than this, if we try to work within the constraints imposed by the current regimes, we are playing into the hands of the existing power structure and are destined to repeat the tragic story of the twentieth-century Left. As Kolakowski (1968) puts it, "Goals unattainable now will never be reached unless they are articulated when they are still unattainable."[20] So long as we do not dare to start constructing a positive, workable utopia, we are doomed never to pose a serious challenge to those who now rule our lives. In that case, we are certain to continue along our current road to intensified military rivalry, to increasingly oppressive and unresponsive government, and to a continuation of the rapid decay of culture, social harmony, and lately even economic productivity which has made so much of this century such a travesty of the ideals of the Left.

Thus the starting point for rebuilding a radical movement, a step that advocates of noncomprehensive planning cannot take, is the recognition of the need for the complete abandonment of the old utopia of planning in order to prepare for the next step: the recon-struction of an alternative vision.

The Left already appears to be taking that first step. Everywhere radical socialists and Marxists are lamenting the "crisis on the Left," searching in desperation for a new intellectual foundation. An editor of *Socialist Review*, for example, now openly advocates a "left plan-ning strategy" that "realizes the dominance of the market," which, she admits, "is actually a fairly efficient mode of transacting a lot of business" (Candace Howes, as quoted in Browning 1983: 56). Such statements are still considered a bit heretical, but it could be argued that heresy on the Left is becoming increasingly common-place. This is a hopeful sign that a major transformation of radical ideas is brewing.[21]

In a challenging article a few years ago in *The Nation*, David Horo-witz incisively described the current crisis on the intellectual Left, a crisis that he says has resulted from the Left's inability or unwilling-ness to learn from, and often even to acknowledge, the catastrophic worldwide failure of planned economies. For too long the Left has applied a double standard to the Soviet Union, China, Cuba, and other socialist nations whose human rights records, after all, bear little relation to the traditional values of the Left.[22] The Left has often and rightly denounced the hypocrisy of conservatives who seem to believe that all evil flows from the Kremlin. It seriously undermines its own case when, as in the uproar over Joan Baez's critical letter to the government of Vietnam, the Left seems to be-lieve, with similar hypocrisy, that all evil flows from Washington. As Horowitz pointed out, the Left is defined by the nature of its utopia—state ownership of the means of production—and because of the human rights violations of socialist governments, "Today, the left's utopia itself is in question. That is the real meaning of the crisis of Marxism."[23]

Probably the most significant self-criticism on the Left has come from Eastern Europe, where the failures of socialist policy are clos-est at hand, and where the first murmurings of a wholesale rejection of planning by radical intellectuals were heard. It is in Eastern Eu-rope where "conservative" means "defender of central planning" and where "liberal" means "proponent of decentralized market institutions." It is there where the stirrings of a grassroots radicalism that fundamentally objects to the whole idea of planning are to be found. In the Hungarian, Czech, and Polish revolts can be found the elements of a new radicalism, which confesses no allegiance to planning but which seems to be groping toward, if not yet clearly articulating, a decentralized alternative.

In his article about the crisis on the Left, Horowitz (1979: 589) quoted Kolakowski, who, though exiled, in many ways epitomizes the embryonic movement in Eastern Europe to replace the planning utopia with something else[24]:

> The experiences of the "new alternative society" have shown very convincingly that the only universal medicine these people have for social evils—state ownership of the means of production—is not only perfectly compatible with all disasters of the capitalist world, with exploitation, imperialism, pollution, misery, economic waste, national hatred and national oppression, but that it adds to them a series of disasters of its own: inefficiency, lack of economic incentives and, above all, the unrestricted role of the omnipotent bureaucracy, a concentration of power never before known in human history.

Kolakowski and the other East European radicals have not yet, to my knowledge, offered a coherent radical alternative to planning, but they have laid the groundwork for such an alternative by rejecting the old utopia of planning without, as do conservative critics of planning, also abandoning the primary aspirations of the Left.

The solution to the crisis on the Left cannot lie in replacing comprehensive with noncomprehensive planning, because noncomprehensive planning is only a minor variation on the status quo. If a new and workable utopia is to fuel a progressive movement, it must be constructed from a firm basis in principled opposition so that the consistent rational application of the principle can be the unifying force for effective change. It is precisely this firm basis in principle that noncomprehensive planning sorely lacks. All this form of planning offers is to replace our present rulers with leaders or representatives of the intellectuals who endorse its policies. All it can promise is that rule by the "good guys" will be more pleasant than rule by the "bad guys." Since it grudgingly concedes the need for market institutions but insists on interfering with them to achieve specific goals, it is a prescription for a continuation of the arbitrary use of power to which the twentieth century has become all too accustomed. Having abandoned the principle put forward by comprehensive planning, it has none left. Instead it recites social priorities that represent a wish list for the progressive-minded, but it has no well-defined standard on what means are to be deemed appropriate to achieve these ends. In short, noncomprehensive planning is not a basis for a radical movement at all. It is politics as usual. It is another plea by messianic political leaders that we should trust them to set things right. The goal of a genuine radicalism must be to transcend this whole level of politics.

As argued in Chapter 2, any socioeconomic system must be founded on one of the three distinct kinds of coordinating process: Tradition, Market, and Planning. These in turn correspond to the three possible forms of "systemic radicalism." One might endorse Tradition and condemn all actions proscribed by ancient customs; one might endorse the Market and condemn all coercive actions intrusive of the competitive process; or one might endorse Planning and condemn all competitive activity itself. Since, except for the occasional romantic anthropologist, nobody in modern political debate is, for good reasons, willing to be a principled advocate of Tradition, the two remaining principles for socioeconomic coordination are Planning and the Market.

But as was argued earlier, the consistent application of planning as a coordinating principle—that is, comprehensive planning—is utterly unworkable. In fact, many of the activities that this ideology must condemn are indispensable for any relatively advanced technological system. For the same reason that science requires freedom and intellectual competition to progress, a modern economy requires economic freedom and market competition. We rely on interpersonal rivalry to give us knowledge about alternative production methods without which most of the present world population would be doomed to starvation.

Thus, because comprehensive planning is built on a principle that is inconsistent with advanced technological production, it has succeeded precisely to the extent that its advocates have *abandoned* the consistent application of their own principles. The tragic attempt by Lenin to take these principles seriously stands as a stern warning to all planners that any principled devotion to their ideology will be catastrophic.

But while there is no example of a society based entirely on the Market as its coordinating principle, the relatively consistent adherence to this principle has proven a most practicable way of organizing society. Rudimentary elements of the rule of law based on some

notions of individual rights can be found in every progressing civilization in human history, and their declines appear to coincide with the
deterioration of these elements. Common law principles accompanied the evolution of free markets in Britain, and some form of property rights prevailed in every nation that participated in the rapid
economic growth known as the industrial revolution. In contrast
to Planning, the instances where the Market principle was more
closely embraced represent among the most successful periods of
human history.[25]

If the best example of an attempt to implement the Planning ideal
was the attempt at comprehensive planning during the War Communism period following the Russian revolution, I would say the best
example of an attempt to realize the Market ideal may have been the
American revolution. While the degree of failure of the former revolution was roughly proportional to the extent to which it stuck to
its ideals, the degree of failure of the latter can be measured by the
extent to which the American revolutionaries shied away from stick-
ing to theirs. What was wrong with the Russian revolution was the
very direction in which it was trying to go, while all that was wrong
with the American one was that its leaders did not carry it far
enough in the *right* direction in which it pointed them. Our task
now, therefore, is to *complete* the American revolution. Unlike the
failed Marxist utopia of Planning, the Jeffersonian Market-guided
society is a workable ideal, an ideal that when properly understood
is far more consistent with the humanitarian and internationalistic
values of the Left.

A certain degree of noncomprehensive planning and certain ex-
ceptions to the principles that otherwise guided that revolution were
allowed which kept America from fully achieving its ideal. For example, equal rights were incompletely extended to women and with-
held altogether from blacks and native Americans. Special monopoly
power over the issuing of currency and special coercive constraints
over the business of banking were allowed. Protectionist trade barriers were erected. New taxes were imposed. Such remnants of coercion were not only inconsistent with the general principles that
fueled the American revolution, but were also ultimately to prove
the causes of most of the nation's problems—and shame—since. It
was this incompleteness that let Americans massacre Indians, enslave
blacks, and restrict the rights of women. It was monopoly control
over money and credit that generated frequent and destructive business cycles and eventually the Great Depression (see Robbins 1934

and Rothbard [1963] 1975). It was the overriding of property rights on behalf of the goals of certain businessmen and political leaders that led to the pollution of rivers, lakes, and air (Horwitz 1977). And at the beginning of this century it was America's tragic entry into the First World War that enabled the corporate and banking elite to secure governmental protection from competition in the form of noncomprehensive planning.

This country was once a shining example of prosperity, admired and emulated throughout the world. It was born in the hope of ending foreign military entanglements and increasing the peaceful and mutually beneficial entanglements of trade. Its dollar was once a symbol of solid value, economic strength, and international harmony. It used to be widely considered the haven where the oppressed, destitute, and downtrodden could flee to start their lives anew.

By now, few remember the Jeffersonian ideals that gave birth to the American revolution. These ideals once called for a basic policy of nonintervention, both into the lives and economic activities of the American people and into the political affairs of other governments. Rather than refine and improve on these ideals, they have been allowed to steadily erode. The United States has debased the dollar that was once the world's symbol of monetary stability. It has taxed its productive economy to the point where the rapid growth once taken for granted has been stifled. It has embarked on insanely destructive wars and sent its marines throughout the globe pretentiously acting as world policemen. It has earned the hatred of millions of oppressed people whose only contact with it is through its support of vicious rulers from Somoza to the Shah of Iran to Marcos. A couple of decades ago all that remained around us of the American revolution's original noninterventionist vision seemed to be entombed in the inscriptions on several buildings in Washington.

Both the modern Left and the conservative Right in this country now take it for granted that this ideology is obsolete. The former reject its policy of economic noninterventionism as applicable only to the simpler times of the hand plow, while the latter reject its policy of military noninterventionism as applicable only to the simpler times of the bayonet.

But the argument can be and is being made that it is precisely the complexity of the modern world that argues for *avoiding* intervention in either domestic economic or foreign political affairs. The principles of noninterventionism both at home and abroad are beginning to come alive again. The battle lines of political struggle are being redrawn. No longer will the alternatives necessarily be restricted to varieties of planning. The option of "none of the above" is starting to be suggested.

To begin again to conceive of the unplanned free-market economy as a radical ideal does, admittedly, require a fairly drastic restructuring of our ideological thinking. Both ardent opponents of the market system and its professed adherents have usually taken it for granted that to support the market is to be for the establishment.

Given such assumptions, it is not surprising that the political choice is seen as being between an antimarket "Left" which has made serious mistakes but whose program at least signifies hope for a democratic, peaceful, and prosperous future, and a pro-market "Right" which combines a rhetoric of free enterprise with a defense of the established order, an intolerance of nontraditional life-styles, and worst of all a rapid build up of the military. The free-market ideal has been found guilty by virtue of its association with clearly reactionary goals.

But this guilt-by-association argument can cut both ways. The origin and practical experience with planning, I have suggested, reveal a profound kinship with the forces of reaction. By contrast, the birth of free-market notions in classical liberalism represents a powerful movement in direct—if not always consistent—opposition to the status quo. This is not to say that so-called defenders of the free market have not themselves often linked the market with reactionary causes. It is only to say that that linkage is arbitrary. Neither the origins nor the essential principles of free-market ideas have anything to do with a defense of any of the established regimes of the world. Quite the contrary, the ideas themselves speak for a fundamental transformation of the world, whatever the often misguided proponents of these ideas may have thought.

The citadels of power are in fact, whether they know it or not, more threatened by the spontaneous forces of the openly competitive market than by any other factor. Power thrives on coercive obstructions to market competition. Ideologies that seek increased governmental intervention into the economy have been only helping the powerful secure better control throughout the world. But an ideology that embraces the spontaneous forces of the market process can yet succeed where all these planning ideologies have failed. The more fully *these* principles are applied, the more the productive elements of the economy are released; the more opportunities for improvement that the competitive discovery process is permitted to uncover, the more the economy grows.

When the central argument of this book, the knowledge problem, was first made some sixty years ago (see Mises [1920] 1935, [1922] 1981), the radical idea of comprehensive planning as a hopeful alternative to the status quo was at its peak. Today the radical ideology of planning is intellectually bankrupt. All that remains are meek suggestions to try yet one more variation on the century's dominant theme of noncomprehensive planning. But this policy does not resolve the knowledge problem; it merely substitutes a form of destructive parasitism on the market process in place of its earlier unachievable goal of dispensing with market processes altogether. The knowledge problem shows that the freely competitive market order makes more effective use of the information that lies dispersed throughout society than can any of its participants. This means that noncomprehensive planning is blind interference into a complex order, interference which *can* succeed in protecting and enhancing monopoly power and privilege, but which *cannot* improve the productive capacity of a modern technologically advanced economy.

Radicals have let their past belief in comprehensive planning push them, by virtue of its utter failure and their unquestioned aversion to free-market institutions, into irreconcilable conflict with their own goals. Their opposition to unregulated competition for fear that it could evolve into monopoly has led them to endorse a policy of government-enforced and protected monopolization. Their restoration to a standpoint of true opposition requires that they finally abandon planning in all its guises and reformulate a radical vision of the free market and a free society.

While the Planning form of radicalism aspires to figure out the one correct way things ought to be done and life ought to be lived, and to reconcile everybody's interests through some sort of democratic process uniting society under a conscious plan, radicalism as such need demand none of this. In my own view, all the cards are not in on what the best way to live life is, and in any case there is no need for us to agree or reconcile our different views of such matters.

There may be much we can still learn from the nineteenth-century radical natural-rights theorist Lysander Spooner ([1875] 1977: 5), who made this point as eloquently as anyone has:

> We all come into the world in ignorance of ourselves, and of everything around us. By a fundamental law of our natures we are all constantly im-

pelled by the desire of happiness and the fear of pain. But we have everything to learn, as to what will give us happiness, and save us from pain. No two of us are wholly alike, either physically, mentally, or emotionally; or, consequently, in our physical, mental, or emotional requirements for the acquisition of happiness, and the avoidance of unhappiness. No one of us, therefore, can learn this indispensable lesson of happiness and unhappiness, of virtue and vice, for another. Each must learn it for himself. To learn it, he must be at liberty to try all experiments that commend themselves to his judgment. . . . And unless he can be permitted to try these experiments to his own satisfaction, he is restrained from the acquisition of knowledge, and, consequently, from pursuing the great purpose and duty of his life.

NOTES TO CHAPTER 7

1. The standard references on this orthodox account of the debate are Bergson (1948) and Schumpeter ([1942] 1950: ch. 16), which are criticized in detail in Lavoie (1981, 1985).

2. See Buick (1975). A good case can be made for the view that if Marx could today be convinced that comprehensive planning is impossible (which is admittedly hard to imagine), he should be expected to retreat not to noncomprehensive planning but to a belief in free-market capitalism. Marx ([1953] 1973: 161) once wrote parenthetically about the market's organizing mechanism:

    > It has been said and may be said that this is precisely the beauty and the greatness of it: this spontaneous interconnection, this material and mental metabolism which is independent of the knowing and willing of individuals, and which presupposes their reciprocal independence and indifference. And, certainly, this objective connection is preferable to the lack of any connection, or to the merely local connection resting on blood ties, or on primeval, natural or master-servant relations.

    Noncomprehensive planning amounts to a retrogression into the same kinds of master-servant relations upon which Marx considered market institutions to have been a definite improvement.

3. For a fascinating restatement and reformulation of this natural rights tradition, see Robert Nozick (1974).

4. See the excellent bibliographic essay by David Hart in the first few numbers of *The Humane Studies Review: A Research and Study Guide* (Institute for Humane Studies, Menlo Park, Calif.).

5. In his definitive three-volume work on the *Main Currents of Marxism*, Kolakowski (1981a: 187) refers to Saint-Simon as "the real founder of modern theoretical socialism, conceived not merely as an ideal but as the outcome of a historical process."

    Halevy (1965: 21) refers to Saint-Simon as "the great precursor" of Marxism. Hayek (1955: 156, 160–63) makes a persuasive case that the influence of the Saint-Simonians was "far greater than is commonly realized." J. S. Mill (1849: 250) argued that Saint-Simonism "during the few years of its public promulgation, sowed the seeds of nearly all socialist tendencies which have since spread so widely in France."

6. This "golden age" of Marxism during the Second International, as Kolakowski noted (1981b: 1), saw a flowering of serious thought because Marxism "was not so rigidly codified or subjected to dogmatic orthodoxy as to rule out discussion or the advocacy of rival solutions to theoretical and tactical problems." The discussion, both in defense of Marxism (as by Bukharin, Hilferding, Bernstein, Plekhanov, Lenin, Tugan-Baranovsky, and Bauer) and in criticism of Marxism (as by Kropotkin, Croce, Simmel, Böhm-Bawerk, Sombart, Struve), reached a far higher level during those years than it has since.

7. The earliest of these models that were widely discussed among economists were written in German in the early 1920s in response to Mises's theoretical challenge. Lange's and Lerner's models were not around until the mid-1930s.

8. See Jan Drewnowski (1961) for the argument that this theory of market socialism bears little relation to the real world. For a general critique of the neoclassical framework upon which Lange's and Lerner's models were based, see Kirzner (1973).

9. See Lavoie (1982) for a critique of modern variants of the Lange-Lerner model.

10. See especially Lippmann (1936: ch. 5). It should be noted, however, that war can only extinguish the *political* difficulties of the planners, in that opposition to planning is defused. The economy continues to face the totalitarian problem and the knowledge problem.

11. In fact, most historians agree that the German war economy mobilized too rapidly. So many resources were withdrawn from agricultural production that, as the war dragged on, food shortages predictably and disastrously resulted. See, for example, Lee (1975).

12. Clarkson was a director of the Council of National Defense.

13. *The Corporate Ideal in the Liberal State* (Weinstein 1968) is a fascinating account of this struggle for monopoly power. Its final chapter is entitled "War as Fulfillment."

14. In an interview in the *Washington Post* (December 5, 1982), Michael Foot, an advocate of national planning and one of the leaders of the British disarmament movement, was asked the question: "Is there any country today, or any point in the past, that you think should serve as a model for the Britain that you envision?" Foot answered in words that one would have thought he'd be ashamed to utter:

> The best example that I've seen of democratic socialism operating in this country was during the second world war. Then we ran Britain highly efficiently, got everybody into a job. It wasn't so difficult then to employ people who were disabled and

in difficulties and all the rest of it. We wanted to use all their efforts and we found the money to do it. We also produced, I would have thought, probably more than any other country including Germany. We mobilized better. The conscription of labor was only a very small element of it. . . . It was a democratic society with a common aim in which many of the class barriers were being broken down.

It is a sad commentary on the demise of the Left when we find people praising the war economy because its trains ran on time or because it gave jobs to the disabled. Of course, Foot knows full well that war has the unfortunate side effect of increasing the supply of the disabled, as well as the demand for them. What he does not realize is that it is not just an ironic coincidence that his ideal case of economic planning happens to be an instance of a war economy.

15.   As Roberts has shown, War Communism was so named only afterwards, in reference to the civil war during which it was imposed. At the time it was simply called communism.

16.   Paul Johnson, in a fascinating chapter on "The First Despotic Utopias," argues that Ludendorff gave Lenin the "practical vision" that was missing in Marxism:

> This was the German war-production machine. One must remember that, during the formative period of the Leninist state, its first twelve months, Russia was first the negotiating partner, then the economic puppet, of Germany. By 1917 . . . the Germans had seized upon the state capitalist model of pre-war Russia and married it to their own state, now run by the military. They called it "war socialism." It looked impressive; indeed in many ways it was impressive, and it certainly impressed Lenin. From then on his industrial ideas were all shaped by German practice. His first industrial supremo, the former Menshevik Larin, was also an enthusiastic exponent of German methods, which of course fitted in perfectly with Lenin's notions of central control. He began to hire German experts. (pp. 89–90)

17.   From " 'Left Wing' Childishness and the Petty-Bourgeois Mentality," published May 9–11, 1918 in *Pravda*; reprinted in Lenin, *Collected Works*, vol. 27 (1965).

18.   For inspiring surveys of many of the amazingly courageous attempts of our ancestors to resist oppression (both violently and nonviolently) see Robert B. Asprey's *War in the Shadows* (1975) and Gene Sharp's *The Politics of Nonviolent Action* (1973).

19.   The New Philosophers in France led by Bernard-Henri Levy seem to reflect this profound pessimism in recognition of the failure of the modern Left.

20.   See the excellent essay "The Concept of the Left" in Kolakowski (1968: 67–83). See also Nozick's "A Framework for Utopia" (1974: 297–334).

21.   Some of what follows has been borrowed from my review that appeared in *The Libertarian Review* (August 1980) of Konrad and Szelenyi's *The Intellectuals on the Road to Class Power* (1979). This book is an excellent example of the emerging libertarian-oriented Left in Eastern Europe. The authors' conclusion that "the growth of a market sector at the expense of

the administered sector . . . could actually reduce the social inequality between workers and the higher strata" (p. 231) represents the kind of statement which would still be considered heretical and even reactionary by radicals in the West but which is increasingly accepted by the radical dissident movement in Eastern Europe. It is significant that Carnoy and Shearer (1980: 128) were irritated by the fact that "even" Eastern European socialist economists concede the superior efficiency of capitalism over economic democracy.

22. The fact that U.S. foreign policy decisions are also to blame for helping to cause these tragedies in Southeast Asia is no excuse for the horrendous crimes against humanity that were committed by followers of Ho Chi Minh and Pol Pot. See Barron and Paul (1977).

23. See for example the soul searching that goes on in the Marxist journal *Monthly Review* over how to characterize and cope with the failure of planning in the Soviet Union. In particular see Paul M. Sweezy (1979: 24), "A Crisis in Marxian Theory," where the situation is described as a Kuhnian paradigmatic crisis "which is now visibly tearing the international revolutionary movement apart."

24. The responses that were published in a subsequent issue of *The Nation* reveal the extent to which the Left is still harboring some dangerous illusions. One went so far as to refer to the Soviet Union's "elimination of unemployment" as "an extraordinary achievement." The rejoinder by Horowitz points out that the title he had given to the original piece had not been "A Radical's Disenchantment" but rather "Left Illusions."

25. For a discussion of the nature of law and its importance for progress and liberty, see Leoni (1961) and Hayek (1973, 1976).

TACIT KNOWLEDGE AND THE REVOLUTION IN THE PHILOSOPHY OF SCIENCE

I believe that science must be understood as a social phenomenon, a gutsy, human enterprise, not the work of robots programmed to collect pure information. I also present this view as an upbeat for science, not as a gloomy epitaph for a noble hope sacrificed on the altar of human limitations. Science, since people must do it, is a socially embedded activity. It progresses by hunch, vision, and intuition.... Facts are not pure and unsullied bits of information; culture also influences what we see and how we see it. Theories, moreover, are not inexorable inductions from facts. The most creative theories are often imaginative visions imposed upon facts; the source of imagination is also strongly cultural. This argument, although still anathema to many practicing scientists, would, I think, be accepted by nearly every historian of science. In advancing it, however, I do not ally myself with an overextension now popular in some historical circles: the purely relativistic claim that scientific change only reflects the modification of social contexts, that truth is a meaningless notion outside cultural assumptions, and that science can therefore provide no enduring answers. As a practicing scientist, I share the credo of my colleagues; I believe that a factual reality exists and that science, though often in an obtuse and erratic manner, can learn about it.

Stephen Jay Gould (1981: 16)

[While] science is without doubt the most powerful revolutionary force in our world, no one directs that force. For science is a process of submission, in which the mind does not dictate to nature but seeks out and then bows to nature's laws, letting its conclusions be guided by that which *is*, independent of our will.

Jonathan Schell (1982: 105)

247

The central argument of this book employs an analogy between scientific and market processes of discovery in which the role of tacit knowledge in both processes was stressed. I relied upon the growth-of-knowledge literature in the philosophy of science in my support of F. A. Hayek's and Michael Polanyi's contention that scientific knowledge rests on foundations that are necessarily tacit.

It must be admitted, however, that many of the writers in this growth-of-knowledge literature have explicitly dissociated themselves from Polanyi's position. Many of the leading new philosophers of science, such as followers of Popper and Lakatos, would strenuously object to the characterization I have given in the text to the significance of their work.[1] The purpose of this appendix is to delve a bit more deeply into these philosophical developments and to show why these writers' work lends support to the theory of tacit knowledge, despite their own statements to the contrary.

Until fairly recently any philosophical discussion of the justification of claims to scientific knowledge was, if not prohibited, at least frowned upon as itself rather unscientific. Philosophy, like the social sciences, was denigrated as one of those "soft sciences" in which the exacting standards of true sciences like physics and chemistry could not be met. Idle philosophical speculation perhaps suited those for whom the rigor of science was too demanding, but it was unbecoming to real scientists. One might be patronizingly tolerant of those who find themselves unable to handle the differential calculus or the delicate and demanding work of the laboratory, and who therefore spend their time spinning theories out of their heads. But surely a real scientist should refrain from joining the philosophers' endless disputes over the nature of "truth" or "goodness."

But by denying legitimacy to all that they deride as metaphysical discussion, indeed even to all examinations of the mind per se, scientists had undermined the foundations not only of dogmatic belief but of scientific belief as well. By retreating from the field of philosophical self-justification in order to get on with the undoubtedly important job of doing their respective science's research, scientists had implicitly relied on a faulty "objectivist" view of knowledge and left themselves and their work extremely vulnerable to a powerful critique from the philosophical flank. As skeptical critics from David Hume to Herbert Marcuse had been charging, the philosophical justification for science that had always been relied upon, whether explicitly or not, has been subject to some rather serious objections that call into question even the most firmly established results of scientific research.

Fortunately, some of the most discerning scientists and historians of science have awakened to this danger and have tried to formulate a justification of scientific knowledge that is immune to the skeptics' critique. In particular, the publication of Thomas Kuhn's *Structure of Scientific Revolutions* launched a thoroughgoing revolution regarding the proper grounds for the legitimacy of scientific methods, which has resulted by and large in a defeat of objectivism within philosophy, if not yet in science as a whole. As is being increasingly recognized, methodological questions cannot be avoided; they can only be begged. When scientists concentrate only on what they are doing, and not on whether their results are valid or why, they thereby endanger the very foundations of the enterprise of science.

Before the recent turmoil in the philosophy of science, the dominant approaches to the justification of knowledge were objectivist, in the sense discussed in Chapter 3; that is, they strove to provide a solid, rational foundation for science that made it immune from controversy, free of any appeals to authority, and altogether independent of personal belief as such. Scientists gather facts, period. They doubt every claim until it has been proven, after which reasonable doubt is impossible. Some such attitude is still prevalent today, if largely implicit, in most practicing scientists' views of their theories' justification. The standard of the complete provability of all science has been, if not that which is either actually practiced or explicitly defended in philosophical circles, nonetheless that to which most scientists still claim allegiance as the ideal.

The basis of this objectivist attitude goes back to the beginnings of modern science, when it was first achieving its welcome victories over religious dogma. It came to be thought that the rise of scientific methods represented the abandonment of *belief*, as such, and its replacement with hard, logically unassailable, and empirically proven facts. A scientist does not merely believe in his theory; he knows it to be true. He refuses in principle—and indeed this is supposed to be his highest principle—to adhere to any idea that has not undergone complete and rigorous testing. Only that which is firmly and unambiguously established, only that which is above mere belief and is clearly demonstrable to any observer, in short, only that which is *objective*, is deemed worthy of the scientists' assent.

Among the exacting standards of scientific objectivity has been the dual insistence upon "complete articulation" and "conclusive testability," that is, in the first instance, the complete articulation of any claim in terms of a rigorous model in which all underlying assumptions have been clearly specified, which then, in the second instance, can be subjected to extensive empirical testing. Only theories that survive the twofold norm of formal logical completeness and extensive empirical verification can ascend to the status of proven scientific knowledge. It is because religious dogmas, ethical systems, and other nonscientific claims to knowledge cannot meet these stringent norms that they are refused entry into the exclusive ranks of science, and it is through this very exclusivity that science has achieved its astonishing progress over the last two hundred years.

Many modern philosophers of science would argue, however, that the kinds of objectivist standards that earlier philosophers had spelled out for physical scientists, and whose obvious violation has earned social scientists that insulting adjective "soft," are in fact so tough that *none* of what we call science, whether "hard" or not, could meet their criteria. Both goals, that of complete articulation of all assumptions and that of thorough empirical testing, are so onerous that were scientists to take them seriously they would be obliged to admit that they have as yet produced no scientific knowledge whatever. But the clear alternative to a retreat into such sterile skepticism is the possibility of substituting a standard for science that is *not* impossibly stringent. Thus, while some of what follows may appear to be an attack against the citadel of science by undermining the standards it uses for justifying its claims to knowledge, it is in fact an attempt to use contemporary work in philosophy to rescue scientists from these false standards.

The first part of this attempt will be to elaborate on the role of "tacit knowledge" in the sciences, thereby overthrowing the requirement of complete articulation. The next part will be to show that the explicit "demarcation" criteria, by which scientists claim they sharply distinguish their empirically founded methods of persuasion from the nonempirical methods of others, do not hold up. What distinguishes science from other pursuits has more to do with certain attributes of the scientists' attitudes and values, and with the evolutionary processes of interaction taking place among members of the scientific community, than it does with any specifiable features or explicit logical criteria of theories or methods. This undermines the criterion of conclusive testability.

The idea that there could be such a thing as scientific knowledge that is unarticulated seems at first to fly in the face of our most basic conceptions of what such knowledge is all about. Surely it is the primary task of any effort aimed at expanding our knowledge, whether it is in the pure sciences, in the applied sciences, or in everyday life, to articulate ideas in a form that can be understood by others. What cannot be articulated cannot be introduced to the community of fellow scientists. It remains a merely personal belief of the person who claims to have this inexpressible knowledge, and cannot be added to what we call the body of science. When a person cannot say what he or she claims to know, why should the rest of the scientific community accredit that person's beliefs with the label "knowledge," a term which, after all, we like to reserve for ideas that we together hold to be true? If a person's beliefs are inexpressible, then we cannot judge their truth content. Indeed, even Polanyi makes it the "essential *logical* difference" between his two kinds of knowledge, that "we can critically reflect on something explicitly stated, in a way in which we cannot reflect on our tacit awareness of an experience." This immunity of inarticulate knowledge to the crucially important process of mutual criticism suggests, even to this leading advocate of the validity of tacit knowledge, that "all the towering superiority of man over animals is due almost entirely to man's gift of speech" (Polanyi 1958b: 13–14).

Given this tremendous importance of articulate knowledge, it was an understandable, if not a strictly logical, development when scientists adopted the objectivist view that we owe all our intellectual achievements to articulate knowledge alone and that "any personal participation in our scientific account of the universe [is] a residual flaw which should be completely eliminated in due course" (Polanyi 1958b: 18). To be completely consistent from this perspective, we ought to deny epistemological legitimacy to any beliefs not *fully* articulated. We should aspire to the reformulation of all sciences into the rigorous language of mathematics so that, like geometry or number theory, all the implicit assumptions underlying any statement in the theory can be made explicit. The ideal theory is seen as the completely formalized model, in which nothing is left to the imagination, in which such elements of primitive science as controversy and interpretation can be forever expunged by the force of the unquestionable certitude and completeness of a mathematical system. The purpose of formalization is taken to be to replace all the subjective or personal elements in scientific discourse. The epitome of such formalization is seen to be a fully axiomatized system such as geometry, in which no hidden assumptions can play havoc with the objective validity of the theory.

But as Polanyi's work has shown, the very process of interpreting, of applying, and of constructing a formal system are creative acts that require active imagination and keen alertness to new insights on the part of the person involved. And, as is being increasingly recognized, creativity is inherently an unformalized process, a process that plays a role in the use of any formal, articulated statement, but the validity of which depends on unformalizable, unarticulated processes. The validity of a formal system or a carefully articulated statement cannot rest on the firm foundations of completely objective criteria of rigorous proof, for no formal system can stand on its own feet. Rather, the validity of all of our articulated knowledge rests on nothing more or less than the personal commitment of the members of the scientific community. Contrary to the objectivist philosophy, science cannot divorce itself from belief by supplying irrefutable statements that can be formally derived from undeniable facts; contrary to that philosophy, controversy is not an embarrassing lack of certitude appropriate to the prescientific state of a discipline. Instead, we should recognize that all science is a consensus of firmly held beliefs on the part of a community that defines itself by its commitment to discovering and articulating scientific truth, and that controversy is a necessary process in such a community for reaching such a consensus.

But surely it should be possible eventually to extend our articulation to override these limitations. Indeed, it has been suggested, this has been done with such fully axiomatized systems in mathematics as number theory and geometry, where every statement is systematically derived from a limited set of fundamental axioms. If this can be done for arithmetic, why not for all systematic knowledge? The answer to this, which came as quite a surprise to the mathematicians themselves, is that not even arithmetic and geometry can boast this achievement of complete articulability.

Alfred North Whitehead's example (cited in Chapter 3) of "$1 + 1 = 2$" (asking if we could know even this if we could not rely on an unarticulated background of knowledge) had been chosen with good reason. He and Bertrand Russell had attempted to provide a completely formalized axiomatic system for number theory in their magnum opus *Principia Mathematica*. But, as the mathematical community now concedes, Kurt Gödel proved not only that Whitehead and Russell's ambitious attempt failed (because there are true statements in number theory that are unprovable within their system). Even more profoundly, he also proved that "the axiomatic method has certain inherent limitations, which rule out the possibility that even the ordinary arithmetic of the integers can ever be fully axiomatized" (Nagel and Newman 1958: 6).

It is certainly one of the great ironies in the development of modern epistemology that just when the formal mathematical mode for the expression of ideas was being emulated by all the sciences as the ideal in certitude, rigor, and completeness, simultaneous developments within mathematics itself rigorously demonstrated the contrary: that no fully formalized system can possibly be "complete," and that the certitude and rigor of any such system have to be established from outside of the formal framework itself. Gödel proved that we cannot decide from within a formal deductive system such as arithmetic or geometry whether any set of axioms composing that system is internally contradictory or not. That is, any formal system is inherently and seriously limited in what it can say about itself; it must rely on analysis from outside itself in order to judge internal consistency of its own foundations. This problem can be temporarily resolved by devising a richer, more encompassing formal system which includes the original one as a subset and which, being more powerful, can answer the questions that are unresolvable within the narrower system. But this only pushes the problem one step further, since this new formal system cannot resolve all the new questions it raises about itself. It turns out that the very complexities one must add to a formal system to make it capable of resolving Gödelian ambiguities will themselves add even more Gödelian ambiguities. In any sufficiently rich formal and consistent system there are an infinite number of statements which are true but which cannot be resolved within that system.

The suggestiveness of Gödel's Proof for the theory of knowledge has been noted by a number of writers, including both Polanyi (1958b: 259-60) and Hayek (1962: 62). The fundamental inability of any formal system to resolve questions that the human mind *can* resolve suggests that our knowledge is in principle unformalizable — that there must always be an inarticulate component even of the most carefully articulated pieces of knowledge. Hayek talks in this context about unspecifiable rules of operation that guide mental processes, while Polanyi refers to tacit maxims of thought underlying the act of articulating an idea, but both are describing the same phenomenon. As Hayek put it, "Gödel's theorem is but a special case of a more general principle applying to all conscious and particularly all rational processes, namely the principle that among their determinants there must be some rules which cannot be stated or even be conscious."

The conduct of the enterprise of science depends entirely on the performance of such tacit skills. Positive rules of proper scientific method have never been satisfactorily written down in a manner that covers everyone from Copernicus to Darwin to Einstein. But although serious mistakes have been made by the scientific community, it is always alert to the exercise of "bad science." Astrology or ESP cannot be *proven* wrong in an objective way; they can only be deprived of *belief* (through persuasion) by scientists. While there is no one correct scientific method, a good scientist can often enough tell—in an inarticulate way—when a crackpot theory is proffered to the scientific community, and the very survival of science depends on what might be called "dogmatic" rejection of theories that are believed *in advance of study* to be fundamentally illegitimate. Scientists cannot afford the time and other scarce resources to chase down every anomaly even in their own work, much less investigate the claims of every psychic researcher and paranormal investigator who decides to challenge the laws of physics. But even this necessary rejection by science of supernatural theories cannot be said to rest on fully articulated proofs, say, that extrasensory perception does not exist; it depends rather on the scientists' skillful judgment that some theories are unworthy of much serious attention.[2]

To say that knowledge has a tacit dimension is not to say that scientists should spend their time articulating arguments of the form, "I assert proposition A not because of explicit evidence $a_1 - a_n$, but simply on the grounds that I have an inarticulate hunch," or "I perceive entity B not as a list of specifiable attributes $b_1 - b_n$, but as an intuitively perceived 'whole'." But as Hayek (1962: 54) pointed out,

> It is entirely consistent, on the one hand, to deny that "wholes" which are intuitively perceived by the scientist may legitimately figure in his explanations and, on the other, to insist that the perception of such wholes by the persons whose interactions are the object of investigation must form a datum for scientific analysis.

It is one thing to recognize that any attempt at articulation is necessarily fated to be incomplete because it inherently rests on tacit assumptions, and quite another to sabotage the attempt to make ideas explicit by substituting intuitive notions into the part of an argument where some articulated statement belongs. The aim of any articulated statement is to render largely inarticulate ideas more explicit in some respect. The person is applying what Polanyi calls a "focal awareness" on some aspects of his understanding by trying to render them as explicit as possible. But in this very process he must be directing his "subsidiary awareness" elsewhere to accomplish this act of articulation. He must employ assumptions and rules or maxims of thought of which he is unaware, or at least only subsidiarily aware, as the means to accomplishing the end of articulation (Polanyi 1958a: 55–57).

One important implication that Polanyi draws from the fact that all articulate knowledge rests on tacit foundations is that the purpose of constructing formal systems must not be viewed as a way of *replacing* inexplicit knowledge with explicit knowledge, or as a way of attaining some sort of fully articulated truth immune from controversy. Rather, building a formal system and explicitly articulating an idea are viewed as ways of enhancing our understanding, of expanding and sharpening our (mostly inarticulate) grasp on reality, and of groping toward an ever elusive truth rather than hoping to finally attain it.

The aim of philosophers of science had originally been to develop a strictly logical foundation for knowing and to dispense with concepts condemned as psychological, such as "belief" and "judgment." This original endeavor can now be pronounced a failure. The collapse of a strict logic of science has been considered a disaster by many philosophers of science, but not so by Polanyi (1969: 156):

> I suggest that we transform this retreat into a triumph, by the simple device of changing camp. Let us recognize that tacit knowing is the fundamental power of the mind, which creates explicit knowing, lends meaning to it and controls its uses. Formalization of tacit knowing immensely expands the powers of the mind, by creating a machinery of precise thought, but it also opens up new paths to intuition; any attempt to gain complete control of thought by explicit rules is self-contradictory, systematically misleading and culturally destructive. The pursuit of formalization will find its true place in a tacit framework.

Thus the aim of this theory of knowledge is by no means to disparage formal theorizing or the clear articulation of ideas, but rather to indicate their proper role as tools for extending human knowledge where the latter is understood to necessarily include unformalized, inarticulate components. For Hayek and Polanyi the main task of science is still the construction and use of formal theories, the explicit rendering of ideas in the form of carefully articulated statements. The point is that little progress can be made entirely from the inside of a formal framework; it is the unformalized *use* of formal systems, the inarticulate judgments about how to articulate, and how to interpret the articulation of others that make formal systems and articulated statements useful in the pursuit of knowledge. As Polanyi (1958a: 83) put it, "The mere manipulation of symbols . . . is effective only because it assists the inarticulate mental powers exercised by reading off their result."

But if it is accepted that all knowledge necessarily rests on tacit foundations, it can be shown that this implies not only that the first objectivist criterion of knowledge—complete articulation—must be abandoned, but also that the second criterion—conclusive testability—will be sabotaged as well. For a test to be conclusive each of its conceivable outcomes must be classifiable in advance as confirming instances, falsifying instances, or irrelevant instances, with respect to the theory being tested. But this, Kuhn ([1962] 1970: 16) has shown, cannot be accomplished

> unless the theory is *fully articulated* logically and unless the terms through which it attaches to nature are sufficiently defined to determine their applicability in each possible case. In practice, however, no scientific theory satisfies these rigorous demands. (Emphasis added.)

Just as the "exalted valuation" of formal, mathematical knowledge was ironically undermined by developments in formal mathematics itself, so was that of conclusive empirical testability ironically undermined by empirical investigations of the history of science. The hypothesis that the empirical testing of hypotheses was the way scientists choose among theories has itself been unable to pass the empirical test. Scientists had claimed, without factual demonstration, that their criteria for selecting one theory over another were firmly grounded in unambiguous, objective, and reproducible laboratory experiments. Recent studies of the history of science such as those conducted by J. B. Conant, Alexandre Koyre, Thomas Kuhn, Imre

Lakatos, Mary Hesse, Stephen Toulmin, and Michael Polanyi have found that the evidence belies this self-image and that in fact scientific theories have always been selected by means of a complex process of persuasion in which clearcut experimental tests play, at best, only a subsidiary role (Lakatos 1970: 151).

Long before this historical evidence had its impact, two philosophical difficulties had plagued objectivist efforts to establish that scientific theories had been selected strictly according to facts derived from empirical tests. The first, the famous problem of induction, questions whether we are logically justified in concluding from repeated empirical results of tests anything at all about the results to be expected from future repetitions of the test. The second and perhaps even more serious problem questions whether there can be any such thing as a fact that is not itself crucially dependent on the theoretical framework used to interpret it, and therefore whether any fact can ever unambiguously decide a conflict between theories. In their efforts to answer these objections, scientists have had to back off from their earlier confident pronouncements that science, as contrasted with all other claims to knowledge, represents strictly proven propositions. Although the aim of these efforts to answer the skeptics was to patch up the wall of demarcation that was supposed to separate established, objective, scientific fact from mere subjective belief, the actual result has been a growing consensus that science itself rests on a particular sort of belief. Thus, the overthrowing of complete articulation and conclusive testability points to an entirely different justification for knowledge claims.

One of the best, and certainly among the most influential, of several attempts to answer the problem of induction was that of Karl Popper (1972). Answering the skeptics on their own terms, Popper not only admitted that we can never be sure our present scientific laws will extend into the future, but he elevated this attitude of universal doubt into a veritable creed of the scientific method. We must never accept theories unless they are amenable to disproof by empirical tests. Those that have so far survived such skepticism are to be held not as certain, but as conjectural knowledge. Skepticism, according to Popper, is not science's adversary but its greatest ally. Nobody, not even a Newton or an Einstein, has the last word in science. And the true scientist is seen as highly dubious even about his own theories. He is obliged to try to come up with theories that show a strong likelihood of being falsified and then to devote the bulk of his effort to refuting them. Only theories that endure this ordeal of sincere and strenuous efforts to falsify them are counted as scientific knowledge.[3] Nonscience, then, is seen as composed of continued belief in theories that had been unambiguously disproven, or of adherence to theories that are empty of empirical content in the sense that they are not falsifiable by any conceivable empirical outcome.

Despite the fact that Popper has gone a long way toward clarifying some important aspects of the scientific attitude, it is not clear that his criterion of falsification is any more objective in practice than the verification approaches it seeks to replace. It is true that a single clear factual counterexample would logically refute a theory while countless clear confirmations cannot logically establish it. But where in practice can we ever find such a clear counterexample? When can we safely abandon the search for intervening factors outside of the experimental system, for example, conditions affecting the accuracy of the instruments? In other words we find ourselves back at our second major problem: Facts are not pure or primitive but are invariably theory-laden, as Popper himself often emphasized. This means that when we try to judge the validity of any given theory, we are not simply testing it against the facts. We are necessarily testing it against other theories, including those that underlie the experimental procedures being used to determine the facts (see Lakatos 1970: 116–22).

But if what is really going on is a judgment between theories, and not factual verification or falsification at all, then a second problem with Popper's approach suggests itself. Is universal skepticism really enough? While a sincere willingness to change his or her mind in the face of intellectually compelling criticism is an indispensable attribute of a true scientist, this is not to say that any amount of positive commitment to one's own theory is undesirable. If we are always weighing theories against other theories, we must, when we doubt some theory, be implicitly denying it on the basis of some other theory in which belief is held. Universal skepticism does not lead to belief in theories that survive grueling empirical tests, but rather to doubts even about the validity of the testing procedures themselves. Yet the attitude of scientists, even as Popper depicts it, seems to be one not simply of doubting but of also positively *believing* (although Popper seems to resist putting it this way) in whatever is considered the best available current theory.

Popper's position may be seen as a halfway retreat from objectivism whereby the personal role of the skillful scientist is permitted but only in one part of scientific activities, in the formation of hypotheses. Any conjecture, however arbitrary, must then be subjected to ruthless, objective criticism in the other activities, in one's attempts to refute one's own hypotheses. Thus, as Polanyi writes, a semblance of objectivism is retained by "dividing the process of discovery sharply into the choice of a hypothesis and the testing of the chosen hypothesis" in which the former "is deemed to be inexplicable by any rational procedure," while the latter "is recognized as a strict procedure forming the scientist's essential task."

This dichotomization of science into two completely separate domains, conjecture and refutation, has done damage to our understanding of both. The logic of scientific discovery, which it was Popper's initial purpose to explicate, becomes not only nonobjective but completely inexplicable, while the logic of theory testing remains wedded to objectivistic standards that can never be met. Moreover, theory testing becomes divorced from discovery processes altogether and loses any relationship to the human imagination, to tacit skills, or to cognitive commitments of any kind.

In the Polanyi view tacit discovery processes play an integral role not only in the initial sighting of a problem and the quest for and drawing of a tentative solution, but also in the acceptance or *holding* of a conclusion to be an established fact. In all these roles, which in any particular instance can be found thoroughly intertwined, the scientist must form expectations based on an intuitive sense of what new evidence future scientific effort may uncover.

To accept a solution as valid is to hold to a specific expectation of future scientific developments—that they will not contradict this solution or define away the problem it was supposed to solve—even though such future developments cannot be known before their time. Hence both conjecture and refutation are deeply imbued with subjective or personal judgments. They both demand a skillful performance on the part of the scientist.

Although from Popper's perspective this conclusion may seem to represent a devaluing of the refutation phase of the scientists' activities, in Polanyi's view it constitutes an elevation of that phase. The testing of hypotheses is not a mechanical procedure in which disinterested scientists subject arbitrary conjectures to clearcut objective challenges. Rather, it involves the active personal participation of the scientists' *imagination*. Indeed, what this view of knowledge intends is not to devalue the refutations phase but to revalue the conjectures phase of scientific efforts. While hypothesis formation is necessarily based on inarticulate elements, it is not thereby arbitrary and entirely inexplicable by the human mind. Popper's approach would leave this crucial phase of scientific work unexamined, claiming it to lie outside the confines of objective science. Polanyi's approach (1972: 45–46) widens those confines:

> The fact that scientists can espy good problems is therefore a faculty as essential to science as is the capacity to solve problems and to prove such solutions to be right. In other words, the capacity rightly to choose a line of thought the end of which is vastly indeterminate, is as much part of the scientific method as is the power of assuring the exactitude of the conclusions eventually arrived at. And both faculties consist in recognizing real coherence in nature and sensing its indeterminate implications for the future.

The influential student of Popper, Imre Lakatos, in the face of the several criticisms of Popper's views, has tried to retreat to a second line of defense of what he seems to think is an objectivist position. In fact, by making the criteria of theory-choice considerably more realistic, he has actually reinforced the very Kuhn-Polanyi type of approach he so stridently condemns. Lakatos rejects falsification and convincingly argues that scientists never judge the validity of a single theory in isolation. Rather, their judgment amounts to a sophisticated weighing of the relative "explanatory power" of competing sets of theories or "research programs," which largely correspond to Kuhn's "paradigms." The *series* of theories constituting a research program can only be assessed as a whole when viewed as a sequence of "problem-shifts," which are described as reformulations of the theory aimed at improving its explanatory power by accounting for former anomalies. Lakatos concedes that it is impossible to judge a given theory as falsified on the basis of any clearcut criteria. Instead, we are urged to refine our explicit criteria for *retrospectively* assessing competing research programs on the basis of a determination as to which alternative contains more "progressive" problem-shifts. Essentially a problem-shift is deemed retrogressive if it seems to be a mere defense of a patched-up theory rather than an improvement that predicts new facts.

The insights Lakatos has given us into the history of science are an indispensable resource for anyone interested in the philosophy of science, but the antiobjectivist implications of his work do not appear to have been noticed by him or by many of his supporters.[4] In fact, his criteria for theory-choice do not represent the objective rules for demarcation that he seems to think they do, but are better understood as important maxims or values that scientists are urged to pursue by means of their own skillful judgments (see Kuhn [1962] 1970: 262).[5] There are no units for objectively measuring explanatory or heuristic power. Neither can we count and compare the "novel facts" that are predicted by two theories without a tacit judgment about what sorts of predicted facts should count as relevant or how to weigh facts of varying significance. Furthermore, Lakatos's admission that his criteria can only be applied with hindsight after research programs have had a fair chance to generate some progressive problem-shifts actually deprives these criteria of their function, if they are supposed to be objective demarcation criteria. The scientific community cannot wait for the historian's perspective in order to make decisions about which potential avenues of research to investigate and which to dismiss without examination.

Thus, although Popper and Lakatos explicitly resist this interpretation of what they have accomplished, I think Thomas Kuhn's assessment ([1962] 1970: 198–99) of Popper accurately applies to Lakatos as well: "I am not clear that what Sir Karl has given us is a logic of knowledge at all. . . . I shall suggest that, though equally valuable, it is something else entirely. Rather than a logic, Sir Karl has provided an ideology; rather than methodological rules, he has supplied procedural maxims."

In any case the study of the history of science reveals that most successful scientists have been passionately committed to their respective theories. Indeed, Polanyi argues that because theories or any articulated knowledge are tools we use for the enhancement of our mostly inarticulate understanding of the world, it is inherent in their nature that we cannot simultaneously use them and criticize them. We *see* the world from within our theories and hence we can *either* study a theory itself, for which we have to rely on some other metatheory, *or* we can trust it and put it to use studying the world. We cannot do both at the same time.

You cannot use your spectacles to scrutinize your spectacles. A theory is like a pair of spectacles; you examine things by it, and your knowledge of it lies in this very use of it. You dwell in it as you dwell in your own body and in the tools by which you amplify the powers of your body. (Polanyi and Prosch 1975: 37)

Similar conclusions have been arrived at in Kuhn's work, in which the history of scientific progress is broken down into two kinds of phases, normal science and extraordinary science. From Kuhn's detailed study of the history of actual scientific practice, it appears that scientists normally view the world through the "spectacles" of a broadly understood and shared paradigm which defines legitimate problems and tools and from within which attempts are made to resolve existing anomalies. But occasionally anomalies turn into analytical monstrosities threatening the paradigm itself, thereby encouraging the formulation of a whole new paradigm and a revolutionary struggle between adherents of the new view of the world and the old. Whereas problem solving *within* a given paradigm can conform to definite standards supplied by that world view, the struggle *between* paradigms is so fundamental that the standards themselves are usually under dispute. They speak from "incommensurable viewpoints." The new paradigm cannot prove its worth by any clear-cut criteria. Rather, "Each party must try, by persuasion, to convert the other" (Kuhn [1962] 1970: 200).[6]

This does not mean that such persuasion is basically nonrational but only that "debates over theory-choice cannot be cast in a form that fully resembles logical or mathematical proof" (Kuhn [1962] 1970: 198–99). Or as Polanyi might put it, debate over basic theories involves tacit judgments on the part of the scientist as to which theory explains better or seems more promising. There are innumerable hints in the new paradigm that suggest to its adherents possibilities for future discoveries, but these possibilities in the nature of the case cannot yet be articulated; if they could they would not be future discoveries. Thus Kuhn concludes,

The man who embraces a new paradigm at an early stage must often do so in defiance of the evidence provided by problem-solving. He must, that is, have faith that the new paradigm will succeed with the many large problems that confront it, knowing only that the older paradigm has failed with a few. A decision of that kind can only be made on faith. (p. 158)

But this ultimate reliance on a kind of faith or belief does not reduce science to arbitrary whim. What makes the enterprise of science successful is not the existence of any formal logical proof of the validity of its results. It rather consists, as Kuhn ([1962] 1970: 8) puts it, in certain "characteristics of the scientific community" and in the processes of "revolutionary competition" between the proponents of different paradigms.[7] Kuhn has not spelled out what these community characteristics should be, but simply urges philosophers of science to pursue this issue. These matters, however, have been investigated by Polanyi and Hayek, and have been explained as a special case of a general theory of "spontaneous order" that may constitute an entirely new kind of justification of scientific, as well as other, forms of knowing.

It might still seem that the significance of these philosophical matters for the possibilities of planning a nation's economy cannot possibly be very great. Perhaps the historian Halevy supplied an important clue to the connection between planning and the philosophy of science when he wrote, "To know positivism and socialism at their source, we must study the school in which the two words were first used." That school was in fact the one that first formulated the ideal of national economic planning: the Saint-Simonians (Halevy 1965: 21). Along with the positivist or objectivist conception of scientific knowledge happened also to come an explicit role for the intellectuals, the *carriers* of such knowledge, as social engineers.

It may have been no accident that objectivist methodologies like positivism and the notion of economic planning were born together. Quite possibly they constitute two inseparable components of a single worldview. If so, it would not be surprising if the defeat of objectivism within the philosophy of science that is now taking place will bring planning down with it.

In particular, it might be argued that it was the intellectuals' belief in objective, certain, fully articulable knowledge that led so many to want to use their supposedly superior knowledge to plan the economy. The ongoing revolution in the philosophy of science may be depriving intellectuals of the justification upon which their rise to a special position of power was based. The justification for raising *the intellectuals* to the position of *The Intelligentsia* is based on an epistemological assumption that is itself under very serious question among philosophers. The intelligentsia were to rule because they could claim to be guiding society according to the latest and most advanced developments of modern science. Their legitimacy, such as it was, was to derive from this knowledge claim. The experts, armed with proven knowledge, could exercise special powers to achieve what they claimed the lay persons could not voluntarily do for themselves.

But if knowledge—whether scientific or economic—is based on tacit skills, if it is inextricably *personal*, and, most important, if it depends upon the free play of open debate and contention, then the intelligentsia's justification for special powers evaporates. For the very freedom of inquiry on which the success of science rests is in this case inconsistent with the bestowal of special powers to anyone, including the scientists themselves.

NOTES TO APPENDIX

1. See, for example, Lakatos (1970: 115) and Lakatos (1978: 112–17), where Kuhn and Polanyi are dismissed as social psychologists and elitists.
2. Scientists do manage to find the time occasionally to carefully consider the claims of "fringe-scientists," as in the pages of *The Skeptical Inquirer*. But it is evident from the very persuasive arguments of that journal that while virtually every claim taken up is found to be ridiculously unfounded, the convincing refutations rarely take the form of a rigorous, objectivist proof. Furthermore, it is admitted by the editors that only a tiny fraction of all the paranormal claims being made every day in the media can ever be explicitly examined by scientists.

   Thus it must be seen as an *essential* function of the scientific community to apply a kind of internal censorship over its own institutions. Its journals must exclude what are deemed crackpot theories from publication if their pages are not to be dominated by valueless writings of no interest to the scientific community. This is not to deny that such exclusion is very risky and has often delayed recognition of genuine contributions of a revolutionary nature. It is only to insist that the scientists cannot afford to allocate resources to the serious consideration of all claims.

   This point can only be denied by ignoring the fact of economic scarcity. For example, Joseph Agassi (1975: 157) rejects the Polanyi–Kuhn view as "authoritarian" because it "supports censorship in order to protect the scientific literature from being flooded by worthless writing." This he finds "unacceptable" on the grounds that while censorship is harmful, "the flood of valueless writings is harmless." This would only be true if worthless publications used up no scarce resources, including the time of scientists, which could be used for alternative purposes. (A former editor of the *Journal of*

Philosophy used to say that not a month went by but that he received at least one article squaring the circle or trisecting the angle.)

It might also be worth mentioning that this kind of censorship has nothing to do with "academic freedom," still less with political freedom. After all, the scientific community is a voluntary community. Those regarded today as crackpots are free to constitute—indeed do constitute—their own communities, in which they will find themselves exercising a similar censorship in their own journals. It is also conceivable that some such group might ultimately vindicate its claims, and find itself willy-nilly accepted as a part of the scientific community. It may be that something of the sort is happening in the case of chiropractic.

3. Lakatos (1978: 151) calls this attitude of trying to refute one's theory with the first contrary evidence that comes along "dangerous methodological cruelty."

4. See Marvin Harris (1980: 19–28), who treats Lakatos as a rescuer of a kind of objectivist view that is then used to justify a highly questionable materialistic conception of social science.

5. Lakatos (1970: 127, 129, 131, etc.) repeatedly uses the word "decision" to refer to judgments which he seems to think are objective, but which in every case I would argue must be tacit.

6. Kuhn has suffered much abuse for using this word "incommensurable" and has explained in response that he does not deny that accurate theory translation from one paradigm to another is always possible in principle. He is only stressing that it is extremely difficult, involving tacit skills on the part of the translator, skills not reducible to a clear-cut formal procedure or algorithm. See also Kuhn (1977: 320–39).

7. See in particular the work of Toulmin (1972: 261–318), who has provided a fascinating evolutionary-sociological analysis of the scientific community which is highly complementary to the Polanyi/Hayek view of science.

REFERENCES

Adler, Mortimer J. 1967. *The Difference of Man and the Difference It Makes.* New York: Holt, Rinehart & Winston.

Agassi, Joseph. 1975. "Genius in Science." *Philosophy of Social Sciences* (June).

Allen, G.C. 1981. *The Japanese Economy.* New York: St. Martin's Press.

Alpern, David M. 1981. "Mr. Fixit for the Cities." *Newsweek*, May 4.

Alperovitz, Gar, and Jeff Faux. 1977. "Building a Democratic Economy." Reprint. *The Progressive.*

Anderson, Martin. 1978. *Welfare.* Stanford: Hoover Institution Press.

Andreski, Stanislav. 1966. *Parasitism and Subversion: The Case of Latin America.* New York: Random House.

Arenson, Karen W. 1982. "On the Frontier of a New Economics." *New York Times*, October 31.

Armentano, Dominick T. 1982. *Antitrust and Monopoly: Anatomy of a Policy Failure.* New York: Wiley.

Asprey, Robert B. 1975. *War in the Shadows: The Guerrilla in History.* 2 vols. Garden City, N.Y.: Doubleday.

Bails, Dale G., and Larry C. Peppers. 1982. *Business Fluctuations: Forecasting Techniques and Applications.* Englewood Cliffs, N.J.: Prentice-Hall.

Barlett, P.F. 1976. "Labor Efficiency and the Mechanisms of Agricultural Evolution." *Journal of Anthropological Research* 32.

Barnett, David L. 1980. "Rebuilding America: It Will Cost Trillions." *U.S. News and World Report*, September 22.

Barrett, William. 1979. *The Illusion of Technique.* Garden City, N.Y.: Doubleday.

Barron, John, and Anthony Paul. 1977. *Murder of a Gentle Land: The Untold Story of Communist Genocide in Cambodia.* New York: Crowell.

Baruch, Bernard M. 1941. *American Industry in the War: A Report of the War Industries Board.* Englewood Cliffs, N.J.: Prentice-Hall.

Bastiat, Frederic. [1850] 1978. "Free Trade and Competition." In *Western Liberalism. See* Bramsted and Melhuish 1978. New York: Longman.

Beckner, Steven K. 1983. "Panel Told Japan's Gains Not Due to MITI Policy." *Washington Times,* July 14.

Bennett, James T., and Thomas J. DiLorenzo. 1982. *Underground Government: The Off-Budget Public Sector.* Washington, D.C.: Cato Institute.

———. 1985. "A New Reconstruction Finance Corporation: Anatomy of an Anti-Industrial Policy." Draft. Forthcoming in *Labor Unions and the State: The Political Economy of Pushbutton Unionism.* Dallas: The Fisher Institute.

Bergson, Abram. 1948. "Socialist Economics." In *A Survey of Contemporary Economics,* vol. 1. Howard S. Ellis, ed. Homewood, Ill.: Richard D. Irwin.

Bluestone, Barry, and Bennett Harrison. 1982. *The Deindustrialization of America.* New York: Basic Books.

Blustein, Paul. 1980. " 'Reindustrialization,' a Vague Idea, Means a Very Clear Profit for Some." *Wall Street Journal,* August 27.

Bowles, Samuel; David M. Gordon; and Thomas E. Weisskopf. 1983. *Beyond the Waste Land: A Democratic Alternative to Economic Decline.* Garden City, N.Y.: Doubleday.

Bradley, Robert L., Jr. 1984. *Oil, Gas and Government: The U.S. Experience.* Draft. Washington, D.C.: Cato Institute.

Bramsted, E.K., and K.J. Melhuish, eds. 1978. *Western Liberalism.* New York: Longman.

Browning, Edgar. 1978. "The Marginal Welfare Cost of Income Redistribution." *Southern Economic Journal* (July): 1–17.

Browning, Frank. 1983. "Neoradicals Rethink Marxism." *Mother Jones,* January.

Buchanan, James. 1969. *Cost and Choice: An Inquiry in Economic Theory.* Chicago: University of Chicago Press.

Buell, John. 1982. "After Reaganomics, What? Democratic Socialism If We Dare." *The Progressive* (July).

Buell, John, and Tom DeLuca. 1977. "Let's Start Talking about Socialism." Reprint. *The Progressive.*

Buick, Adam. 1975. "The Myth of the Transitional Society." *Critique* 5.

Burton, John. 1981. "The Thatcher Experiment: A Requiem?" Research Monograph no. 1. *Journal of Labor Research* (August).

Business Week. 1980. "The Reindustrialization of America." Special Issue reprint from *Business Week,* June 30.

Caldwell, Bruce. 1982. *Beyond Positivism: Economic Methodology in the Twentieth Century.* London: Allen and Unwin.

Campbell, Jeremy. 1982. *Grammatical Man: Information, Entropy, Language and Life.* New York: Simon and Schuster.

Caplan, Arthur L., ed. 1978. *The Sociobiology Debate: Readings on Ethical and Scientific Issues.* New York: Harper & Row.

Carnoy, Martin, and Derek Shearer. 1980. *Economic Democracy: The Challenge of the 1980s.* Armonk, N.Y.: M.E. Sharpe.

Carnoy, Martin; Derek Shearer; and Russell Rumberger. 1983. *A New Social Contract: The Economy and Government After Reagan.* New York: Harper & Row.

Casement, Richard. 1982. "The Innovative Japanese." *Economist,* June 19.

Chibnik, M. 1980. "Working Out or Working In: The Choice Between Wage Labor and Cash Cropping in Rural Belize." *American Ethnologist* 7.

Chomsky, Noam. 1963. *Syntactic Structures.* The Hague: Mouton.

Chomsky, Noam, and Edward S. Herman. 1979. *The Washington Connection and Third World Fascism.* Boston: South End Press.

Clark, Grahame. 1977. *World Prehistory in New Perspective.* Cambridge, England: Cambridge University Press.

Clarkson, Grosvenor B. 1923. *Industrial America in the World War.* Boston: Houghton Mifflin.

Clarkson, Kenneth W. 1976. *Catalog of Research Issues for Understanding National Economic Planning.* Coral Gables, Fla.: Law and Economics Center, University of Miami.

Cliff, Tony. 1978. *Lenin.* Vol. 3, *Revolution Besieged.* London: Pluto Press.

Coase, Ronald H. 1959. "The Federal Communications Commission." *Journal of Law and Economics* (October).

Coffin, Howard E. 1916. "Industrial Organization for National Defense." *World's Work* (May).

Cohen, Stephen F. 1974. *Bukharin and the Bolshevik Revolution.* London: Wildwood House.

Cohn-Bendit, Daniel, and Gabriel Cohn-Bendit. 1968. *Obsolete Communism: The Left-Wing Alternative.* Translated by Arnold Pomerans. New York: McGraw-Hill.

Comptroller General. 1982. *Industrial Policy: Japan's Flexible Approach.* ID-82-32, U.S. General Accounting Office, Washington, D.C.

Conquest, Robert. 1972. *V.I. Lenin.* New York: Viking.

Counts, George S.; Luigi Villari; Malcolm C. Rorty; and Newton D. Baker. 1932. *Bolshevism, Fascism and Capitalism.* New Haven, Conn.: Yale University Press.

Crombie, A., ed. 1963. *Scientific Change.* New York: Basic Books.

Crosland, C.A.R. 1957. *The Future of Socialism.* London: Macmillan.

Crotty, James R., and Raford Boddy. 1975. "Who Will Plan the Planned Economy?" Reprint. *The Progressive* (February).

Cuff, Robert D. 1973. *The War Industries Board: Business–Government Relations During World War I.* Baltimore: Johns Hopkins University Press.

Daly, C. B. 1968. "Polanyi and Wittgenstein." In Langford and Poteat 1968.

Daly, John Charles, moderator. 1980. "Reindustrialization, Boon or Bane?" *AEI Forum*, September 30.

Diamond, Edwin; Norman Sandler; and Milton Mueller. 1983. *Telecommunications in Crisis: The First Amendment, Technology, and Deregulation.* Washington, D. C.: Cato Institute.

DiLorenzo, Thomas J. 1984. "The Myth of America's Declining Manufacturing Sector." *Heritage Foundation Backgrounder*, no. 321. Washington, D. C.: Heritage.

Djilas, Milovan. 1957. *The New Class: An Analysis of the Communist System.* New York: Praeger.

Domhoff, G. William. 1970. *The Higher Circles: The Governing Class in America.* New York: Random House.

Drewnowski, Jan. 1961. "The Economic Theory of Socialism: A Suggestion for Reconsideration." *Journal of Political Economy* (August).

Dreyfus, Hubert L. 1979. *What Computers Can't Do: The Limits of Artificial Intelligence.* New York: Harper & Row.

Estrin, Saul, and Peter Holmes. 1983. *French Planning in Theory and Practice.* Boston: George Allen and Unwin.

Etzioni, Amitai. 1983. *An Immodest Agenda: Rebuilding America Before the Twenty-First Century.* New York: McGraw-Hill.

Fetter, Frank A. 1977. *Capital, Interest, and Rent: Essays in the Theory of Distribution.* Kansas City, Kans.: Sheed Andrews & McMeel.

Friedman, Milton. 1953. "The Methodology of Positive Economics." In *Essays in Positive Economics.* Chicago: University of Chicago Press.

Friedman, Milton, and Anna J. Schwartz. 1963. *A Monetary History of the United States: 1867–1960.* Princeton: Princeton University Press.

Gelwick, Richard. 1977. *The Way of Discovery: An Introduction to the Thought of Michael Polanyi.* New York: Oxford University Press.

Gier, Nicholas F. 1981. *Wittgenstein and Phenomenology: A Comparative Study of the Later Wittgenstein, Husserl, Heidegger, and Merleau-Ponty.* Albany: State University of New York Press.

Gilder, George. 1982. "The Entrepreneur." *Manhattan Report*, October.

Ginsburg, Woodrow. 1982. "An Economic Recovery Program." Washington, D. C.: Americans for Democratic Action.

Gladwin, C. H. 1979. "Production Functions and Decision Models: Complementary Models." *American Ethnologist* 6.

Goldstein, Walter, ed. 1978. *Planning, Politics, and the Public Interest.* New York: Columbia University Press.

Goodman, John C. 1980. *The Regulation of Medical Care: Is the Price Too High?* Washington, D. C.: Cato Institute.

Gould, Stephen Jay. 1980. *The Panda's Thumb: More Reflections in Natural History*. New York: W.W. Norton.

_____. 1981. *The Mismeasure of Man*. Excerpts reprinted in *Skeptical Inquirer* 7 (Winter 1982/1983).

Grant, James. 1983. *Bernard Baruch: The Adventures of a Wall Street Legend*. New York: Simon and Schuster.

Gray, John. 1984. *Hayek on Liberty*. Oxford: Basil Blackwell.

Greer, Colin, and Frank Riessman. 1981. "If Not Now, When?" Review of Carnoy and Shearer 1980. *Social Policy* (January/February).

Grinder, Walter E., and Alan Fairgate. 1975. "The New Deal's RFC Rides Again." Council for a Competitive Economy, Perspectives on Public Policy Series. Reprint. *Reason* (July).

Gross, Bertram. 1979. "Anti-Inflation for Progressives." *Nation*, June 23.

Halevy, Elie. 1965. *The Era of Tyrannies*. Garden City, N.Y.: Doubleday.

Hardin, Clifford M., and Arthur T. Denzau. 1981. "The Unrestrained Growth of Federal Credit Programs." Center for the Study of American Business, Formal Publication no. 45. St. Louis: Washington University, December.

Harrington, Michael. 1965. *The Accidental Century*. New York: Macmillan.

_____. 1982. "A Path for America: Proposals from the Democratic Left." *Dissent* (Fall).

Harris, Marvin. 1980. *Cultural Materialism: The Struggle for a Science of Culture*. New York: Vintage.

Hattiangadi, Jagdish N. 1973. "Mind and the Origin of Language." *Philosophy Forum* 14.

Hayden, Tom. 1982. *The American Future: New Visions Beyond the Reagan Administration*. New York: Washington Square Press.

Hayek, F.A. [1931] 1935. *Prices and Production*. New York: Kelley.

_____. [1933] 1966. *Monetary Theory and the Trade Cycle*. New York: Kelley.

_____. 1935. *Collectivist Economic Planning: Critical Studies on the Possibilities of Socialism*. London: Routledge.

_____. [1939] 1975. *Profits, Interest and Investment*. New York: Kelley.

_____. 1944. *The Road to Serfdom*. Chicago: University of Chicago Press.

_____. 1948. *Individualism and Economic Order*. Chicago: University of Chicago Press.

_____. [1952] 1963. *The Sensory Order*. Chicago: University of Chicago Press.

_____. 1955. *The Counter-Revolution of Science: Studies on the Abuse of Reason*. New York: Free Press of Glencoe.

_____. [1960] 1972. *The Constitution of Liberty*. Chicago: University of Chicago Press.

_____. [1962] 1967. "Rules, Perception and Intelligibility." In Hayek 1967.

_____. 1967. *Studies in Philosophy, Politics and Economics*. Chicago: University of Chicago Press.

_____. 1973. *Law, Legislation and Liberty.* Vol. 1, *Rules and Order.* Chicago: University of Chicago Press.

_____. 1976. *Law, Legislation and Liberty.* Vol. 2, *The Mirage of Social Justice.* Chicago: University of Chicago Press.

_____. 1978. *New Studies in Philosophy, Politics, Economics and the History of Ideas.* Chicago: University of Chicago Press.

_____. 1979. *Law, Legislation and Liberty.* Vol. 3, *The Political Order of a Free People.* Chicago: University of Chicago Press.

_____. 1982. "The Ethics of Liberty and Property." Mont Pelerin Society meetings. Forthcoming as chap. 4 in *The Fatal Conceit.*

Hazlitt, Henry. 1973. *The Conquest of Poverty.* New Rochelle, N.Y.: Arlington House.

Heilbroner, Robert. 1982. "Does Capitalism Have a Future?" *New York Times Magazine,* August 15.

Henderson, David R. 1983. "The Myth of MITI." *Fortune,* August 8.

Hilferding, Rudolf. 1981. *Finance Capital: A Study in the Latest Phase of Capitalist Development.* London: Routledge, Kegan & Paul.

Hoff, Trygve J.B. [1949] 1981. *Economic Calculation in the Socialist Society.* Indianapolis: Liberty Press.

Hofstadter, Douglas R. 1979. *Gödel, Escher, Bach: An Eternal Golden Braid.* New York: Random House.

Holton, Gerald. 1969. "Einstein, Michelson and the 'Crucial Experiment.'" *Iris* 60.

Hoover, Herbert. [1920] 1941. "Introduction." In William C. Mullendore, *History of the United States Food Administration.* Stanford, Calif.: Stanford University Press.

Horowitz, David. 1971. *The Free World Colossus.* New York: Hill and Wang.

_____. 1979. "A Radical's Disenchantment." *Nation,* December 8.

Horwitz, Morton J. 1977. *The Transformation of American Law: 1780–1860.* Cambridge, Mass.: Harvard University Press.

Hunt, Morton. 1982. *The Universe Within.* New York: Simon and Schuster.

Hurwicz, Leonid. 1973. "The Design of Mechanisms for Resource Allocation." *American Economic Review* (May).

Johnson, Chalmers. 1982. *MITI and the Japanese Miracle.* Stanford: Stanford University Press.

Johnson, Paul. 1983. *Modern Times: The World from the Twenties to the Eighties.* New York: Harper & Row.

Jones, Basset. 1934. *Horses and Apples: A Study of Index Numbers.* New York: John Day.

Jones, Jesse H. 1951. *Fifty Billion Dollars: My Thirteen Years with the RFC 1932–1945.* New York: Macmillan.

Kirkland, Lane. 1982. "An Alternative to Reaganomics." *USA Today* magazine (May).

Kirzner, Israel M. 1973. *Competition and Entrepreneurship.* Chicago: University of Chicago Press.

_____. 1979. *Perception, Opportunity and Profit: Studies in the Theory of Entrepreneurship.* Chicago: University of Chicago Press.

Kline, Morris. 1980. *Mathematics: The Loss of Certainty.* New York: Oxford University Press.

Koestler, Arthur. 1964. *The Act of Creation.* New York: Macmillan.

Kolakowski, Leszek. 1968. *Toward a Marxist Humanism: Essays on the Left Today.* Translated by Jane Z. Peel. New York: Grove.

_____. 1981a. *Main Currents of Marxism.* Vol. 1, *The Founders.* Translated by P.S. Falla. New York: Oxford University Press.

_____. 1981b. *Main Currents of Marxism.* Vol. 2, *The Golden Age.* Translated by P.S. Falla. New York: Oxford University Press.

Kolko, Gabriel. 1963. *The Triumph of Conservatism.* New York: The Macmillan Company, The Free Press of Glencoe.

Konrad, George, and Ivan Szelenyi. 1979. *The Intellectuals on the Road to Class Power.* Translated by A. Arato and R.E. Allen. New York: Harcourt Brace Jovanovich.

Kristol, Irving. 1978. *Two Cheers for Capitalism.* New York: Basic Books.

Krueger, Anne O. 1974. "Political Economy of the Rent-Seeking Society." *American Economic Review* (June).

Kuhn, Helmut. 1968. "Personal Knowledge and the Crisis of the Philosophical Tradition." In Langford and Poteat 1968.

Kuhn, Thomas S. [1962] 1970. *The Structure of Scientific Revolutions.* 2d ed. Chicago: University of Chicago Press.

_____. 1970. "Logic of Discovery or Psychology of Research?" and "Reflections on My Critics." In Lakatos and Musgrave 1970.

_____. 1977. *The Essential Tension: Selected Studies in Scientific Tradition and Change.* Chicago: University of Chicago Press.

Lachmann, Ludwig M. 1973. "Macro-economic Thinking and the Market Economy." Hobert paper no. 56. London: Institute of Economic Affairs.

_____. 1978. *Capital and Its Structure.* Kansas City, Kans.: Sheed, Andrews and McMeel.

Lackner, J.R., and M. Garrett. 1973. "Resolving Ambiguity: Effects of Biasing Context in the Unattended Ear." *Cognition*: 359–72.

Lakatos, Imre. 1970. "Falsification and the Methodology of Scientific Research Programmes." In Lakatos and Musgrave 1970.

_____. 1978. *Philosophical Papers.* Vol. 2, *Mathematics, Science and Epistemology.* New York: McGraw-Hill.

Lakatos, Imre, and Alan Musgrave, eds. 1970. *Criticism and the Growth of Knowledge.* Cambridge, England: Cambridge University Press.

Lange, Oskar. [1938] 1964. *On the Economic Theory of Socialism*, edited by B.E. Lippincott. New York: McGraw-Hill.

Langford, Thomas A., and William H. Poteat, eds. 1968. *Intellect and Hope: Essays in the Thought of Michael Polanyi*. Durham, N.C.: Duke University Press.

Lavoie, Don. 1981. "A Critique of the Standard Account of the Socialist Calculation Debate." *Journal of Libertarian Studies* (Winter).

———. 1982. "The Market as a Procedure for Discovery and Conveyance of Inarticulate Knowledge." Center for the Study of Market Processes, Working Paper no. 2. Fairfax, Va.: George Mason University.

———. 1983. "Some Strengths in Marx's Disequilibrium Theory of Money." *Cambridge Journal of Economics* 7.

———. 1985. *Rivalry and Central Planning: The Socialist Calculation Debate Reconsidered*. New York: Cambridge University Press.

Leakey, Richard E., and Roger Lewin. 1978. *People of the Lake: Mankind and Its Beginnings*. Garden City, N.Y.: Doubleday.

Lee, Joe. 1975. "Administrators and Agriculture: Aspects of German Agricultural Policy in the First World War." In Winter 1975.

Leijonhufvud, Axel. 1981. *Information and Coordination: Essays in Macroeconomic Theory*. New York: Oxford University Press.

Lekachman, Robert. 1978. "The Inevitability of Planning." In Goldstein 1978.

———. 1982. *Greed Is Not Enough: Reaganomics*. New York: Pantheon.

Lenin, Vladimir Ilyich. [1918] 1965. *Collected Works*. Translated by Clemens Dutt, vol. 27. Moscow: Progress.

Lens, Sidney. 1974. "Running Out of Everything." Reprint. *The Progressive*.

———. 1980. " 'Reindustrialization': Panacea or Threat?" *The Progressive* (November).

Leoni, Bruno. 1961. *Freedom and the Law*. Los Angeles: Nash.

Leontief, Wassily. 1966. *Input-Output Economics*. New York: Oxford University Press.

———. 1973. "Sails and Rudders, Ship of State." *New York Times*, March 16. Reprinted in *Capitalism: The Moving Target*, ed. Leonard Silk. New York: Times Books, 1974.

———. 1976. "The Alternative to Not Planning May Be Chaos: A Conversation With Wassily Leontief." *Business and Society Review* 17.

———. 1977a. *Essays in Economics: Theories, Facts, and Policies*. vol. 2. White Plains, N.Y.: M.E. Sharpe, Inc.

———. 1977b. *The Future of the World Economy: A United Nations Study*. New York: Oxford University Press.

———. 1981. "The Case for National Economic Planning." *Journal of Business Strategy* (Spring).

———. 1982a. "Academic Economics: Letter to *Science* magazine." *Science* 217.

———. 1982b. "What Hope for the Economy?" *New York Review of Books*, August 12.

Lerner, Abba. 1944. *The Economics of Control: Principles of Welfare Economics*. New York: Macmillan.

Levy, Bernard-Henri. 1979. *Barbarism with a Human Face*. Translated by George Holoch. New York: Harper & Row.

Lindblom, Charles E. 1959. "The Science of 'Muddling Through'." *Public Administration Review* 19.

Lippmann, Walter. 1936. *The Good Society*. New York: Grosset & Dunlap.

Lutz, Vera. 1969. *Central Planning for the Market Economy: An Analysis of the French Theory and Experience*. London: Longman, Green.

Macrae, Norman. 1980. "Must Japan Slow?" *Economist*, February 23.

Magaziner, Ira C., and Robert B. Reich. 1982. *Minding America's Business*. New York: Harcourt Brace Jovanovich.

Mahoney, David J. 1983. "Beyond the Free Market." *New York Times*, February 7.

Marx, Karl. [1867] 1967. *Capital*. Vol. 1, *A Critical Analysis of Capitalist Production*. New York: International.

_____. [1953] 1973. *The Grundrisse: Foundations of the Critique of Political Economy*. Translated by Martin Nicolaus. New York: Vintage.

_____. [1871] 1974a. "First Draft of 'The Civil War in France'." In Marx 1974c.

_____. [1875] 1974b. "Critique of the Gotha Programme." In Marx 1974c.

_____. 1974c. *Political Writings*. Ed. David Fernback. Vol. 3, *The First International and After*. New York: Vintage.

McClelland, P., and A. Magdovitz. 1981. *Crisis in the Making*. Cambridge, England: Cambridge University Press.

McCloskey, Donald N. 1983. "The Rhetoric of Economics." *Journal of Economic Literature* (June).

Menger, Carl. [1870] 1981. *Principles of Economics*. Translated by J. Dingwall and B.F. Hoselitz. New York: New York University Press.

Mill, John Stuart. 1849. *Principles of Political Economy*. 2d ed., vol. 1.

Mises, Ludwig von. [1912] 1980. *The Theory of Money and Credit*. Translated by H.E. Batson. Indianapolis, Ind.: Liberty Press.

_____. [1920] 1935. "Economic Calculation in the Socialist Commonwealth." Translated by S. Adler. In Hayek 1935.

_____. [1922] 1981. *Socialism: An Economic and Sociological Analysis*. Translated by J. Kahane. Indianapolis: Liberty Press.

_____. [1949] 1966. *Human Action: A Treatise on Economics*. 3d ed. Chicago: Henry Regnery.

Müller, Ronald E. 1980. *Revitalizing America: Politics for Prosperity*. New York: Simon and Schuster.

Murray, Charles. 1984. *Losing Ground: American Social Policy, 1950–1980*. New York: Basic Books.

Nagel, Ernest, and James R. Newman. 1958. *Gödel's Proof*. New York: New York University Press.

Nelson, Richard R., and Sidney G. Winter. 1982. *Evolutionary Theory of Economic Change*. Cambridge, Mass.: Harvard University Press.

Nozick, Robert. 1974. *Anarchy, State and Utopia*. New York: Basic Books.

_____. 1977. "On Austrian Methodology." *Synthèse* 36.

Nutter, G. Warren. 1983. *Political Economy and Freedom*. Indianapolis, Ind.: Liberty Press.

O'Driscoll, Gerald P., Jr. 1977. *Economics as a Coordination Problem: The Contributions of Friedrich A. Hayek*. Kansas City, Kans.: Sheed Andrews and McMeel.

Olson, Mancur. 1982. *The Rise and Decline of Nations: Economic Growth, Stagflation and Social Rigidities*. New Haven, Conn.: Yale University Press.

Park, Robert E. 1931. [review of Sombart's *Die drei Nationalökonomien*], *American Journal of Sociology* 36 (May).

Parry, Albert. 1966. *The New Class Divided: Science and Technology Versus Communism*. New York: Macmillan.

Paul, Ron, and Lewis Lehrman. 1982. *The Case for Gold: A Minority Report of the U.S. Gold Commission*. Washington, D.C.: Cato Institute.

Peterson, Russell W. 1981. *Statement of the President of the National Audubon Society*. Hearings before the House Committee on Energy and Commerce Subcommittee on Oversight and Investigations and the Subcommittee on Energy Conservation and Power, 97th Cong., 1st sess.

Piaget, Jean. 1971. *Biology and Knowledge: An Essay on the Relations Between Organic Regulations and Cognitive Processes*. Translated by B. Walsh. Chicago: University of Chicago Press.

Piven, Frances Fox, and Richard A. Cloward. 1971. *Regulating the Poor: The Functions of Public Welfare*. New York: Random House.

Polanyi, Karl. 1957. *The Great Transformation: The Political and Economic Origins of Our Time*. Boston: Beacon Press.

Polanyi, Michael. [1946] 1963. *Science, Faith and Society*. Chicago: University of Chicago Press.

_____. 1951. *The Logic of Liberty*. Chicago: University of Chicago Press.

_____. 1958a. *Personal Knowledge: Towards a Post-Critical Philosophy*. Chicago: University of Chicago Press.

_____. 1958b. *The Study of Man*. Chicago: University of Chicago Press.

_____. 1962. "The Republic of Science: Its Political and Economic Theory." In Polanyi 1969.

_____. 1969. *Knowing and Being*. Chicago: University of Chicago Press.

_____. 1972. "Genius in Science." *Encounter* (January).

Polanyi, Michael, and Harry Prosch. 1975. *Meaning*. Chicago: University of Chicago Press.

Popper, Karl R. 1972. *Objective Knowledge: An Evolutionary Approach.* Oxford: Oxford University Press.

Reese, David A. 1980. "Alienation and Economics in Karl Marx." Ph.D. diss., Department of Economics, Virginia Polytechnic Institute, Blacksburg, Va.

Reich, Robert B. 1983. *The Next American Frontier.* New York: Times Books.

Richman, Sheldon. 1981. "War Communism to NEP: The Road from Serfdom." *Journal of Libertarian Studies* (Winter).

Robbins, Lionel. 1934. *The Great Depression.* New York: Macmillan.

Roberts, Paul Craig. 1971. *Alienation and the Soviet Economy.* Albuquerque: University of New Mexico Press.

Roberts, Paul Craig, and Matthew Stephenson. 1973. *Marx's Theory of Exchange, Alienation, and Crisis.* Stanford, Calif.: Hoover Institution Press.

Rohatyn, Felix G. 1980a. "Strong Medicine." *Across the Board*, May.

_____. 1980b. "The Coming Emergency and What Can Be Done About It." *New York Review of Books*, December 4.

_____. 1981a. "A Matter of Psychology." *New York Review of Books*, April 16.

_____. 1981b. "An RFC Could Help New York Transit." *New York Times*, June 29.

_____. 1982a. "The State of the Banks." *New York Review of Books*, November 4.

_____. 1982b. "Alternatives to Reaganomics." *New York Times Magazine*, December 5.

Rosch, Eleanor. 1977. "Human Categorization." In *Advances in Cross-Cultural Psychology*, vol. 1. London: Academic Press.

Rothbard, Murray N. [1962] 1970. *Man, Economy and State: A Treatise on Economic Principles.* Los Angeles: Nash.

_____. [1963] 1975. *America's Great Depression.* Kansas City, Kans.: Sheed and Ward.

Rothenberg, Randall. 1983. "An RFC for Today: A Capital Idea." *Inc.*, January.

Ryle, Gilbert. 1945. "Knowing How and Knowing That." *Proceedings of the Aristotelian Society.*

Sahlins, Marshall. 1972. *Stone Age Economics.* Chicago: Aldine.

Sakoh, Katsuro. 1983. "Industrial Policy: The Super Myth of Japan's Super Success." Heritage Foundation Asian Studies Center Backgrounder. Washington, July 13.

Schell, Jonathan. 1982. *The Fate of the Earth.* New York: Alfred A. Knopf.

Schumpeter, Joseph. [1942] 1950. *Capitalism, Socialism and Democracy.* New York: Harper & Row.

Serrin, William. 1981. "Rohatyn, 'Going National,' Doubts Free-Market Future." *New York Times*, April 21.

Sharp, Gene. 1973. *The Politics of Nonviolent Action.* Boston: Porter Sargent.

Shaw, Jane S. 1981. "The RFC: A Born-again Lender under Reagan?" *Business Week*, April 13.

Silk, Leonard. 1976. *The Economists.* New York: Basic Books.

_____. 1983. "Structural Joblessness." *New York Times*, April 6.

Simon, Julian L. 1981. *The Ultimate Resource.* Princeton: Princeton University Press.

Sowell, Thomas. 1980. *Knowledge and Decisions.* New York: Basic Books.

_____. 1981. *Ethnic America: A History.* New York: Basic Books.

Spooner, Lysander. [1875] 1977. *Vices Are Not Crimes.* Cupertino, Calif.: TANSTAAFL.

Stilwell, Joe. 1983. "Deficits and the Economy." Cato Institute Policy Analysis, no. 24. Washington, May 26.

Sunwall, Mark. 1983. "Is MITI Responsible for Japan's Industrial Success?" Unpublished paper, Center for the Study of Market Processes, George Mason University, Fairfax, Va.

Sweezy, Paul M. 1979. "A Crisis in Marxian Theory." *Monthly Review* (June).

Thomas, Lewis. 1974. *The Lives of a Cell: Notes of a Biology Watcher.* New York: Bantam Books.

Thorpe, William Homan. 1963. *Learning and Instinct in Animals.* Cambridge, Mass.: Harvard University Press.

Toulmin, Stephen. 1972. *Human Understanding: The Collective Use and Evolution of Concepts.* Princeton: Princeton University Press.

Trebilcock, Clive. 1975. "War and the Failure of industrial Mobilization: 1899 and 1914." In Winter 1975.

Trezise, Philip. 1982. "Industrial Policy in Japan." In *Industry Vitalization: Toward a National Industrial Policy*, ed. Margaret E. Dewar. Elmsford, N.Y.: Pergamon Press.

Tullock, Gordon. 1967. "The Welfare Costs of Tariffs, Monopolies, and Theft." *Western Economic Journal* (June).

_____. 1983. *Economics of Income Redistribution.* Boston: Kluwer-Nijhoff.

Vanek, Jaroslav. 1971. *The Participatory Economy: An Evolutionary Hypothesis and a Strategy for Development.* Ithaca: Cornell University Press.

Villari, Luigi. 1932. "The Economics of Fascism." In Counts et al. 1932.

Vorhies, W. Francis. 1982. "Marx and Mises on Money: The Monetary Theories of Two Opposing Political Economies." Ph.D. diss., Economic Institute for Research and Education, University of Colorado, Boulder.

Walsh, Annmarie Hauck. 1978. *The Public's Business: The Politics and Practices of Government Corporations.* Cambridge, Mass.: MIT Press.

Weber, Christopher. 1983. *Bailing Out a Bankrupt World.* San Francisco: Investment Insights Publishing.

Weinstein, James. 1968. *The Corporate Ideal in the Liberal State: 1910–1918.* Boston: Beacon Press.

White, Lawrence H. 1984. *Free Banking in Britain.* Cambridge, England: Cambridge University Press.

Whitehead, Alfred North. [1947] 1968. *Essays in Science and Philosophy.* New York: Greenwood.

Wilson, David E. 1980. *The National Planning Idea in U.S. Public Policy: Five Alternative Approaches.* Boulder, Colo.: Westview Press.

Wilson, Edward O. 1971. *The Insect Societies.* Cambridge, Mass.: Harvard University Press.

_____. 1975. *Sociobiology: The New Synthesis.* Cambridge, Mass.: Belknap Press.

Winpisinger, William W. 1982. "Rebuilding America." *USA Today* magazine (May).

Winter, J.M., ed. 1975. *War and Economic Development: Essays in Memory of David Joslin.* Cambridge, England: Cambridge University Press.

Zaid, Charles, compiler. 1973. *Preliminary Inventory of the Records of the Reconstruction Finance Corporation, 1932-1964.* National Archives and Records Service, U.S. General Services Administration. Washington.

INDEX

abstract wholes, 57–8, 61–2, 93,
  254–5
Adler, Mortimer J., 26
advertising, 132–3, 162–3, 164–5
Agassi, Joseph, 264
aggregation, 92, 93–4, 102–12,
  115–16, 121–2, 134
aggregative planning, *see* planning,
  noncomprehensive
agricultural society, 33–4, 47, 52, 142
alienation, 18, 41, 140, 146, 213, 218
Allen, G. C., 194
Allied Purchasing Commission, 225
Alpern, David M., 173, 178, 183
Alperovitz, Gar, 126–8, 137, 143–4,
  155, 161, 164–5, 168–71
American revolution, 238–9
Americans for Democratic Action, 126
anarchy of production, 68, 132, 214
Anderson, John, 201
Anderson, Martin, 167
Andreski, Stanislav, 162
antitrust, 74, 194
Arenson, Karen W., 202
Armentano, D. T., 205
articulation, 59, 62, 69, 71, 76–7, 81,
  85, 251, 255–6, 261
  complete, 250–6, 263
  dynamic limitation to, 60–1, 79,
    83–5, 190, 253–5

static limitation to, 60–1, 79–83,
  190, 253–5
Asprey, Robert B., 244
Austrian economics, 44, 73–4, 205
awareness
  focal, 61, 71–2, 81, 84, 255
  subsidiary, 62–3, 71–2, 80–1, 83–4,
    255

Bach, J. S., 165
Baez, Joan, 235
Bails, Dale G., 122
Barlett, P. F., 48
Barnett, David L., 204, 207
Barone, Enrico, 88
Barrett, William, 89
Barron, John, 245
Baruch, Bernard M., 220, 223–6, 232
Bastiat, Frederic, 51
Bauer, Otto, 243
Bauer, P. T., 205
Bazard, S.-A., 217
Beckner, Steven K., 195
Bennett, James T., 171, 206
Bergson, Abram, 242
Bernstein, Eduard, 243
biology, 92, 108
Bismarck, Otto von, 221
Blanc, Louis, 217
Blustein, Paul, 208

Bluestone, Barry, 126–31, 133, 137, 141, 144, 147–50, 152, 162–4, 168–70, 175, 178–9, 185, 199, 201–2, 204
Boddy, Raford, 126, 130, 138, 149, 155, 161, 164
Böhm-Bawerk, Eugen von, 109, 243
Bowles, Samuel, 162
Bradley, Robert L., Jr., 166
Braverman, Harry, 130
Browning, Edgar, 167
Browning, Frank, 235
Brozen, Yale, 205
Buchanan, James, 123, 205
Buell, John, 126, 129–31, 137, 139, 143, 147, 149, 160–4, 166
Buick, Adam, 242
Bukharin, Nicolai, 228, 229, 243
Burton, John, 205

calculation argument, see knowledge problem, as a critique of comprehensive planning
calculation debate, 24, 88, 213, 243
Caldwell, Bruce, 23
Campbell, Jeremy, 90
capital structure, 92, 103–4, 105, 185, 195, 209
Caplan, Arthur L., 46
Carey, Hugh, 191
Carnoy, Martin, 7, 126–31, 134, 139, 143, 145–7, 149, 151–2, 155–9, 162, 164, 166–7, 169, 170–1, 245
Carr, E. H., 222
Carter, Jimmy, 174, 201, 207, 208
Casement, Richard, 195–6
Castro, Fidel, 213
Chibnik, M., 48
Chomsky, Noam, 22, 90
Clark, Grahame, 34, 48
Clarkson, Grosvenor B., 243
Clarkson, Kenneth W., 121
classical economics, 44, 213
Cliff, Tony, 142
Cloward, Richard A., 167
Coffin, Howard E., 223
Cohen, Stephen F., 229
Cohn-Bendit, Daniel, 233
Cohn-Bendit, Gabriel, 233
Committee on Public Information, 225

competitive discovery processes, 6, 68–70, 73, 78–9, 85–6, 88, 98, 242, 248
market, 5, 6, 18, 21–2, 37–9, 48, 52, 54, 73–86, 95, 98, 104, 114–16, 128, 132, 134–7, 140, 158–9, 163, 181, 185–6, 190, 193, 195, 199–200, 205, 214, 216, 221, 225, 228, 237, 240–1, 248, see also coordination principles, market and evolution, economic
scientific, 5, 6, 12–17, 19, 59, 63–6, 76–86, 92, 115, 237, 243, 247–8, 250, 252, 259, 262–4, 265
sociobiological, 5, 27, 46, 66, 67–73, 76–8, 91, 115, see also mass communication
complexity
as an obstacle to aggregation, 103–4
as an obstacle to planning, 46–7, 52, 55, 86, 94, 104, 118, 146, 166–7, 180, 189, 239–40
as a remediable problem for planning, 55, 66, 100–2, 121, 144–6, 166–7
attained by competitive processes, 36–8, 72, 86, 116, 119
methodological implications of, 108, 253
of the capital structure, 92, 105
of individual human beings compared with insects, 70
of market processes compared with that of insect societies, 66, 70, 72, 86
of market processes compared with that of scientific processes, 79, 86
of relative price effects of inflation, 209
of society relative to the individual, 27–8
compositive theory, 68, see also explanation of the principle
computers
and artificial intelligence, 55, 59, 90, 118–19, 123–4
and economic forecasting, 104
as allegedly threatening jobs, 118
as analogous to economies, 117–18
as complementary to market processes, 54

as tools for comprehensive planning, 49, 54–5, 74–5
as tools for noncomprehensive planning, 138
Comte, August, 15
Comte, Charles, 216
Conant, J. B., 256
conclusive testability, 250, 256–63
Congressional Research Service, 121
Conquest, Robert, 222
conscription, 212, 222, 244
conservatism
  as backward-looking, 144
  as not opposed to national economic planning, 142, 204, 231, 237
  contrasted with radicalism, 1, 15–16, 236, 239–240
  failed policies of, 188–9, 205
  hypocrisy of, 235
  populist, 174
consumer sovereignty, 38–9, 43, 81, 132, 134, 164–5, 176, 181, 185, 197, 207–8, 210
coordination principles, 5, 26–30, 35–7, 40, 46, 52, 76–7, 185, 188, 190, 218, 237, 242
  Market, 29, 34–9, 40–6, 52, 54–6, 75, 86, 181–2, 221, 237–8, 242, see also competitive discovery processes, market and evolution, economic
  Planning, 29, 36, 39–44, 46, 52, 56, 75, 86, 216, 237–8, 241, 263, see also planning
  Tradition, 29, 30–4, 36, 39, 41, 45–6, 52, 54, 86, 221, 237, see also evolution, cultural
Copernicus, Nicolaus, 254
copyright laws, 85
corporate planning, 125–32, 139, 142–4, 146, 152, 162, 168–9, 174, 176, 186–7, 197, 201–2, 205, 220–23, 225, 230, 239, see also war planning
corruption, 12, 131, 193–4
Council of National Defense, 223, 243
crime, 12
Croce, Benedetto, 243
Crombie, A., 89
Crosland, C.A.R., 151
Crotty, James, 126, 130, 138, 149, 155, 161, 164

Crusoe, Robinson, 71
Cuff, Robert D., 224–6
Custer, George Armstrong, 167

Daly, C. B., 89
Daly, John Charles, 202
Darwin, Charles, 25, 122, 182, 254
data, 6, 52–65, 66, 77, 119
data gathering, 55–6, 77, 87, 94–105, 111–12, 122–3, 160, 210
Da Vinci, Leonardo, 21
Dawes, Charles, 193–4
debt
  private, 132, 164, 184, 192, 196, 204–5
  public, 98, 120, 133, 141, 149, 151, 154, 164, 188–9, 191–3, 196–8, 206, 209
DeLuca, Tom, 126, 129–31, 137, 139, 143, 147, 149, 161–4, 166
democracy, 17–18, 20–1, 44, 125–7, 135, 137–8, 140, 146, 152, 160, 201–2, 204, 208, 213, 217, 225, 230, 232–3, 240–1
Demsetz, Harold, 205
Denzau, Arthur T., 164
Department of Agriculture, 87
Department of Energy, 99
DiLorenzo, Thomas J., 171, 203, 206
Dilthey, Wilhelm, 123
Dissent, 126
Djilas, Milovan, 229
Dobzhansky, Theodosius, 31
Domhoff, G. William, 23
Dreyfus, Hubert L., 90, 124
Dunoyer, Charles, 216

econometrics, 102–5, 122
economic democracy, see planning, noncomprehensive
Einstein, Albert, 12, 22, 254, 257
energy, 2, 99, 134–5, 153, 166–9, 171, 208, 231
Enfantin, B.P., 217
Engels, Frederick, 212, 220
environment, the, 2, 99, 134, 145, 153, 168–9, 198
Environmental Protection Agency, 99
epistemology, see philosophy of science and knowledge
Estrin, Saul, 123

ethology, 59, 90
Etzioni, Amitai, 23, 122, 165, 174,
    197, 199–200, 204, 207–8
Euclidean geometry, 59
evolution
    biological, 25, 28, 30–2, 34–5, 40,
        43, 45, 46–7, 108–9, 182
    cultural, 25, 28, 31–2, 34, 40, 43,
        45–7, 62, 91, 144, 265
    economic, 35–6, 39, 40, 42, 43,
        45–6, 91, 181–2, 188, see also
        competitive discovery processes,
        market
existentialism, 89
experts, rule by the, 138, 183, 186,
    190–6, 200, 205–6, 216, see
    also intelligentsia
explanation of the principle, 108–9,
    117, 122, 144, see also composi-
    tive theory

Fairgate, Alan, 202, 207
fascism, see corporate planning
Faux, Jeff, 126–8, 137, 143–4, 155,
    161, 164, 166, 168–71
Federal Reserve System, 87, 150, 160,
    164, 169, 198, 202–3, 209
feudalism, see rigidification, economic
Feuerbach, Ludwig, 217
financial transactions, 132–3, 163–4
firm, the, 38, 71, 74, 76, 95, 103, 128,
    145, 224
fiscal policy, 100, 102, 149–50, 196,
    see also deficits, taxes, and govern-
    ment expenditures
Fonda, Jane, 164
Food and Fuel Administrations,
    224–5
Foot, Michael, 243–4
Ford, Henry, 202
Fourier, Charles, 217
freedom
    economic, 38, 73–4, 84–5, 129,
        131, 145, 179, 200, 203, 205,
        212, 220, 221–2, 237–9
    intellectual, 63–4, 84–5, 92, 212,
        237, 264, 265
Friedman, Milton, 23, 167, 188, 205

Gandhi, Mohandas, 21
Garrett, M., 90
Gelwick, Richard, 89

general equilibrium, 73, 88, 103, 121
Gier, Nicholas F., 89
Gilder, George, 195
Ginsburg, Woodrow, 126, 129, 139,
    155, 163, 169
Gladwin, C. H., 48
Gödel, Kurt, 253–4
Goldstein, Walter, 161
Goodman, John C., 167
Gordon, David M., 162
Gould, Stephen Jay, 25, 247
government expenditures, 121, 128,
    131, 135, 139, 143, 150, 152–4,
    158–9, 167, 169–71, 180–4,
    188, 195, 197–8, 208–9
Grant, James, 225
Gray, John, 87
Greer, Colin, 127
Grinder, Walter, 202, 207
Gross, Bertram, 167
growth of knowledge literature, 58,
    88–90, 248–63

Halevy, Elie, 217, 242, 263
Hardin, Clifford M., 164
Harrington, Michael, 7, 11, 126, 129,
    130, 138, 142, 148–9, 152–3,
    155, 159, 160–1, 163–4, 166–7,
    169–70, 199, 200
Harris, Marvin, 47, 265
Harrison, Bennett, 126–9, 131, 133,
    137, 141, 144, 147–50, 152,
    162–4, 168–70, 175, 178–9, 185,
    199, 201–2, 204
Hart, David, 242
Hart, Gary, 201
Hattiangati, Jagdish N., 90
Hayden, Tom, 23, 125–7, 129–30,
    149, 161–9, 199–200
Hayek, F.A.
    on conservatism, 205
    on cultural evolution, 25–6, 32, 47
    on decentralized planning, 125
    on ideology and utopia, 16, 211
    on monetary theory and policy, 150,
        210
    on property rights, 48, 245
    on spontaneous order, 66, 90, 94,
        263
    on the knowledge problem, 23–4,
        44, 65, 92, 94

on the nature of knowledge, 56, 58,
    61–3, 65, 79, 87, 89–91, 108,
    122, 248, 253–4, 256, 265
on the price system, 72–3, 80–1
on the totalitarian problem, 24, 44,
    217–18, 242–3
Hayes, Alfred, 202
Hazlitt, Henry, 168
health care, 2, 145, 148, 153, 167–70,
    197–8, 208, 231
Hegel, Georg W.F., 217
Heilbroner, Robert, 126, 143–4, 149,
    155, 161–3, 167, 171
Henderson, David R., 195, 207
Herman, Edward S., 22
Hess, Moses, 217
Hesse, Mary, 257
Hicks, John, 130
Hilferding, Rudolf, 243
Hitler, Adolf, 232
Ho Chi Minh, 245
Hoff, Trygve J.B., 24
Hofstadter, Douglas R., 124
Hollings, Fritz, 201
Holmes, Peter, 123
Holton, Gerald, 22
Hoover, Herbert, 224, 226
Horowitz, David, 23, 235–6, 245
Horwitz, Morton J., 239
Howes, Candace, 235
Hume, David, 89, 248
Humphrey, Hubert, 96, 147, 169
Humphrey-Hawkins bill, 96, 120, 169
Humphrey-Javits bill, 96, 120
Hunt, Morton, 90
hunter-gatherer society, 30, 33, 47
Hurwicz, Leonid, 49, 92
Husserl, Edmund, 89

ideology, 16–17, 211, 215, 221, 226,
    228, 231–4, 237, 240
incentives, 148, 168, 170, 182–3, 197,
    207
indicative planning, 121
individual intelligence, 26–7, 76, 79,
    115, 116, 136–7, 186, 189, 193,
    see also social intelligence and
    organizational intelligence
induction, problem of, 257–8
Industrial Preparedness Committee,
    223

inequality, 218–19, 245
    economic, 2, 97, 131, 138, 153, 202
    political, 1, 17–18, 131, 215–16,
        233–4, 238, 242
inflation, 12, 130, 133–4, 141, 145,
    148–50, 154–5, 164, 166, 167,
    169, 196, 198, 206, 208–10
infrastructure, 182–3, 204, 208
Initiative Committee for National
    Economic Planning, 96, 126
input-output method, 96–8, 105–12,
    123
insect societies, see competitive dis-
    covery processes, sociobiological
institutions, 31
intelligentsia, 216–18, 236, 263–4,
    see also experts, rule by the
interest rates, 150, 154–5, 159, 169,
    198, 207, 209–10
Internal Revenue Service, 155, 168
International Monetary Fund, 184,
    192
investment, 8, 12, 129, 132–3, 145,
    150–1, 157–8, 160, 163, 164,
    170, 176, 181, 185, 193–200,
    203, 207
investment-guiding agency, 159–61,
    175, 177–86, 189, 191–6, 198–9,
    202, 206, 209, 222
    as insulated from political rivalry,
        175–6, 191–4, 202–4
    as open to political scrutiny, 175–6,
        194–6
    futurist, 176–7, 180, 185–6, 194–6,
        199–200
    preservationist, 176–7, 178, 180,
        182–6, 196, 199–200, 204

Jasinowski, Jerry, 207
Jefferson, Thomas, 1, 238–9
Johnson, Chalmers, 207, 223, 227
Johnson, Paul, 228, 244
Jones, Bassett, 109
Jones, Jesse H., 193–4, 206–7
Journal of Philosophy, 264–5

Kaiser, Henry, 194
Kant, Immanuel, 89
Kirkland, Lane, 179
Keilin, Eugene, 181
Kemp, Jack, 174

Keynes, John Maynard, 102, 147, 149–50, 167, 174, 196, 198, 202, 209
Khomeini, Ayatollah Ruholla, 165
Kirzner, Israel M., 73, 91, 121–3, 205, 243
Kline, Morris, 90
knowledge
  as contextual, 41, 77, 93, 113–15
  as dispersed, 52, 56, 77–8, 113–14, 241
  as embodying commitment, 84, 258, 261–2
  as embodying presuppositions, 60–1, 252–3, 260
  as embodying skillful judgments, 55–6, 71, 78, 91, 98, 130, 254–6, 259, 261–5
  as involving appeals to authority, 64, 249
  as involving expectations, 63, 77, 83, 98, 109, 113, 115, 133, 157, 177, 259, 262
  as involving imagination, 78, 83, 91, 118, 247, 251–2, 259–60
  as involving the use of analogy, 62, 66–7
  as involving values, 58, 63–5, 250, 261
  as personal, 58–9, 63, 83–4, 86, 88–90, 249, 251–2, 259–60, 264
  dissemination of, 72, 115, 134–6, 140, 158–9, 185, 188, 237, 242, see also competitive discovery processes
  inarticulate, 5–6, 14, 58–65, 71, 77–83, 86, 89–91, 110, 113–14, 135–6, 189–91, 198, 247–65
  interpretive dimension of, 13–14, 58–9, 251–2, 256–8, 260–2
  objectivist view of, 56–60, 64, 87, 89, 248–52, 259–65
  of productive techniques, 77–84, 88, 130–1, 134–5
  scientific, 57–8, 63, 77–86, 247–65
knowledge problem
  aggregation as a solution to, 86, 93–5, 102–12, 115–16, 134–5
  and the principle of mass communication, 27, 65–76
  as a critique of comprehensive planning, 4–5, 8–9, 44, 52, 54–7, 59, 65, 75–6, 86, 89, 94

  as a critique of noncomprehensive planning, 5, 8–9, 55–7, 76, 86–7, 94–6, 101, 111–12, 136, 157, 160, 171, 198, 207, 243
  as addressed by Leontief, 96–7, 99, 117–18
  as analogous to the case for intellectual freedom, 76–86, 237, 263–4
  as ignored by most proponents of planning, 8, 20, 166, 198
  as independent of the issue of motivation, 21
  as related to totalitarian problem, 201
  channeling of investment to selected sectors as a solution to, 86, 160, 180–1, 188, 190, 193–4, 200
  decentralization of decision making as a solution to, 86, 100, 125, 135–7, 160–1
  original formulations of, 23–4, 88, 241
  the nature of the problem, 51–65
Kolakowski, Leszek, 217, 234, 236, 242–4
Konrad, George, 229, 244
Kopkind, Andrew, 157
Koyre, Alexandre, 256
Kristol, Irving, 23
Kropotkin, Peter, 243
Krueger, Anne O., 17
Kuhn, Helmut, 89
Kuhn, Thomas S., 88–90, 245, 249, 256, 260–5

Lachmann, Ludwig M., 51, 92–3, 103
Lackner, J. R., 90
Lakatos, Imre, 90, 248, 256–8, 260–1, 264–5
Lamarck, Jean Baptiste Monet de, 25, 31
Lange, Oskar, 24, 88, 213, 220, 243
language, 32, 61–2, 79–80, 89, 124, see also linguistics
Larin, Yuri, 244
Lassalle, Ferdinand, 217
Lavoie, Don, 23, 24, 49, 242, 243
law, 62, 94, 237–8, 245, see also property rights and inequality, political
Leakey, Richard, 33, 47
learning, 57–8
Lee, Joe, 243

Left, the, *see* radicalism
Lehrman, Lewis, 245
Leijonhufvud, Axel, 90, 167
Lekachman, Robert, 7, 125-6,
    129-30, 136, 142, 145, 147, 149,
    152, 155, 160-4, 167-9
Lenin, Vladimir Ilyich, 13, 49, 138,
    141-2, 213, 219, 227-9, 237,
    243-4
Lens, Sidney, 201
Leoni, Bruno, 245
Leontief, Wassily, 2, 7, 55-6, 66, 77,
    93-124, 126, 132, 140, 143, 146,
    149, 160, 166, 185
Lerner, Abba, 213, 220, 243
Levy, Bernard-Henri, 202, 244
Levy, Gustave, 203
Libertarian Review, 244
linguistics, 59, 90
Lippmann, Walter, 165, 222, 230, 243
Lloyd George, David, 220, 223, 226
Locke, John, 89
Louis XVIII, 217
Ludendorff, Erich Friedrich Wilhelm,
    220, 222, 226-9, 244
Lutz, Vera, 98, 120-1

Macrae, Norman, 195
Maeterlinck, Maurice, 67
Magaziner, Ira C., 203
Magdoff, Harry, 163
Magdovitz, A., 206
Mahoney, David J., 203
Maine, H. S., 48
Mao Tse-Tung, 213
Marcos, Ferdinand, 239
Marcuse, Herbert, 248
Market, *see* coordination principles
market failure, 74
market socialism, 24, 88, 213, 220,
    243, *see also* planometrics
Martin, William McChesney, 202
Marx, Karl, 1, 3, 18-19, 23, 36, 40-3,
    46, 49, 56, 68, 72, 91, 101, 109,
    122, 140-4, 163, 212-20, 227-9,
    232-3, 235, 238, 242-5
mass communication, 27, 65-76, 115
mathematics, 13-14, 59, 90, 251-4,
    256
McClelland, P., 206
McCloskey, Donald N., 23
meaning, 58, 107-12, 114, 123
Medicaid and Medicare, 148, 170

Mendel, Gregor, 31
Menger, Carl, 47-9
mercantilism, 215, 221
mergers and acquisitions, 132-3,
    163-4, 176, 203
methodology of economics, *see* com-
    positive theory *and* explanation of
    the principle
Meyer, Eugene, 193, 226
Michelson-Morley experiment, 22
militarism
    and the free market, 167, 240
    as the main problem of our time,
        1-2, 11-13, 15, 120, 203
    economic democracy advocates
        critical of, 130, 138, 147, 153
    planning as a proposed means for
        our emancipation from, 2, 208
    planning as a proposed means of
        promoting, 192, 208, 211-32, 240
    planning as modeled after, 165,
        211-32, 240, 243-4
    reindustrialization advocates mildly
        critical of, 198
Mill, John Stuart, 243
Ministry of International Trade and
    Industry, 2, 174, 194-6, 207
Ministry of Munitions (British), 221,
    223, 226
Mises, Ludwig von, 23-4, 44, 53, 73,
    88, 109, 121, 156, 205, 241, 243
Mondale, Walter, 167, 201
monetary policy, 100, 102, 149-51,
    154, 167, 169, 187, 196, 198,
    209-10, 232, 238-9
money, 34, 43, 47, 49, 70-2, 109,
    121, 149, 150, 214, 218, 229
monopolization, 138, 212, 215-16,
    220, 224-9, 231, 238-9, 241, 243
Monthly Review, 245
Morgan, J. Pierpont, 171, 193-4
Müller, Ronald E., 175, 196, 199, 205
Municipal Assistance Corporation,
    175, 191, 206
Murray, Charles, 167
mysticism, 65

Nagel, Ernest, 253
Napoleon I, 217
Napoleon III, 218
Nation, The, 235, 245
nationalism, 212, 219

nationalization, 151, 155–7, 166, 169–71
Nazi Germany, 226
Nelson, Richard R., 91
neoclassical economics, 38, 49, 73–4, 80, 91, 102, 105, 112, 123, 187–8, 213, 220, 243
New Philosophers, 244
new RFC, see investment-guiding agency and Reconstruction Finance Corporation
New York Times Magazine, 161
Newman, James R., 253
Newton, Isaac, 12, 15, 90, 109, 257
Nozick, Robert, 122, 242, 244
Nutter, G. Warren, 49

O'Driscoll, Gerald P., Jr., 205
Olson, Mancur, 166
Ong, John O., 203
ordering processes, see coordination principles
organizational intelligence, 76, 92, see also social intelligence and individual intelligence

Pareto, Vilfredo, 73
Park, Robert E., 123
Parry, Albert, 92
patent laws, 85
Paul, Ron, 245
Peppers, Larry C., 122
perfect competition, 38, 73, 91, 129–32, 145, 220
Peterson, Russell, 173
phenomenology, 89
pheromones, 28, 68–70, 72–3, 76, 85
philosophy of science, 6, 13–15, 22–3, 57–65, 77–8, 83, 87, 88–91, 212, 245, 247–65
physics, 59, 90, 91, 106–8
Piaget, Jean, 90
Piven, Frances Fox, 167
Planning, see coordination principles
planning, alleged inevitability of, 140–6, 156, 160, 205
planning, comprehensive
  abandonment of, 3, 20, 49, 111, 212–14, 225, 232, 236, 241–2
  and the knowledge problem, 4, 6, 46, 52, 54, 57, 59, 65, 75–8,

86–7, 89, 94–5, 101–2, 209, 241, 263–4
  as a reactionary diversion of the radical movement's aspirations, 9, 216–19, 231
  as involving the abolition of all market institutions, 3–4, 6, 18–19, 29, 44, 75, 102, 214, 227
  as the most consistent and coherent form of planning, 19, 43, 49, 232, 236–7, 241
  contrasted with insect societies, 67–8
  contrasted with noncomprehensive planning, 3–4, 6, 42, 94–5, 111, 201, 213–14, 225, 228, 236, 242
  defined, 3, 29, 120–1
  initial aspirations of, 18–20, 39–40, 46, 65, 75, 86, 147, 216–19, 241, 263–4
  planometric variant of, 54–6
planning, noncomprehensive, 3–4, 6, 9, 20, 42, 52, 55–7, 76, 86, 94–5, 113, 120–1, 201, 211–45
  aggregative variant, 7–8, 86, 93–124, 139
  economic democracy variant, 7–8, 86, 97, 100, 123, 125–72, 174–8, 186–8, 190, 196–8, 210, 245
  reindustrialization variant, 8, 86, 133, 160–6, 173–210, 226, see also corporate planning
planometrics, 49, 54–5, 72–3, 80, 92, 220, 243, see also market socialism
Plekhanov, Grigorii V., 243
Pol Pot (Tol Saut), 245
Polanyi, Karl, 48
Polanyi, Michael
  on aggregation, 93, 111
  on freedom and truth, 212
  on knowledge, 56–64, 71, 81, 84, 87–92, 114, 248, 251–65
  on property rights, 48
  on the differences and similarities among the sciences, 22–3
  on the Soviet-type economy, 49
  on spontaneous order, 48, 51, 66
political power, 1, 12, 99, 131, 136, 137, 162, 176, 201, 206, 212, 225, 233–4, 263–4, see also totalitarian problem
Popper, Karl R., 248, 257–61

poverty, 2, 147–8, 167, 204
Pravda, 244
price controls, 85, 143, 151, 154–6,
    167, 198, 206, 210, 222
prices
    as signals influenced by choice, 54,
        70, 72–3, 75–6, 81, 83–6, 88,
        130–2, 135–6, 140, 156, 210
    as signals influencing choice, 54,
        70–6, 80–3, 85–6, 88, 109, 114,
        132, 136, 156, 166, 210
    as tools of corporate power, 129,
        130, 132, 152, 220, 224
    as tools of national economic plan-
        ning, 102, 110–11, 214, 229
    in equilibrium, 73–5, 104, 187–8
private sector vs. public sector, 17–18,
    21–2, 99–100, 131, 143, 154,
    169, 233
productivity, 12, 148–9, 203, 210,
    234
profit and loss accounting, 35–43, 45,
    54, 71–2, 81–6, 92, 119–20,
    128, 142, 147, 155–6, 162, 167,
    170–1, 180–1, 185, 189, 193,
    200, 218, 221, 224, 229
Progressive, The, 2, 126, 161
property rights, 34, 48, 62, 84–5, 94,
    101, 187, 214, 238–9
Prosch, Harry, 64, 91, 262
Prussian war ministry, 221–3, 227–9,
    244
psychology, 59, 89, 90
public corporations, 151, 156, 158–9,
    171, 191–2, 206, *see also* Recon-
    struction Finance Corporation

radicalism, 1–2, 9, 12, 15–16, 19, 99,
    125–7, 134, 137, 146–7, 151,
    174, 184, 186, 196, 199–200,
    203, 208, 211–45, 247
    libertarian, 117, 123, 143–6, 167,
        181, 186–9, 200–1, 215–19,
        231–42, 244–5
    socialist, 140, 144, 155, 169, 185,
        202, 241
Rand, Ayn, 87
Reagan, Ronald, 98, 123, 142, 144,
    147, 161–2, 167, 188, 197–8,
    201, 205, 208–9, 231–2
recessions, *see* unemployment

Reconstruction Finance Corporation,
    1, 2, 125, 160, 171, 174–86, 189,
    198, 206–11, 226, *see also*
    investment-guiding agency
Reese, David A., 23
Reich, Robert B., 8, 23, 160, 164,
    173–210, 211
reindustrialization, *see* planning, non-
    comprehensive
Reissman, Frank, 127
Richman, Sheldon, 49
Right, the, *see* conservatism
rigidification, economic, 213, 215,
    217–18, 224, 228–30, *see also*
    monopolization
risk, 35, 128, 133, 193, 225
rivalry
    economic, *see* competitive discovery
        processes, market
    political, 85–6, 97, 125, 135–6,
        139–40, 166, 171, 176, 183–4,
        190–1, 194, 199–201
    scientific, *see* competitive discovery
        processes, scientific
Robbins, Lionel, 238
Roberts, Paul Craig, 23, 49, 92, 244
Rogers, Will, 194
Rohatyn, Felix G., 8, 125, 142, 147,
    160, 173–210, 226
Rosch, Eleanor, 90
Rothbard, Murray N., 153, 239
Rothenberg, Randall, 181, 207
Rowley, Charles, 205
Rumberger, Russell, 162
Russell, Bertrand, 252–3
Ryle, Gilbert, 62

Sahlins, Marshall, 47
Saint-Simon, Claude Henri de, 15,
    216–18, 221, 242
Sakoh, Katsuro, 195
Samuelson, Paul, 202
scarcity, 4–5, 28, 48, 54, 71–2,
    79–80, 82, 166, 184–5, 196, 210,
    254, 264
Schell, Jonathan, 11, 12, 15, 247
Schumpeter, Joseph, 242
scientific socialism, 216–17, 229
Serrin, William, 202
Shah, Mohammed Reza Pahlavi, 239
Shapiro, Irving, 203
Sharp, Gene, 244

Shaw, Jane S., 204
Shearer, Derek, 7, 126–31, 134, 139, 143, 145–7, 149, 151–2, 155–9, 162, 164, 166–7, 169, 170–1, 245
Silk, Leonard, 118, 120
Simmel, Georg, 243
Simon, Julian L., 166
Skeptical Inquirer, The, 264
Slawson, David W., 155
Smith, Adam, 221
social intelligence, 26–8, 30, 52–5, 66, 70, 75, 79, 86, 95, 115–16, 136, 186, 189, 193, *see also* individual intelligence *and* organizational intelligence
Social Policy, 126
Social Security, 148, 208
socialism, *see* radicalism *and* planning
Socialist Review, 235
sociobiology, *see* competitive discovery processes, sociobiological
sociology, 123
Solzhenitsyn, Alexander, 231
Sombart, Werner, 243
Somoza, Anastasio, 239
Soviet economy, 42, 49, 127, 141–2, 173, 213, 222, 227–31, 238, 244, 245
Sowell, Thomas, 61, 80, 84–5, 205
specificity of factors of production, 53, 75
speculation, 132–3, 157, 163
spontaneous order, 66, 69, 76, 86, 90, 94, 108, 116, 119, 186, 189, 190, 216, 240, 242, 263, *see also* coordination principles *and* social intelligence
Spooner, Lysander, 241
Stalin, Joseph, 3, 92, 213, 215, 227, 229–30, 232, 243
Stein, Herbert, 149
Stephenson, Matthew, 23, 49
Stevenson, Adlai, III, 171, 202
Stigler, George, 205
Stilwell, Joe, 164
Strauss, D. F., 217
structuralism, *see* planning, non-comprehensive, reindustrialization
structure metaphor, 174–5, 178–80, 182, 184–6, 204
Struve, Peter B., 243

substitutability of factors of production, 53, 75
Sunwall, Mark, 195
Sweezy, Paul M., 245
Szelenyi, Ivan, 229, 244

taxes, 12, 98, 131, 133–4, 145, 148, 150–1, 152–4, 159, 163, 164, 167–8, 176, 180, 182, 184, 188, 192, 193, 195–8, 204, 206–10, 238–9
technical vs. economic choice, 53–4
Tennessee Valley Authority, 159
Thatcher, Margaret, 188–9, 205
Thierry, Augustin, 216
Thomas, Lewis, 46, 91
Thorpe, William Homan, 90
Tiegs, Cheryl, 164
totalitarian problem, 7, 20–1, 24, 44, 99, 137–40, 193, 201, 211–45
Toulmin, Stephen, 257, 265
Tradition, *see* coordination principles
Trebilcock, Clive, 223
Trezise, Philip, 195, 207
Trotsky, Leon, 142
truth, 83–4, 92, 212, 247, 248, 251, 255
Tugan-Baranovsky, Michael, 243
Tullock, Gordon, 17, 167

uncertainty, 44, 81, 100, 133, 193, 208, 221
unemployment, 12, 118, 129–30, 145, 148–51, 153–4, 169, 196–8, 204, 209, 210, 238, 243–4, 245
United States Railroad Administration, 225
utopia, 16–17, 140, 231, 235–8, 244

value, 53–4
Vanek, Jaroslav, 127
Villari, Luigi, 205
Vorhies, W. Francis, 49

wage and price controls, *see* price controls
Wagner, Richard, 205
Walker, Charls E., 204
Walras, Leon, 29, 88
Walsh, Annmarie Hauck, 159
War Finance Corporation, 211, 225–6

War Industries Board, 221, 223–6
war planning, 214, 220–32, 240, 242,
    244, *see also* militarism
Washington Post, 243
Weber, Christopher, 205
Weber, Max, 123
Weinstein, James, 23, 224, 243
Weisskopf, Thomas E., 162
welfare programs, 147–9, 152, 167,
    184, 197, 208
White, Lawrence H., 210
Whitehead, Alfred North, 60–1,
    252–3
Wilson, David E., 226

Wilson, Edward O., 27, 32, 67–9
Wilson, Woodrow, 223
Winpisinger, William W., 179
Winter, Sidney G., 91
Wittgenstein, Ludwig, 89
Woodcock, Leonard, 96
workers' control, 127–8, 176
World War I, 211, 219–26, 239
World War II, 226, 243–4

Young Hegelians, 216–17

Zaid, Charles, 207

ABOUT THE AUTHOR

Don Lavoie is currently Assistant Professor of Economics at the Center for the Study of Market Processes at George Mason University and adjunct scholar at the Cato Institute. He has an undergraduate degree in computer science and received his Ph.D. from New York University. He is the author of *Rivalry and Central Planning: The Socialist Calculation Debate Reconsidered.*